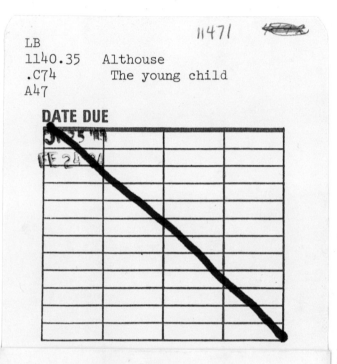

the young child

learning with
understanding

Rosemary Althouse

the young child

learning with understanding

Teachers College, Columbia University
New York and London   1981

Published by Teachers College Press, 1234 Amsterdam Avenue, New York, New York 10027

Library of Congress Cataloging in Publication Data

Althouse, Rosemary, 1932–
    The young child.

    Bibliography: p. 250
    Includes index.
    1. Creative activities and seat work.   2.   Lesson
planning.   3.   Preschool tests.   4.   School discipline.
I.   Title.
LB1140.35.C74A47   372'.21   81–4600
ISBN 0–8077–2658–3   AACR2

Manufactured in the United States of America

86   85   84   83   82   81   1   2   3   4   5   6

to James and Jonathan,
a continual source of joy

contents

6. children are creative: music and art   152

7. children are talkative: language arts   190

preface

This book is written from a cognitive-interactional point of view. To me both nature and nurture play an important part in the child's growth and development. This point of view is congruent with that of many national preschool models that have developed since 1965. The Responsive Environment, High Scope, and the Bank Street model consider both nature and nurture to be important. The outstanding behavioral models are the Engelmann-Becker model and the Behavior Analysis model. The Open Education model and many Head Start programs are influenced to a greater extent by the maturational point of view. Although a variety of preschool models exist, no one model is represented in this book. I have taken an eclectic approach using the knowledge gained from an examination of models, learning theories, developmental theories, and experience.

The questions most often asked by students of child development and early childhood are "What are young children like?" and "What can we do about it?" Teachers must know how the child grows and develops in order to plan an effective program. Teachers must also know how the environment can best meet the needs of the growing child. The chapters in this book are based upon the outstanding characteristics of young children and their implications for planning the curriculum.

acknowledgments

The author wishes to thank Winthrop College, its School of Education and School of Consumer Science and Allied Professions for providing laboratory facilities. She is especially indebted to Joel Nichols, campus photographer, for the photographs that illustrate this book.

the young child

**learning with
understanding**

1
good teachers are planners

Teachers who plan prepare for the future. Teachers who do not plan are at the mercy of fate. Planning begins with goals or purposes. Alice in Wonderland, when asked by the Cheshire Cat, "Where are you going?" replied, "I don't know." The cat remarked, "Then any road will get you there." Indeed, if teachers do not know where they are going, any path will do. Success will be purely accidental.

objectives

Before teachers can plan effectively for the school year, they must decide what it is they want children to learn. This approach necessitates formulating goals or educational objectives. Frost and Kissinger (1976) state: "Educational objectives in early childhood programs encompass all aspects of development—psychomotor, cognitive, affective, and social. These aspects of development are inextricably mixed in the educative process so that development in one area is intertwined with development in the other areas" (p. 178).

One of the best ways to plan is to decide first on broad, general goals for the school year. The following are broad, general goals helpful in planning:

COGNITIVE DOMAIN. A child:

1. Develops sensory and perceptual acuity
2. Develops new concepts and modifies and expands existing concepts
3. Develops communicative skills
4. Develops problem-solving ability
5. Develops creative thinking ability
6. Develops his or her potential for good health and establishes good health habits

SOCIAL DOMAIN. A child:

1. Develops a positive self-concept
2. Progresses from egocentric ways to more sensitive feelings for others
3. Develops self-control
4. Learns responsibility

AFFECTIVE DOMAIN. A child:

1. Enlarges aesthetic appreciation of the environment
2. Shows an interest in learning
3. Shows an openness to new ideas.

PSYCHOMOTOR DOMAIN. A child:

1. Develops body coordination and is able to use the body effectively
2. Develops eye-hand coordination
3. Develops eye-foot coordination

From these broad, general goals or objectives teachers can formulate specific behavioral objectives. Behavioral objectives help teachers by forcing them to ask, "What is it I want to teach?" Behavioral objectives also serve as guides for evaluating outcomes. Teachers can return to stated objectives and ask, "Does this child exhibit the behaviors stated? To what extent?"

It is relatively easy to establish behavioral objectives for the cognitive domain (intellectual skills) and the psychomotor domain (physical skills) because these learning outcomes may be readily observed. It is more difficult to create objectives in the affective domain (attitudes, emotions, interests, and values) and in the social domain (self-concept and relationships with others). Assessment of these objectives is possible only when a child openly expresses thoughts and feelings. Another limitation of behavioral objectives is that performance is evaluated in terms of what a child can do in a specific situation, not what a child will do in another situation at another time. In order to form a more accurate picture of a child's total growth, stated objectives must be evaluated throughout the year, not just at the beginning and end of the year.

Even when behavioral objectives are used, the value of a teacher's subjective judgment must not be underestimated. The teacher knows children in the class well and has knowledge about them that cannot be learned elsewhere. The teacher can obtain information about the children from developmental checklists, anecdotal records, time samplings, children's work, and Piagetian tasks. These kinds of evaluations allow for subjective judgment while at the same time controlling for subjectivity by centering the teacher's attention on specific aspects of growth and development.

learning centers

Teachers must know not only where they are going but also how to get there. One of the best ways to organize a classroom for optimum learning is through learning centers.

Learning centers occupy separate areas of the room, and what happens there does not occur solely by chance. The activities encountered help reinforce and broaden concepts—moving from basic to more complex activities. In a good learning center there is "a constant flow of both planned and spontaneous activity" (Althouse and Main, 1974, p. 223).

A teacher's role is not passive but active. In the learning process the teacher becomes the child's partner, with a responsibility to observe, listen, make appropriate comments, ask thought-provoking questions, and present materials that encourage further learning.

indoor learning centers

Children need ample space to move freely about the room. There should be a minimum of 35 to 40 square feet (3.25 to 3.7 square meters) per child, preferably 60 to 70 square feet (5.6 to 6.5 square meters), in each classroom.

Centers typically found in the classroom are a dramatic-play center for family living; a block center; a music center; an art center; a library center; a sand and/or water center; and a woodworking center. Other centers that have been added in the past 10 years are a science center, a language arts center, an indoor movement center, and a writing center.

Centers should be evenly distributed throughout the room so that children are not crowded into any one area. In arranging learning centers teachers must first consider the permanent properties of the classroom. These are the characteristics that cannot be changed, such as location of toilets, sinks, doors, windows, and electrical outlets. Next teachers should examine the existing equipment and supplies. They must know what they have to work with in order to organize centers for optimal learning and, if possible, order other items they feel are needed. Next teachers may make a scaled drawing of the room with scaled, cutout furniture. They can then reorganize the room on paper until a feasible arrangement is found. The art and science centers are messy, require running water, and stimulate a lot of activity. If possible they should be placed near running water and on a vinyl floor. Centers that are more active and noisy are the block, dramatic-play, and indoor movement centers. Quieter centers are the library, manipulative, and language arts centers. Quiet centers may be placed near each other and the more active, noisy centers in another area of the room.

The types of centers found in a classroom will vary from room to room. Those that meet the needs of a particular group of children should be chosen. A writing center may be inappropriate for children who have never been to school, cannot write their names, and are still in the scribbling stage of their art development. On the other hand, a writing center is a must for children who are writing their names, recognize letter names, and are interested in copying words and sentences. Centers are sometimes combined when there is limited class-room space. The manipulative and mathematics centers and the library and language arts centers contain similar materials that can be combined satisfac-torily.

Centers that follow the interests of one child or a small group of children may be added. One group of children became interested in dinosaurs and brought books, fossils, and dinosaur models to school. A part of the science area was set aside as a dinosaur center. Another group of children became interested in color. A small table designated as the color table was placed near a window. Each week the color of the objects on the table changed. First there were red objects, then blue, yellow, orange, green, purple, and, finally, brown and black.

When space is limited it may be desirable to remove a center for a week or weeks and replace it with another center. The woodworking center can be replaced by a sand or water center and the dramatic-play center by a career-education center. Centers change with children's interests. A group of nursery school children visited a grocery store to buy fruit to make fruit salad. When they returned to their room they began to rearrange the furniture in the dramatic-play center to resemble a grocery store. The refrigerator became a cold-storage box, the cupboard, store shelves filled with foods, and the stove, a checkout counter. The teacher provided a cash register and play money that had until now been in the storeroom. Fresh meat was made from play dough colored red with food coloring. Fruits and vegetables were made from earth clay and painted with tempera paints. The grocery store bore little resemblance to the previous dramat-ic-play center.

Children need an area of the room where they can go when they want to be alone. In a few preschools there is a separate room off the main classroom which serves as an isolation area for sick children and as a place where children can go to be alone. Doors are left open so that children can see and be seen by teachers. When a separate room is not available a teacher should examine the classroom for an area that can be arranged to accommodate children comfortably. A part of the library center may be set aside by a screen or other partition. A large pillow and a shelf with books make this an inviting setting for a child who wants privacy.

EQUIPMENT AND SUPPLIES.   Equipment and supplies for centers must be chosen with great care. In selecting equipment a teacher must ask, "Can I explain to anyone who asks me why I have this piece of equipment in my classroom?" A teacher who is knowledgeable about a piece of equipment can think of many different ways it can be used. Pegs and pegboards can be used to develop eye-hand coordination; knowledge of color names; one-to-one correspondence; rote counting; enumeration; creative design; counting by 1's, 2's, 5's, and 10's; simple addition and subtraction; and solution of such problems as, "Do you have a green peg for every red peg?" and "How many pegs will it take to finish this row?"

Sometimes teachers neglect to try out new equipment and supplies before presenting them to children. One teacher ordered new doll clothes with buttons instead of snaps. Her purpose was to help children develop eye-hand coordination through buttoning and unbuttoning. She found that these children preferred to dress their dolls in the old clothes. Puzzled, she decided to dress the dolls herself, and discovered that the buttons were too big for the buttonholes.

CHOICE BOARDS.   A Choice Board is used to limit the number of children in a center and to relieve congestion in some centers. Children learn to plan ahead since they must think about the center they want to choose and the activities available to them. Unless the room is small—less than 35 square feet (3.25 square meters) per child—and/or the children are having difficulty selecting centers, however, the use of a Choice Board may seriously hamper the movement of children and interfere with their spontaneous interests and creative impulses. A group of children were observed in a music center pretending to be insects as they moved to a musical selection. Other children wanted to enter but were unable to take part since the Choice Board limited the center to five children. On another occasion a child was standing in front of a Choice Board with her name tag in her hand. When she did not seem to know what to do the aide asked, "Can I help you?" The child replied, "I want to go to the science center to see the butterfly, but there is no room for me. All the other children and the teacher are there." This child was confused and frustrated because the Choice Board had been disregarded by the teacher and the other children. In another classroom children in the science center were fascinated as they watched a gerbil run a maze made from blocks. Any child who was interested could watch the gerbil. Since there was no Choice Board, no child was asked to leave the center. If these children had been required to wait for a turn they might have missed the activity or lost interest altogether. Teachers must decide for themselves whether the advantages of a Choice Board outweigh the disadvantages.

outdoor learning centers

The outdoor play area should adjoin the indoor area or be within easy access to it and the bathroom. From 100 − 200 square feet (9.3 to 18.6 square meters) per child is recommended. The area should be fenced in on all sides by a four-foot

(1.22-meter) fence with gates that can be locked when necessary. If possible there should be large grassy areas and hillsides, for rolling, jumping, and climbing. When there are not enough trees for adequate shade, a shelter with a storage room at one end may be built. This shaded area may be used with paints, blocks, and/or woodworking.

Centers usually found outdoors are woodworking, block, sand and/or water, and a variety of large-muscle-development areas. In warmer climates and when adequate space and storage are available, outdoor areas may include a library, art, gardening, and science center. Where it is impossible to make these centers permanent, they may be set up as temporary centers. An easel can be carried outside for outdoor painting and books taken outdoors to read. The resourceful teacher will make the outdoor environment an extension of the indoor environment as much as possible.

EQUIPMENT AND SUPPLIES. Large, permanent pieces of equipment may be ordered from supply houses specializing in outdoor equipment. Choose strong metal apparatus; wooden structures are attractive but many splinter. Portable equipment is highly desirable since it can be moved to shady areas during hot weather and sunny ones during colder days. Children can move the portable equipment and arrange their own movement centers.

Small pieces of equipment may be kept in storage units and brought outside by children. With their help it is possible to bring some larger indoor pieces outside. Children can carry nesting chair blocks outside with the understanding that they will be returned to the classroom.

scheduling the day

Most public schools have a morning and an afternoon session of kindergarten, with 20 to 30 children in each session. It is unfortunate that some classrooms have as many as 30 children per session. This is unfair to young children, who need individual attention, and frustrating to teachers, who want a good program. One public school teacher commented, "I have 30 children in one section and 26 in the other. It is a waste of the taxpayers' money, my time, and the children's time." The recommended maximum number of children per teacher is 10 five-year-olds, 8 four-year-olds, and 6 three-year-olds. Fortunately in most preschool groups there are two adults, a teacher and an aide. A teacher should never be left alone with young children. This practice is unsafe since one adult cannot adequately care for a group of children.

Most public school kindergarten sessions are two and one-half to three hours in length. A few states have a single session of kindergarten from approximately 8:30 A.M. to 2:30 P.M. Many Head Start programs are similar to day-care programs: children may come as early as 7:00 A.M. and stay until 5:00 P.M. Other Head Start programs are half-day sessions. Laboratory schools connected with colleges and universities usually have half-day sessions for three's, four's, and five's and, in some cases, day-care infant and toddler programs. These schools may also have multiage groups with children from three to five years old.

Most of a young child's day should be spent in self-directed activities. The allotted blocks of time will vary with the length of the session, the climate, and the children. There are days when children will be outdoors for most of the day; other days they will remain outside for short periods of time. In mild places such as Florida and California, children were observed carving jack-o'-lanterns out-doors in October and wading in outdoor pools in March.

Children themselves control the schedule to some extent. If children are involved in special projects during learning-center time, the teacher may extend the period and omit a scheduled group activity. Changes in schedule should be explained to children, and whenever possible they should know of a change ahead of time. One teacher omitted snack time when she took four-year-olds on a field trip. When they returned several children refused to eat lunch because they had not had their snack.

It is not advisable to send children home immediately after outdoor play or other vigorous exercise. Children in morning sessions may be too excited to eat lunch. Some parents and bus drivers report that they have more behavior problems when children are overstimulated.

Daily schedules vary with the length of the session, the group of children, and the type of center. The following are suggested schedules for a variety of preschool situations.

suggested schedules for preschool groups

1. Schedule for a double-session kindergarten (three-hour) facility with adjoining fenced outdoor area:

8:30	Arrival.
8:35 to 9:50	Indoor learning centers—individual and self-paced small-group activities.
9:15 to 9:45	Staggered snack.
9:50 to 10:00	Cleanup.
10:00 to 10:15	Group activities—stories, music, finger plays, planning.
10:15 to 11:00	Outside learning centers—individual and self-paced small-group activities.
11:00 to 11:10	Cleanup.
11:10 to 11:25	Quiet time and preparation for dismissal.
11:25 to 11:30	Dismissal.

The afternoon schedule follows the same time allotments for a three-hour session. It begins at 12:30 P.M. to give teachers time to set up for the afternoon session and eat lunch. Indoor learning-center activities and outdoor learning-center activities may be switched in either session.

The above schedules may be used with three- and four-year-olds; however, younger children take longer to carry out activities such as washing hands and putting on outdoor clothing. The blocks of time must be flexible enough to meet the needs of this age group and of the individual children within the group. Even when children are approximately the same age, some mature more slowly than others and need more supervision and time to finish routines.

2. Suggested schedule for a six-hour kindergarten, 8:30 A.M. to 2:30 P.M.

8:30	Arrival.
8:35 to 10:15	Indoor learning centers—individual and small-group activities.
9:45 to 10:15	Staggered snack.
10:15 to 10:20	Cleanup.
10:20 to 10:35	Group activities—stories, music, finger plays, etc.
10:35 to 11:15	Outdoor learning centers—individual and small-group activities.
11:15 to 11:25	Cleanup.
11:25 to 11:45	Group activities—music, stories, planning. Preparation for lunch.
11:45 to 12:15	Lunch.
12:15 to 12:30	Preparations for rest—tooth brushing, toileting.
12:30 to 1:30	Rest. Individual needs vary. Children who are not asleep after 20 minutes may engage in quiet self-directed activities. Children who need to may rest until 2:00 P.M.
1:30 to 2:00	Snack—available on a staggered basis indoors or outdoors. Children who sleep longer may have snack when they wake up.
1:30 to 2:10	Outdoor or indoor learning centers.
2:10 to 2:20	Cleanup.
2:20 to 2:30	Quiet time. Preparation for going home.

3. Suggested schedule for a full-day child development program, 7:30 A.M. to 5:00 P.M.

7:30	Arrival.
7:45 to 8:15	Breakfast—served on a staggered basis.
8:15 to 8:40	Tooth brushing, toileting, washing.
8:40 to 10:00	Indoor learning centers—individual and small-group activities.
10:00 to 10:10	Cleanup.
10:10 to 10:25	Group activities—stories, music, planning.
10:25 to 11:15	Outdoor learning centers—individual and small-group activities.
11:15 to 11:25	Cleanup.
11:25 to 11:40	Group activities—stories, music, planning. Children prepare for lunch.
11:45 to 12:15	Lunch.
12:15 to 12:30	Preparation for rest. Tooth brushing, washing up, toileting.
12:30 to 1:30	Rest. Individual needs vary. Children who need a longer rest period may sleep until 2:00 P.M.
1:30 to 2:00	Snack—available on a staggered basis. Children who sleep longer may have snack when they wake up.

1:35 to 2:30	Indoor or outdoor learning centers.
2:30 to 2:40	Cleanup.
2:40 to 3:00	Quiet time—stories, music, filmstrips.
3:00 to 5:00	Children play indoors or outdoors. Parents begin picking up children. Each child has 10 minutes of quiet activity before going home. Before going home, each child puts away what he or she has played with.

staggered entrance

A staggered entrance for the first week of school will help children adjust to other children, the teachers, and the school. There are many kinds of staggered entrances. All are feasible and a teacher's choice will depend on the particular situation and the children's backgrounds. Three types of staggered entrance for a half-day session are (assume 20 children in each group):

1. *Monday and Wednesday:*
   A.M.   10 children from the morning group
   P.M.   10 children from the afternoon group
   Tuesday and Thursday:
   A.M.   Remaining 10 children from the morning group
   P.M.   Remaining 10 children from the afternoon group
   Friday:
   A.M.   All the morning children
   P.M.   All the afternoon children
   Suggested time schedule:
   A.M.   group from 8:30 to 11:30 A.M.
   P.M.   group from 12:30 to 3:30 P.M.
2. *Monday, Tuesday, Wednesday*—shortened schedule for all children:
   8:30 to 10:00 A.M.   10 children from the morning group
   10:00 to 11:30 A.M.   Other 10 children from the morning group
   12:30 to 2:00 P.M.   10 children from the afternoon group
   2:00 to 3:30 P.M.   Remaining 10 children from the afternoon group
   Thursday and Friday: All children follow the regular schedule
3. *Monday:*
   Seven children in the morning
   Seven children in the afternoon
   Tuesday:
   Seven new children are added to the Monday morning group and seven to the afternoon group
   Wednesday:
   Six new children are added to the 14 who came on Tuesday morning and 6 to the 14 who came on Tuesday afternoon
   Thursday and Friday:
   All children in the morning group come in the morning
   All children in the afternoon group come in the afternoon

Suggested schedule:
8:30 to 11:30 A.M.
12:30 to 3:30 P.M.

Schedule 3 has several advantages over schedules 1 and 2. First, all children come to school every day after their first day. A child who is eager to go to school finds it difficult to wait a whole day to go back whereas a child who has difficulty adjusting may find it more difficult to come back to school after being at home. Second, children who have already been in school a day or more often help new children adjust to the classroom. Third, teachers can focus on the children who are new while aides work with children who have been to school the day(s) before. With a change in time schedules six-hour kindergartens can use the above suggestions for staggered entrance.

grouping

indoor grouping

SMALL GROUPS.   To many teachers the term "grouping" is synonomous with "all the children." Grouping may mean 12, 5, or as few as 2 children. Usually a large preschool group is from 10 to 12 and a small group from 4 to 8 children. Group size will vary with the maturity level of the children and the teacher's purpose for grouping.

Children are sometimes expected to sit still and not interrupt. It is surprising that adults expect from children what they do not expect from themselves. Few adults can sit for over 30 minutes without squirming, and they "tune out" a speaker who speaks over an hour even when their interest is high. Why should young children who are very active and whose large and small muscles are not yet developed be expected to sit still for 30 to 45 minutes?

Since young children are egocentric and have difficulty seeing things from a point of view other than their own, they are more interested in what they have to say than in what their classmates say. Small groups (four to six) give children the opportunity to express themselves and also encourage them to entertain other points of view. Since they have ample opportunity to express themselves and are not so concerned with "my turn," they are better able to listen to other children. Opportunity for language development is optimum in small groups but almost extinct in large groups. A few children who are more verbal and less shy monopolize the conversation in a large group. They and the teacher do most of the talking.

One of the best ways to provide for small-group activities is during the learning-center time. Small-group activities may be planned around a current interest. Children in a kindergarten were very interested in their pet gerbil. One of the children suggested taking pictures of the gerbil with the class's Polaroid camera. As an outgrowth of the children's interest, photographs were taken at different times during the day.

The photographs of the gerbil were placed on the science table, and the teacher and children discussed them. This small-group activity continued throughout learning-center time. Children entered and left the center as they chose. The teacher made a note of each child who entered. It was found that over half the children participated. This activity continued for several days as more pictures of the gerbil were taken. The children talked about the different activities of the gerbil. The teacher wrote what they said in a large book. Each child dictated at least one sentence, and the child's name was written under the contribution.

At the same time small groups were discussing the gerbil other centers requiring less teacher interaction were set up. Small plastic animals were placed in the mathematics center for the children to classify by "putting together the animals that belong together." Felt figures of different-size dogs and their corresponding doghouses were placed on the flannel board. Children were encouraged to arrange the dogs from the smallest to the largest and find the corresponding house for each dog. These centers required only occasional supervision by the aide, freeing the teacher to work with small groups.

TOTAL GROUP. Children enjoy a true sense of belonging to a group—a class of children. Singing, telling and reading stories, and discussing topics of interest lend themselves to whole-group activities. During an energy crisis the lights in a classroom went out suddenly. The children were surprised to learn that the principal had turned off the lights and asked the teacher to use fewer lights in the future. The teacher called the children together to discuss the energy crisis and the reasons why they would not be able to burn as many lights.

How often children come together in a group depends on the needs, ages, and maturity of the group. Even when children are five years of age, it is best to limit group time to 10 to 15 minutes. Some teachers of three- and four-year-olds limit their group time to 5 to 10 minutes. It is not necessary to come together in a total group more than once a day. In some cases it is not necessary to meet every day.

Children should be comfortable when they sit in groups. They may be given a choice of sitting on a rug or in chairs. When given a choice changes in seating are infrequent and children appear less restless. When chairs are used they should be the proper height for children. Chair seats should be 12 inches (0.30 meters) high with a few 10 inches (0.25 meters) for smaller children.

Although children's attention span increases with age and maturity, a teacher must continually guard against requiring children to sit too long. A teacher who is sensitive to the needs of children will tell by their behavior when they are ready to change activities. Two five-year-old boys taught a kindergarten teacher a valuable lesson. They asked her what makes day and night. She immediately got the standard flashlight and ball. In a darkened room she began her explanation. Soon both boys left her alone in the room. One boy called back, "Thanks, teacher, that's enough."

outdoor grouping

Children group themselves naturally outdoors just as they do indoors. When a teacher wants children to practice certain motor skills, the teacher can set up an environment that encourages participation. If children need help in walking a balance beam, teachers can place a rope on the ground for the children to walk on. If some children are afraid to jump, a low balance board can be set up a few inches off the ground.

first day of school

The first day of school is crucial. Careful planning helps ensure success.

learning centers

The first day of school should be one of activity for children. Most of the day may be spent in exploring the room and the outdoor area. It may take several weeks to become acquainted with the centers and the equipment found in each. A tour of the room on the first day may be confusing to a child. There is too much to see and too much to learn. It is sometimes best to allow children to explore freely with a minimum of teacher intervention. Some children may stay in one or two centers for the first day or two. Only when a child continues to play in one center for several weeks should the teacher encourage the child to choose other centers. Very few children stay with one center after the first few weeks of school.

equipment and supplies

Few pieces of equipment should be put out on the first day. A few challenging and more difficult pieces, however, should be included for children with previous preschool experiences. Also, it is desirable to put out some equipment with which the majority of the children are not familiar. Interest is high when a totally new toy is discovered. Disadvantaged children may need more direction and help with equipment. The teacher must not assume, however, a disadvantaged child is not ready for more advanced equipment. Watch and see how children use materials and then guide them to those most appropriate for them.

restrooms

Teachers should show each child the restroom soon after the child arrives at school. Strange bathrooms can be frightening. Some toilets flush noisily, and some have doors to which children are not accustomed. Toilets should be child-size, about 13 inches (0.33 meters) in height. It is important to tell the child when the restroom may be used. If it is in the classroom, children may be told that they may go to the restroom at any time and it is not necessary to tell the teacher. When children must use a bathroom outside the classroom, the teacher or another adult should accompany them. It is always advisable for children to have an extra change of clothing at school in case of accidents.

cleanup

Cleanup should be a time when both children and teachers help. At first a teacher may want to suggest something for each child to put away. Later in the year children can be asked to put away whatever they find out of place.

Putting the blocks away.

It is best to tell children when it is 5 or 10 minutes before cleanup time. This gives them a chance to finish what they are doing. In some cases children should be allowed to finish their work and clean up later. If a child is painting a picture and cannot finish in five minutes, he or she can be allowed to finish, put materials away, and then join the group.

Although children should help in keeping the room neat, it is the responsibility of the teacher to keep the room in order. Rugs should be vacuumed each day, the vinyl floor mopped at least twice a week. Teachers should constantly look for safety hazards, such as splintered blocks and scissors lying on the floor. Broken toys should be removed at once.

lockers

There should be a locker or cubbie for each child's clothing and personal possessions to give each child something that is his or her own. Instead of lockers being assigned each child can be allowed to choose a locker. A method that has been used with success allows a child to choose a locker by chance. Cards with pictures (balloon, duck, cat, sun) on them are placed in a box with a hole large enough for a child's hand (a sense and tell box). Each child draws a card. The teacher writes the child's name on the card while the child watches. The child finds a locker by matching the picture on the card with the identical picture on a locker. This becomes his or her locker since no other child has a locker with the same picture. The name card may be worn until the child goes home or, if necessary, left in the locker to be worn the next day.

Meeting in a small group for a story.

group time

At the beginning of the year group time should be brief, not over 5 to 10 minutes. The main purpose of group time should be to help children get to know each other and become familiar with the room. Songs, finger plays, and short stories are appropriate. When group times are interesting and activities appropriate, hesitant children eventually join in small- or large-group activities. When children continue to refuse to enter any type of group activity, it may be because they are developmentally immature and are not yet ready to be part of a group. Other reasons for this behavior may be more serious, such as emotional or physical problems. A teacher should then seek help from available professionals.

snack time

A staggered snack is desirable with most groups of children. During snack time, food may be placed on a trolley or tray near an empty table. Children can get their food and take it to a table. Drinks can be poured from plastic pitchers by the children. The snack may be left out for approximately 30 to 40 minutes, giving all the children an opportunity to eat. A staggered snack avoids the problem of sitting too long and waiting for other children to be served or to finish their snacks. When children wait unnecessarily they become restless and irritable.

through the year

A teacher should gradually help children become more independent in their choices and uses of materials. A kindergarten child asked to make a game she

We pass food to each other.

called "Fishing." The teacher provided the child with the materials she wanted: sticks, construction paper, felt pens, string, paper clips, small magnets, and a large container. Sue made paper fish and put a paper clip on each nose. Then she put all the fish in the container and filled it with water. She was upset when the fish fell apart. The teacher told her to think of something she could do to keep the fish from coming apart. Sue decided to wrap each fish in Saran wrap. This method was satisfactory for several days, and Sue was very pleased with what she called "my good game." Independent thought, problem-solving ability, and the desire to experiment and learn through trial and error are characteristics teachers should strive to develop in children. This is often a slow process and should not be hurried.

Equipment that has been stored should be introduced gradually as the children's abilities and interests dictate. One year a group of nursery school children became interested in colors. They accidentally discovered that a round jar filled with water would make colors in the sunlight. They asked for more jars, which the teacher supplied. Several prisms and other items of cut glass (perfume bottles, ash trays, earrings) were placed on the science table. The children discovered that certain kinds of glass and sunlight make a rainbow.

Often teachers plan activities around themes or topics such as holidays and seasons. This is a good approach provided the topics relate to the children and/or grow out of their interests. When teachers are tuned in to children's ideas, topics often develop from their interests. At Halloween a group of kindergarten children became interested in weighing pumpkins. The teacher suggested weighing the pumpkins before and after they were cut. This activity led to an interest in comparing the weights of many small objects in the room. An equal-arm balance was introduced so that the children could compare masses as well as weights of objects.

meeting goals

One of the best ways for teachers to evaluate is to refer back to their behavioral goals and ask, "Am I planning significant learnings around my objectives?" A college teacher guiding graduate students in a practicum with young children became concerned when activities were being planned without objectives. She was relieved when one of the students asked, "When are we (the class) going to have a focus? We are doing piecemeal teaching." Careful consideration of the relationships of objectives to activities and activities to objectives will help a teacher plan appropriately for children.

Each of the following chapters contains suggestions for evaluating pupil learning in a systematic and objective manner. The value of the teacher's subjective judgment is not ignored.

2
children
are active

movement education

All healthy children are active. This is perhaps their most outstanding characteristic. A visitor once asked a kindergarten teacher, "Are children ever still? When I walk into a kindergarten, I feel like I've stepped into the middle of an anthill." The teacher laughingly replied, "No, it is unnatural for children to be still for very long."

Charles (1974) says, "Children must act. Seldom are they inactive for more than a few minutes during their waking hours" (p. 27). Activity is very important to the total development of young children. It is their way of learning about themselves and their world. Yardley (1974) says:

The child uses movement as an aid to satisfying his personal needs. Movement gives him great pleasure and plays an essential role in social contact. It is through his own actions that a child becomes aware of himself as a separate entity. The child uses bodily movement as a means of expressing and recording impressions and reactions. Movement is an ever ready medium through which the child can find a creative outlet. Most important of all, the child moves in order to explore a world which in his early years extends for him only as far as he can reach. (pp. 18 –19)

Throughout the history of preschool education an emphasis has been placed upon the child as an active learner. Froebel, the father of the kindergarten, devised a curriculum for active learning based upon his observations of children. In his school the child acted upon objects that were called "gifts." The child was told exactly how to use the gifts. This method of direct instruction is a far cry from the learning through self-activity advocated by educators today;

18

however, the idea of an "active learner" was revolutionary in Froebel's time (Weber, 1969, pp. 1–17).

Montessori speaks of children's "intense motivation toward [their] own self-construction" (Lillard, 1972, p. 31) which motivates them to perform a task until they have mastered it. Children move at their own pace, choosing those tasks best suited to meeting their needs. They leave a task that is too difficult or too easy for them. Montessori did not leave the environment to chance, but created a "prepared environment." She invented over 1,400 didactic materials designed to meet the needs of young children. She felt that each child should work at his or her own pace, and was the best judge of when he or she had finished with a piece of equipment (had mastered the task) and was ready to move on to a more complex task (Montessori, 1965, pp. 37–189).

Dewey also stressed children's activity. He saw children as active agents in their own learning. Children learn by doing. Dewey thought of the schoolroom as a miniature society where children solved problems that came from their own interactions. Young children learn best through involvement with other children in a realistic environment that resembles the family and the community (Weber, 1969, pp. 60 – 64).

Perhaps no person has stressed the importance of learning by activity more than the Swiss psychologist Jean Piaget. His theories of learning have had tremendous impact on every aspect of early childhood education. Piaget feels that for growing children, knowledge comes from their own activites on objects and in situations (Ginsburg and Opper, 1969, pp. 221–223).

"Movement education" is closely related to the activity of children. The

19

idea of educating children through movement has become part of the physical education program in many elementary schools and is rapidly becoming part of preschool programs. Certain aspects of movement education are familiar to early childhood educators. Provisions for large- and small-muscle development, outdoor play on large pieces of equipment, rhythms, and creative dance have all been part of the preschool curriculum. It is almost as if the advocates of movement education have taken movement experiences long associated with the education of young children and combined them to create a new area of the curriculum. Perhaps the main difference lies in the concept of planned movement experiences. Gallahue (1977) states:

Contributing to the physical development of the child is certainly a worthy objective of any preschool program, but the vast majority of early childhood educators are: (1) poorly informed as to why development of these abilities is important, (2) poorly informed as to what forms of physical activity to include, and (3) poorly informed as to how to go about such a task. As a result the psychomotor development of the young child is often taken for granted or dealt with solely through loosely supervised free play. . . . Although free play activities can and should play a part in the nursery school and kindergarten experience, it is not enough to assume that the purchase of expensive pieces of indoor and outdoor equipment will effectively aid in the development and refinement of the child's movement abilities. Too often children are turned loose on various forms of apparatus and expected magically to develop efficient forms of movement behavior on their own. Only through wise guidance, thoughtful interaction, and careful planning can we assure the proper development of the young child's movement abilities. (p. 59)

Block (1977) agrees with Gallahue; he states, "Free and spontaneous play is not the same as movement exploration. The latter is a guided program; free play is relatively limitless" (p. 24).

Kirchner et al. (1970) describe three methods of teaching movement education, the direct, indirect, and limitation methods (pp. 22–25). In the direct method the teacher chooses the activities and prescribes what and how each child shall execute them. The teacher decides that the children will practice hopping. A hopping demonstration is given by the teacher, who tells the children to hop as shown. Each child imitates the teacher as he or she hops. In the indirect method the children choose the movement activity. Various pieces of apparatus are available for them to use as they choose. A class using the indirect method would resemble children in a free-activity classroom. The limitation method is a compromise between the direct and indirect methods. The choice of the activity is limited in some way by the teacher, for example, the teacher might say, "Move to the end of the room lying on your backs." The children are free to use their own creativity in their movements. One child may use both arms and legs in the movement; one child may use legs only; and another child may use only the arms. The teacher can analyze the various movements, since a similar type of movement is demonstrated by all the children (Kirchner et al., 1970, pp. 22–24).

The indirect method and the limitation method are more appropriate for young children, who need freedom to use their bodies in order to discover what their bodies can do. They do need guidance in order to develop more refined motor skills. Herkowitz (1977) discusses the value of planned movement experiences for the young child: "Planned movement experiences encourage normal physical development. At no time in the life of the human being is physical development more dramatic than from birth to six years of age" (p. 15). He feels that movement experiences benefit the young child in the following ways:

1. Lay the foundation for later skills.
2. Provide physical activities for children in urban settings.
3. Provide risk-taking behavior in a controlled, supervised environment.
4. Develop a positive self-concept.
5. Help to orient children in space. May be the foundation upon which complex cognitive concepts are built.
6. Give the child joy and pleasure.
7. Help improve verbal communication skills—language of movement.
8. Develop social skills. (p. 16)

Little research has been done with young children and movement education, but research has been conducted in the area of young children's physical development. When children are given similar opportunities, the differences that occur are related to age and less clearly to sex role, intelligence, and school achievement. Sinclair and other authors summarize the findings as follows:

1. Age: Children improve in movement as they grow older (Sinclair, 1973, p. 53). Readiness for motor learning is a result of maturation and learning (Godfrey and Kephart, 1969).
2. Sex: At age four boys move ahead of girls in strength and throwing ability (Sinclair, 1973, p. 55). Boys forge ahead in speed, power, and endurance (Milne, Seefeldt, and Reuschlein, 1976, pp. 716 –730).
3. Race: Children of the black race achieve a higher degree of motor proficiency than whites (Sinclair, 1973, p. 58; Milne, Seefeldt, and Reuschlein, 1976, pp. 726 –730).
4. Intelligence: A positive but low correlation has been found between intelligence and motor skills (Sinclair, 1973, p. 59).
5. Reading readiness: Movement education may be indirectly related to reading or other achievements. Results of research are contradictory. The movement characteristics most often related to reading proficiency are balance, mixed or delayed dominance, and eye-hand coordination (Sinclair, 1973, p. 59).

It is clear from the above discussion and the findings of research that movement education contributes to the total development of young children. This chapter will concentrate primarily on children's psychomotor development. Gallahue (1976) states:

Psychomotor development is at the very heart of the movement education program and should be viewed as an avenue by which both cognitive and affective competencies can also be enhanced. Psychomotor development refers to *learning to move* with control and efficiency through space. (p. 2)

After a careful consideration of suggested movement education programs for young children, movement activities are discussed under the following headings:

1.   Basic movements: acquiring skills in fundamental locomotor abilities, such as walking, running, hopping, galloping, and skipping
2.   Body awareness: learning what the body can do and how to make the body do it
3.   Spatial awareness: learning to orient the body in space
4.   Temporal awareness: getting the body parts to work together smoothly and in the proper sequence

physical characteristics of young children

Before formulating goals for movement education it is necessary to review the physical characteristics of young children. Listed in table 2–1 are physical characteristics of young children from three to six years of age. They represent general characteristics of young children and *do not* represent the characteristics of any one child; each child has an individual built-in rate of growth.

table 2–1
representative physical characteristics
of young children

From About 3 Years	to About 6 Years of Age
1. Catches ball, arms straight	1. Catches ball, elbows at sides
2. Copies circle; draws straight lines	2. Copies square, triangle, diamond, designs, a few letters and numerals
3. Unbuttons; puts shoes on	3. Fastens buttons he or she can see, zips zippers, is learning to tie shoes
4. Spills from spoon	4. Eats with fork and spoon without spilling; is learning to eat using knife
5. May walk on tiptoes	5. Walks with feet close together (narrow stance)
6. Rides tricycle	6. Learning to ride bicycle
7. Goes up and down stairs foot to foot	7. Alternates feet going up and down stairs
8. Tears paper	8. Cuts and folds paper
9. Runs, climbs, gallops	9. Is learning to skip
10. Grasps brush, crayons in fist	10. Holds brush, crayon, pencil between thumb and forefinger
11. Hand preference is more firmly established; may be ambidextrous	11. Hand preference is usually established
12. Large-muscle development is more advanced than small	12. Small-muscle control is refined
13. Weight is about 32 pounds (14.5 kilograms)	13. Weight is about 48 pounds (21.8 kilograms)
14. Height is about 38 inches (0.97 meters)	14. Height is about 49 inches (1.24 meters)

goals of movement education

The following goals for development through movement education have been chosen as realistic ones for a teacher to select since they can be achieved by the majority of children from ages three to six. Since physical development and skills affect the development of the whole child, objectives are written in the psycho-motor, cognitive, affective, and social domains. It is important to remember that not all the objectives will be reached by the time a child is five or six. The objectives are listed as a guide for a teacher in planning and as one source for evaluating physical development.

PSYCHOMOTOR DOMAIN.   The child:

1. Alternates feet going up and down steps
2. Runs with speed using limbs in opposition
3. Jumps for a distance of about 3 feet (0.91 meters)
4. Jumps for a height of about 1 foot (0.30 meters)
5. Hops 8 to 10 times on the same foot (6 times for four's, 3 times for three's)
6. Gallops, combining a walk and leap, with the same foot leading through-out (gallops more skillfully by age five)
7. Skips skillfully about 20 percent of the time (one-footed skip at four, skips well by five-and-a-half to six-and-a-half)
8. Throws a ball with forearm and body rotated (from five to six years); steps forward with leg on same side as throwing arm
9. Catches the ball using hands only (using arms and body at three and four years)
10. Kicks the ball and follows through (after three no longer kicks at the ball)
11. Strikes an object by rotating trunk and hips and shifting body weight forward (four to five years—swings in horizontal plane and stands to the side of the objects)
12. Walks on a 2-inch or a 3-inch beam alternating feet
13. Balances on one foot from 3 to 4 seconds (five years)
14. Bounces a ball 6 consecutive times
15. Carries a weight of 10 pounds (4.5 kilograms) for three-year olds, 12 pounds (5.4 kilograms) for four's, 16 pounds (7.3 kilograms) for five's, 20 pounds (9.09 kilograms) for six-year-olds.
16. Uses various joints to move through a full range of motions (bending, twisting, turning)
17. Buttons, unbuttons, zips, and snaps clothing (four to five years)
18. Puts on and takes off most of his or her outer clothing (three to five years)
19. Ties own shoes (five-and-a-half to six-and-a-half years)
20. Places pegs in a pegboard and large beads on a string (three- to four-year-olds)
21. Holds a paintbrush, pencil, or crayon between thumb and forefinger (five-and-a-half to six-and-a-half years)
22. Hangs from a support for at least 12 seconds
23. Pulls an object with hands from 4 to 6 feet (1.2 to 1.8 meters)
24. Has the proper eye-hand coordination to write name in manuscript letters (five to six years)

COGNITIVE DOMAIN.   The child:

1.   Names and locates the parts of the body
2.   Correctly uses parts of the body required for a specific motor activity
3.   Determines the location of an object relative to the place where he or she is standing (far away, beside, near)
4.   Determines the location of objects relative to their proximity to other nearby objects without regard to the location of child's own body (go through the hall to get to the gym; go outside to climb on the jungle gym; find the part of the room that is shown in the picture; follow the picture map to the treasure)
5.   Responds to and uses directional cues such as right-left, front-back, above-below, up-down, forward-backward
6.   Combines body movements in a unique way in order to create own movements
7.   Adjusts body movements to accompany a contrasting rhythm (slow-fast, light-heavy, even-uneven)

AFFECTIVE DOMAIN.   The child:

1.   Shows through actions and words that he or she is open to new ideas involving movement
2.   Shows through actions and words that he or she can do many things with the body and has confidence in own abilities
3.   Shows an interest in movement education by asking questions, making comments, and participating eagerly in activities

SOCIAL DOMAIN.   The child:

1.   Shares equipment and materials involved in movement activities
2.   Contributes ideas and displays feelings while interacting with other children in movement activities
3.   Shows by words and actions that he or she is not prejudiced toward other children in the group because they are different from the majority of the group

indoor learning centers

Indoor learning centers that relate most closely to the development of eye-hand coordination, eye-foot coordination, and fine- and large-muscle development are the manipulative center and the indoor movement center. Centers that relate indirectly to psychomotor development are the block center, the woodworking center, the music center, the art center, and the writing center. (This center is included when a teacher feels it is appropriate.) The manipulative center and the indoor movement centers will be described in detail.

manipulative center

The main purpose of the manipulative center is to develop eye-hand coordination and the small muscles. Every area of the preschool curriculum—spatial,

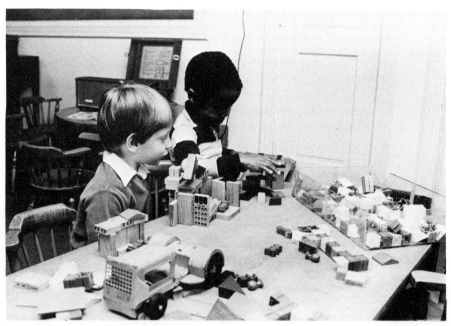

Making buildings.

relations, numbers, temporal relations, language—is taught here, however. It is true that no center can be exclusive, developing concepts from only one area of the curriculum. A teacher must be aware of the concepts from other disciplines which children can learn.

LOCATION.   The manipulative center is relatively quiet and may be placed by other quiet centers, such as the library, mathematics, or language arts centers. An ideal location is next to the mathematics center. Most mathematics equipment is manipulative, and equipment in the manipulative center can be used to teach mathematical concepts. Placement of the center will depend on the physical characteristics of the classroom and the other centers to be included.

EQUIPMENT AND SUPPLIES.   Large equipment may include:

Dividers—pegboards, low screens, backs of shelves (stationary or portable), teacher-made screens (covered with contact paper or decorated by the children).
Large pillow(s) or bean bag(s).
Chairs.
Tables—recommended height, 20 to 22 inches (0.51 to 0.56 meters); space between top of table and chair seat, 10 inches (0.25 meters). Only one table is necessary if space is provided to work on the floor.

   Small equipment may include:

Pegboards and pegs.
Beads and strings.

Hammer and nail sets.
Unit table blocks.
Construction toys—Lego blocks, Lincoln logs, plastic squares and disks, snap
    blocks.
Puzzles—7 to 26 pieces.
Nesting blocks.
Small colored blocks.
Combination chalk and magnetic board.
Flannel boards.
Felt and magnetic figures—geometric shapes, letters, numerals.
Lacing boards.
Sorting boxes.
Form boards.
Sort and match sets.
Design boards—mosaics, tiles, parquetry blocks.

This is only a limited list since there is a wide variety of good manipulative
material available.

TEACHER'S ROLE.   Equipment should be chosen that encourages group activities (Lego blocks, unit blocks, construction toys, Lincoln logs) and individual
activities (puzzles, beads and laces, form boards, gadget boxes). Clear plastic
boxes are best for storing equipment on low, open shelves. Children can see at a
glance the equipment they want to use.

    A teacher must evaluate children's activities carefully in order to know
when to remove equipment and put out new equipment. Children who have
learned to place pegs in a pegboard and to string beads are ready for more
difficult manipulative equipment, such as gadget boards, hammer and nail sets,
and lacing boards. Children who have difficulty placing pegs and stringing
beads need less complicated equipment, such as nesting blocks or an oversize
pegboard with large pegs.

    Sometimes teachers will take a more directive role in children's activities.
They may ask questions or make comments to stimulate further learning. A child
puts all the red pegs in the pegboard. The teacher asks, "Did you use all the red
pegs? Do you have enough blue pegs to fill the empty holes?" Another child uses
the hammer and nail set. The teacher comments, "I see you're using the hammer
and nails today. You are holding the hammer close to the head. What would
happen if you moved your hand to the end of the hammer handle? Could you hit
the nail harder?"

    Children should be encouraged to use equipment and should be shown
how to use it when necessary. A teacher should not, however, do the work for
the children or make models from construction toys for them to copy. Children
know then that the work is not theirs, and the satisfaction of "I can do it myself!"
is taken away.

indoor movement center

LOCATION.   The main purpose of the indoor movement center is the development of large muscles. It also serves as a place where children can go to get rid of

excess energy and release frustrations. The center should be placed near other active centers, such as the block center, the dramatic-play center, or the science center. It is desirable to carpet the area or put mats under larger pieces of equipment. The center may be no larger than 8 feet by 10 feet (2.44 meters by 3.0 meters). If the room is small, the center may be set up only on rainy days. When the room is large (more than 40 to 60 square feet per child, 3.7 to 5.6 square meters) this center may be permanent.

EQUIPMENT AND SUPPLIES. A small center may have one or two pieces of equipment; a large center will have more. The equipment should be portable so that it may be changed as the children's needs dictate. Two sawhorses and one board with cleats are portable and may be made into a seesaw, a bridge, a jumping board, or an inclined plane. A mirror placed in the center will give the children opportunities to observe themselves in movement activities.

Large equipment may include:

Boards with cleats
Tumbling mats
Punching bags
Balance beams
Sawhorses
Nesting bridges
Carpet squares
Rocking boat
Low stilts
Mats
Mirror

Small equipment may include:

Play hoops
Yarn balls
Jump ropes
Bean bags
Tiles shaped like footprints

For information on making indoor and outdoor equipment for movement education, consult *Motor Development in Early Childhood* by Betty Flinchum (1975).

TEACHER'S ROLE. A teacher must be familiar with each piece of equipment and cognizant of the possibilities for psychomotor development. Children need guidance in order to use their bodies effectively. A child who cannot walk across a three-inch beam placed slightly off the floor needs experiences walking a rope or tape placed on the floor. On the other hand, a child who has adequate balance needs to be challenged by more difficult equipment and activities. A teacher may suggest walking on the beam sideways, backward, to the right, to the left. This child is now ready for a two-inch beam balance. A teacher should know what each child can do and can be expected to do next.

outdoor learning centers

LOCATION.   Permanent outdoor equipment may include concrete pipes, a slide, a large jungle gym, or a multipurpose unit. Apparatus should be spaced so that no child is in danger of falling from one piece onto another. Portable pieces of equipment may be moved from place to place and put together in a variety of ways.

EQUIPMENT AND SUPPLIES.   Equipment for large-muscle development should be abstract or neutral in its form. Children can use their imagination and creativity to turn the structure into anything from a house to a rocket. There should be more portable than permanent pieces of equipment to allow children to create their own movement centers for climbing, jumping, walking, crawling, sliding, hopping, running. When portable equipment is used, it is not necessary to invest a great deal of money in expensive pieces of permanent equipment such as teeter-totters, jungle gyms, and slides.
     Portable pieces of equipment may include:

Portable nesting climbers
Lightweight ladders
Balance beams
Large drag boxes with provision for pulling
Inner tubes for rolling, sitting, stacking
Tumbling mats
Sawhorses and boards with cleats
Portable nesting bridges
Punching bag
Wooden cable spools—several sizes, obtainable free from utility or construction
     firms
Trampoline—commercial, or fasten canvas over a tire
Blocks and posts—various heights and widths for stepping from one to the other
Bouncing boards—10 to 12 feet (3 to 3.7 meters) long, placed a few inches off
     the ground
Metal tunnels for crawling

     Pieces of small portable equipment that can be purchased or easily made may include:

Balls—6 to 10 inches (0.15 to 0.25 meters) in diameter
Bean bags
Yarn balls—teacher-made by twisting yarn around stiff paper, tying in the
     middle, and cutting ends
Walking clogs
Wobbles—medium-size
Individual jump ropes—of proper lengths

Jumping high.

Play hoops—medium size
Toss games—commercial or teacher-made

Permanent pieces of equipment may include:

Multipurpose unit
Three-way ladder
Rope ladder
Heavy cement drainpipes for crawling through—available from manufacturers
Jungle gym
Slide

When nursery schools and kindergartens are connected with public schools, there may be no provision for permanent large equipment. All of the above small portable equipment may be kept indoors and brought out as needed.

TEACHER'S ROLE.   A teacher's first concern is the safety of the children. Children should have both hands free for climbing; proper clothing should be worn (long dresses or smooth-soled shoes are inappropriate); and broken, unsafe equipment must be removed at once.

A teacher should assess the physical abilities of the children as they use the permanent and portable equipment. Do all the children climb? Are any children afraid of heights? Do any have coordination problems? How serious are these problems? Should these children be referred for testing? Are there children who lack sufficient muscle tone to hang from bars? As teachers assess each child's ability they can plan strategies for helping individual children. Informal practice games, such as throwing a ball back and forth, walking a balance beam, lifting a board with cleats, walking on a tape maze, help improve skills. Suggestions and comments help the child to improve skills: "Good! You climbed to the second bar. Can you climb to the third bar?" "Can you go all the way across the ladder?" "Try again, you almost did it last time."

Obstacle courses can be set up to challenge children. Portable equipment may be arranged in a variety of ways, increasing in difficulty as the child moves through the course: (1) "Crawl through the barrel, walk across the walking beam, and jump off. Then climb over the box." (2) "Slide down the slide. Step in and out of four tires." (3) "Climb in and out of a barrel." (4) "Climb up and walk across the bridge, jump off, and then slide down a board." Children love obstacle courses and will try feats they might avoid in other situations.

Children should be encouraged to use their imagination in arranging portable equipment. A teacher may make a suggestion by beginning an arrangement which the children can add to or take away from until they are satisfied. The advantages of portable equipment are its flexibility and the opportunities it gives children to arrange their movement centers.

scheduling

indoor centers

Activities in the manipulative and indoor movement centers occur during learning-center time. Occasionally teachers may ask individual children who need help with a special skill to use a particular center.

outdoor centers

Activities in outdoor movement centers occur at a scheduled time each day. This schedule may vary as the weather changes. Children may go outside as soon as they come to school in warm weather, or, if the playground is shared with other groups, outdoor play may be scheduled at the beginning, middle, or end of the day. Children in full-day programs usually play outside more than once a day.

grouping

natural grouping

During learning-center time outdoors and indoors, children will group themselves according to their interests and abilities. This is natural grouping, and it occurs spontaneously in various centers. It is usually initiated by children and not by the teacher. Natural grouping is controlled by the children themselves as they move from center to center.

small groups

Movement activities can be carried out in small groups of 10 to 12 children. There are many ways to divide into groups by chance: Each child draws a card with the numeral 1 or 2 printed on it, or with a blue or a red design, or with a Hula hoop or a ball on the card. There are times when a teacher may want a child in a particular activity or group. The teacher designates the child or, if possible, stacks the deck of cards in such a way that the child draws the activity that he or she needs most. Children accept group division much better when it occurs by chance and they do not feel put into a particular group or with a particular teacher.

After groups are formed, a teacher can work with one group and an aide the other. When both groups have finished their activities, the groups can switch. Most movement activities may be enjoyed outdoors, indoors (with furniture pushed back), or in a gymnasium.

One way to begin a movement activity is to ask children to hold hands and make a circle, then drop hands and sit down. This is a quick way to get children in a circle. When children are in a circle, a teacher can begin a bean bag activity by throwing a bean bag to each child, asking the group to stand up, put the bean bags on their heads, and walk around in a circle. Say "Walk slowly. Walk fast. Stop." Then ask the children to move (no longer in a circle) with the bean bags on the backs of their hands, on their feet, shoulders, or knees. Ask them to move the bean bags from one hand to the other, one foot to the other, or one knee to the other. This is difficult, and there is much laughter as the bean bags fall and are recovered. After planned activities, children have free play with the bags. An activity like this lasts about 10 to 15 minutes. Group movement activities should not last over 15 to 20 minutes for older children (five to six years) and 5 to 10 minutes for younger children (three to five years).

first day of school

manipulative center

A few pieces of equipment should be put on the shelves the first day of school. Good selections are beads to string, pegs and pegboards, hammer and nail sets, Lego blocks, puzzles (8 to 20 pieces), construction sets, and lacing frames. A teacher's main responsibility is to observe how the equipment is used. How is the child's eye-hand coordination, visual discrimination? Is he or she right-handed, left-handed, ambidextrous? Is the equipment familiar? Is it challenging? Is it too hard? Too easy?

indoor movement center

This center may be set up if space allows. Only one or two pieces of equipment should be in the center—a board with cleats and sawhorse made into a slide, punching bag, board with cleats and two sawhorses, balance beam, or maze made of tape on the floor. This center may be introduced on the first day of school or later, when children have become familiar with the other centers.

outdoor movement center

Few pieces of equipment should be out on the first day of school. Additional equipment can be added later. Good selections are a sawhorse and one board with cleats, two sawhorses and one bridge, three drag boxes to climb or jump off, and a sawhorse and two boards with cleats.

movement activities through the year

Since movement in the guise of movement education is somewhat new to the field of preschool education, activities designed to increase basic movements, body awareness, spatial awareness, and temporal awareness are listed for the year, moving from simpler to the more complex. These activities should be carried out with small groups (8 to 12 children). All movement activities may be carried out indoors or outdoors.

basic movements

These motor patterns form the basis for skilled movement:

Locomotor: crawling, walking, running, skipping, jumping, galloping
Nonlocomotor: pushing, pulling, stretching, turning, swinging, bending, twist-
     ing, balancing

    I.   Turning, stretching, twisting, swinging, bending.
         A.   Turn, stretch, twist, swing, bend different parts of your body (legs, arms, hands, fingers).

    B.   Turn (repeat all directions in A) in different positions (lying down, standing up, kneeling, sitting up).

    C.   Turn (repeat all directions in A) as many different ways as you can (to the left, to the right, up, down, to one side, to the other).

    D.   Turn (repeat all directions in A) the same body parts as the child facing you.

    E.   Turn (repeat all as in A) to music.

    F.   Turn (repeat all as in A) hanging from a bar.

II. Walking and running.

    A.   Walk and run with your hands in different positions (above your head, by your sides, stretched in front of you, behind you, etc.).

    B.   Walk and run in as many ways as you can (fast, slowly, softly, loudly, high, low).

    C.   Walk and run with music—fast, slowly, softly, loudly.

    D.   Follow the leader and walk as he or she does.

    E.   Pretend to be an animal and move as the animal moves—rabbit, kangaroo, horse, frog.

III. Balancing.

    A.   Balance on a board with one foot, with both feet.

    B.   Balance with a bean bag on one foot, the other foot, one hand, the other hand, the head, your arm, shoulder.

    C.   Touch various parts of your body while balancing.

    D.   Balance on various objects (balancing board, inner tube, trampoline, teeter-totter).

IV. Pushing and pulling.

    A.   Push and pull large boxes, blocks, inner tubes, wagons, etc.

    B.   Fill box with objects (blocks, books, bean bags) and try to push and pull them. Can you? Can you with the help of a friend? With the help of five friends?

    C.   Play games such as Tug-of-War, rope pull, London Bridge.

V. Skipping and galloping. Some children will not be able to skip until first grade.

    A.   Hop on one foot and then the other. (This movement helps children learn to skip).

    B.   Skip and gallop in different directions (front, back, sideways).

    C.   Skip and gallop in different ways—slowly, fast, high, low. Skip in a pattern on the floor such as a triangle, circle, square.

    D.   Skip with different objects—skip rope, skip and bounce a ball, skip while throwing and catching a bean bag or yarn ball, skip and hit a balloon and keep it swinging.

VI. Crawling and jumping.

    A.   Crawl and jump like an animal (snake, caterpillar, ant, toad, grasshopper, bear).

    B.   Crawl under obstacles—broom handle between two chairs, rope, nesting bridge, chair, slide.

    C.   Jump over obstacles—rope, board, box, hoop, wide piece of paper taped to the floor, stick, candle (play Jack Be Nimble, etc.).

D.   Jump off an obstacle—box, step, rung of a ladder, jungle gym.
E.   Jump and crawl in different ways—fast, slowly, forward, backward, with one hand on head, hands behind back, touching parts of the body.

body awareness

A child learns the names of body parts and discovers what they can be made to do.

I.   Place objects on different parts of the body.
   A.   Put the bean bag on your shoulders, head, arm, knee, feet.
   B.   Put your finger on your head, nose, chest. Play "Simon Says."
   C.   Hold up your finger. Touch it with your knee, arm, hand.
   D.   Close your eyes and touch your foot, your head, your shoulder.
II.   Propel objects with different parts of the body.
   A.   Hit the balloon with your head, shoulder, knee, hand.
   B.   Move the bean bag from one foot to another without using your hands, from one hand to another, from one arm to another.
III.   Trace the outline of your friend on a piece of paper. Have a friend or teacher trace yours.
   A.   Draw in the features and the clothes.
   B.   Paint or color the outline. (Painting is less fatiguing for the child.)
IV.   Explore the different ways body parts move.
   A.   Move the parts of your body—elbows, legs, fingers, hands—in as many ways as you can
   B.   Look in the mirror. Observe your body parts as they move. "Does the image in the mirror change when you move your body?"
   C.   Lie on your back. Put your feet in the air.
      1.   In how many ways can you use your feet—to make circles, squares, numbers, letters?
      2.   How many ways can you move your feet-up and down, sideways, backward, forward?
      3.   What can you make your hands do? (Clap, touch, shake, squeeze.)
   D.   Lie on your stomach.
      1.   What can you do with your feet? Legs? Arms?
      2.   Move your left leg out. Put your right arm up.
      3.   Move your right leg out. Move your left arm up.
      4.   Move your left leg out. Move your left arm up.
      5.   Move your right leg out. Move your right arm up.
      6.   Move your right arm up. Move your right leg out.
V.   Use creative movements.
   A.   Make yourself tall, small, thin, wide.
   B.   Pretend to be a tree, dog, ball, clown.
   C.   Roll like a dog, hop like a rabbit.
   D.   Move from one end of the room to the other on your back, on your stomach, on your side, with your feet still, with your arms still, on your hands and knees.

I can make myself as tall as a tree.

VI. Discover the size of body parts.
   A. Move your hand down your arm, leg, face. Where does the body part start and where does it stop?
   B. Put your hand around your wrist. Do your fingers meet?

spatial awareness

The child learns how much space the body occupies and how it relates to other objects in space.

I. Draw geometric shapes on the playground or indoors with chalk or tape on the floor.
   A. Walk around the shapes, inside, over, beside.
   B. Make yourself as small as you can inside the shape, as large as you can.
   C. Walk from one shape to another.
      1. Put one hand inside the circle and one foot inside the square.
      2. Put your right hand in the square and your left foot in the triangle.
   D. Walk backward and forward from one shape to another.
II. Place your body inside a box.
   A. Find a box that is big enough for you. Make yourself as small as you can.
   B. Find a box that you and your friend(s) can fit inside. How many children will fit inside the box?

III.   Make a shape with your body.
    A.   Make a big circle, little circle, big triangle, little triangle.
    B.   Make a snake, snowman, letter S, tree, and the letter O.
    C.   Make anything you want to make. Let us guess what it is.

IV.   Throw objects at different shapes.
    A.   Throw bean bags, yarn balls, darts at different shapes drawn or painted on a stand-up or suspended board.
    B.   Throw objects at shapes drawn on the floor or ground. At Halloween this could be a jack-o'-lantern with triangles for eyes, a square for a mouth, and a circle for a nose. Try a Santa Claus face, a heart face, an Easter rabbit, a snowman.

V.   Move among objects without touching them.
    A.   Move through a maze of objects. Move between, over, under, inside, and around objects.
    B.   Move through a maze walking, jumping, sliding, hopping.

VI.   Complete an obstacle course (preferably on the playground).
    A.   Walk on footprints or carpet squares placed on the floor or ground. Step inside shoe boxes.
    B.   Crawl, climb, walk through large pieces of equipment. Crawl through a tunnel, jump into a tire, climb into and out of a box, walk over a board, climb a ladder, slide down a board and land on two feet. The obstacle courses should be changed often.
    C.   Memorize a short obstacle course. Try to move through it with your eyes closed. (Teacher must be nearby to help.)

VII.   Judge the distance from one object to another.
    A.   Throw a bean bag backwards and try to hit a waste paper basket, a box, or a target drawn on the floor.
    B.   Estimate the number of steps to a point on the floor, an object, a line.
        1.   How many small steps does it take?
        2.   How many running steps does it take? Hops? Jumps? Skips?

VIII.   Go on a treasure hunt.
    A.   Use a picture map indoors with clues from 1 to 5. Follow the clues:
        1.   Start at the door and take three hops forward.
        2.   Crawl through the tunnel.
        3.   Take four steps forward.
        4.   Jump inside the circle.
        5.   Climb up the ladder to find the treasure (pretty rock, seashell, seed).
    B.   Go outside and follow the picture map.
        1.   Walk to the big tree.
        2.   Jump to the slide.
        3.   Look under the slide; the treasure is here.
    C.   Follow the picture map—showing lines drawn between each familiar object in the playground.
        1.   Go to the tree.
        2.   Go to the water table.

           3.   Go to the slide.

           4.   Go back to the tree.

           5.   Go to the sandbox and find the treasure.

IX. Move your body through space.

    A.   Run, walk, hop, jump; slide across the room from one point to another, from one object to another, from one color to another.

    B.   Explain different ways to move in space. Which are faster, slower, easier, more difficult?

X. Follow directional commands.

    A.   Use a walking board, a balance beam, or a ladder lying flat on the floor or ground.

        1.   Walk backward (two spaces on the ladder, etc.).

        2.   Walk forward (three spaces).

        3.   Walk sideways.

        4.   Turn around on the board, etc.

        5.   Walk forward, turn around, come back, walk backward.

    B.   Use an object such as a ball, balloon, a bean bag.

        1.   Throw the ball *over* your shoulder.

        2.   Throw the ball *in front of* you.

        3.   Throw the ball *to the left.*

        4.   Throw the bag *between* your legs.

        5.   Throw the ball *to the right.*

        6.   Etc.

    C.   Use your body to move in different ways.

        1.   Creep forward, backward, sideways (left hand with left knee, right hand with right knee).

        2.   Walk (starting on left foot with left hand pointing to left toes, right hand stretched behind, then pointing to right toes).

        3.   Hop (on the left foot, right foot, to the left, right, forward, backward).

        4.   Jump over a rope. (Raise rope slightly on each try.) Go under rope. (Lower rope with each try.)

        5.   Lie on your back. Throw a bean bag with your left hand and catch it with your left hand, right hand; throw with your left hand, catch with your right.

        6.   Run (forward 10 steps, backward 3 steps, to the right 5 steps, to the left 6 steps).

temporal awareness

A child develops a time structure within the body and learns to coordinate movements. "Eye-hand coordination" and "eye-foot coordination" refer to a child's ability to coordinate movements.

    I. Move to a drumbeat.

        A.   The teacher beats the drum in an even rhythm.

            1.   Clap your hands with the beat (in place).

       2.   Move parts of your body—arms, head, hands—with the drumbeat (in place).

       3.   Move several parts of your body—feet and legs, head and hands—with the drumbeat (in place).

       4.   Move your body in space—walk, slide, hop—with the drumbeat. (Move faster when beat is faster.)

  B.   The teacher beats the drum in an uneven rhythm. Do steps 1 to 3 as in A.

       4.   Move your body in space (skip, hop).

  C.   The teacher varies the drumbeat. Do steps 1 to 4 as in A.

  D.   Play a rhythm instrument with even and uneven drumbeats.

  E.   Move your body to uneven and even beats played with various rhythm instruments.

  F.   Respond rhythmically to a piano selection or record. (Beat may change but must be distinct; a piano recording is best.)

II. Make up your own responses to rhythms.

  A.   Make up your own beat.

  B.   Move around the room to your own beat.

  C.   Listen and respond to the beats of other children.

III. Free body movements.

  A.   Move around the room, gym, or outdoor area in any way you choose (a few children at a time).

  B.   Move around the room avoiding physical obstacles.

  C.   Move around room, stop on command, "freeze," "clap hands." Begin on command, "start" or "begin," "clap hands."

  D.   Move freely to a rhythmic selection (distinct tempo).

  E.   Repeat B through D. (Teacher may take record off or stop piano in repeat of C.)

IV. Throw objects at a moving target or targets.

  A.   Try to toss an object into a waste basket, box, or barrel while it is moving. (Teacher can attach string and pull.)

  B.   Throw bean bag or balls through a swinging hoop, rolling hoop, or rolling tire.

V. Act out pretend activities (in sequential order). These activities may be done in the room or outside in small groups.

  A.   Fly a kite.

  B.   Slide down a slide.

  C.   Put on clothes.

  D.   Ride a tricycle or bicycle.

  E.   Throw a ball.

  F.   Take a bath.

  G.   Go to the store.

  H.   Wake in the morning.

VI. Act out pretend activities to a musical selection. (Make up your own activities.) These activities may be carried out in the classroom, gym, or outside if there is an extension cord for a record player.

  A.   Be a child going to sleep, waking up on Christmas morning, and finding toys under the tree.

We're rockets going to the moon.

    B.   Be a rabbit hiding Easter eggs. Run behind a bush and watch children finding the eggs.

    C.   Be a child going for "Trick or Treat" on Halloween night.

    D.   Be a child on the moon, on Mars, or out in space.

VII.   Use your hands and eyes together (eye-hand coordination).

    A.   Bat a balloon or yarn ball with a nylon paddle or with your hand. Keep it up in the air. Bat the balloon with different parts of your body.

    B.   Bounce a ball as many times as you can.

    C.   Throw a ball to a friend or to a teacher and catch it when he or she throws it back.

    D.   Toss a ball or a bean bag into a bucket, a waste basket.

    E.   String beads, put puzzles together, place pegs in a pegboard, put construction toys together, place nesting blocks on top of each other, stack as many blocks as you can without letting them fall.

    F.   Hit a plastic or yarn ball extended from a string. Keep the ball moving with your hand or with a stick.

VIII.   Use feet and hands together (eye-foot coordination).

    A.   Kick a balloon with your foot. Keep it in the air as long as you can.

    B.   Kick a yarn ball; keep kicking it as it moves along the floor. See how long you can keep it moving.

    C.   Kick a football as far as you can, as high as you can.

    D.   Kick a suspended ball. See how long you can keep it moving.

    E.   Jump over a moving rope. Move faster as the rope moves faster.

    F.   Jump off a low box, a higher and higher box.

    G.   Jump over a rope. Jump higher as the rope is raised higher.

    H.   Keep your eyes closed. Jump as high as you can. Hop on one foot,

then the other. Kick a football in front of you, back of you, to one side of you.
l.   Climb up a box, jungle gym, ladder, steep hill.

meeting goals

The teacher makes a checklist for each child. The behavioral objectives or goals determined prior to instruction (Goals of Movement Education, p. 23) are checked as the child reaches the objective. The chart on page 41 is an example of a checklist using the objectives for movement education in this chapter.

The checklist serves as a record of behavior. In order to record the child's behavior accurately and efficiently, a teacher must use a combination of methods for collecting data.

methods for collecting data

learning centers

Teachers may keep a notebook and pencil in each learning center. They and their aides record specific kinds of behaviors that occur in various centers. Such as the child's choice and use of equipment, the child's conversation(s), and the length of time spent in the center. Notebooks should be analyzed each week and pertinent information recorded on the checklist. Not all information gathered will refer to behaviors spelled out by the behavioral objectives. The information may be, in some cases, more important than that recorded on the checklist: A child commented in the indoor movement center, "I don't want to sit on the floor. I might get my clothes dirty." After careful observations the teacher discovered that this was Jimmy's defense against failure. The checklist would not have given the teacher a clue to Jimmy's problem.

samples of children's work

Keep a file of each child's work. Collect work samples on a regular basis, such as weekly, biweekly, or monthly. This method eliminates the chance that the work represents the child's poorest or best efforts. The area of movement education includes samples such as drawings of animals and objects in motion, stories dictated by the child about his or her movement experiences, and photographs taken by the teacher of the child engaged in movement activities.

videotapes

One of the best ways to evaluate a child's work in the psychomotor domain is to videotape him or her engaged in movement activities. A teacher can watch for specific types of motor behavior and record a child's progress. Tapes may be made on a regular basis and children's earlier movement activities compared with later activities. Pertinent information may be recorded on a child's checklist.

Movement education checklist

Name: John Brown   school: Ebenezer Avenue
date of birth: 4/10/72   year: 1977

psychomotor domain	Oct. 15	Jan 15	May 15	comments
1. Alternates feet	✔			
2. Runs using limbs in opposition		✔		
3. Jumps distance of 3 feet			✔	
4. Jumps height of 1 foot		✔		
5. Hops 50 feet in 11 seconds			✔	
6. Etc.				
cognitive domain				
1. Names and locates parts of body	✔			
2. Uses body for specific motor activities	✔			*Skilled in following directions and moving body*
3. Determines location of objects relative to self	✔			
4. Determines location of objects relative to their proximity to other objects		✔		
5. Etc.				
affective domain				
1. Open to new ideas		✔		*No longer critical of other children*
2. Confident in abilities	✔			*Very proud of accomplishments*
3. Accepts limitations				*Confident; brags somewhat*
4. Shows prejudice				*More accepting of others; confident but seldom brags*
5. Etc.				
social domain				
1. Shares equipment				*Less dictatorial*
2. Contributes words and feelings				*Able to listen to ideas of others as well as contribute own*
3. Etc.				

teacher-made informal tests

These are not written tests at the preschool level, nor should the children think of them as tests. A teacher devises a set of tasks to assess particular objectives. A teacher may want to find out if a child knows the names of the parts of the body. The teacher can play a game by asking each child to "find your nose," "find your elbow," "find your knee." If a teacher wants to know whether or not a child can skip, a Hula hoop may be placed on the floor. To begin, the child is asked to show all the ways he or she can move around the hoop. If the child makes no attempt to skip, the teacher may say, "Now walk around the hoop; run; skip." The child may follow directions with a one-legged skip or a natural skip.

anecdotal records

An anecdotal record is a description of what a child says and does. A teacher's interpretation of what happened is written later and is *separated from* the anecdote. Teachers should record behaviors that are desirable and undesirable, usual and unusual. Anecdotal records often reveal regression and/or progress in behavior.

time sampling

A time sampling is a direct record of anything a child does or says at a specific time during a given period. A child's behavior may be recorded for three minutes at 8:30 A.M. and at 10:30 A.M. each day for a week. The advantages of time samplings are that they reveal consistencies and inconsistencies in behavior.

running record

A running record is similar to a time sampling; however, behavior is recorded at any time of day and for any length of time. A direct record is kept of what a child says and does. The main advantage of this method is that a complete record of a single episode is recorded.

The anecdotal record, time sampling, and running record are all useful methods of recording behavior. When one or more of these methods is chosen, they should be used regularly and systematically. One system teachers may use is to observe a few children each day. A class of 20 children may be divided into 5 groups of 4 children. Each group is observed on a different day of the week. To remove the chance that the day of the week (bad Monday or exciting Friday) may have an effect on some children, the groups may be moved up a day each week—Monday's group to Tuesday and Friday's group to Monday. This process may continue throughout the year.

Data supplied by any of the methods suggested in this section may be analyzed and used to complete the checklist. Some data will not fit the items on the checklist. This information about the child should help a teacher make a more complete evaluation of behavior. Information, including the checklist, should be kept in a cumulative record file. This information identifies problem areas, shows improvement in behavior, and provides a springboard for parent-teacher conferences. It is crucial that no child be labeled "thief," "mentally ill," or "incorrigible" on paper or verbally. This kind of labeling may be dangerous and can do irreparable damage to children. Parents have a right to look at their children's records (according to the Buckley Amendment) and may challenge record data they feel are inaccurate, inappropriate, or misleading (Gee and Sperry, 1978, pp. R-3 to R-7).

Piagetian tasks

The Swiss psychologist Jean Piaget developed cognitive tasks dealing with moral development, number, space, time, seriation, and classification. Children's responses have been recorded and analyzed. Several tasks in the areas of spatial relations and time relations will help a teacher know how a child is thinking about space and time. One of the best ways a teacher can learn how children think of themselves and objects in space is to examine their drawings. Does a child draw a person as a large circle with two to four lines extending from it? Does he or she draw body parts, such as eyes, hands, mouth, neck, waist? Is there a baseline for the placement of objects? Can a child sight a line between two points (Task-Projection of a Straight Line)? If not, the child may have difficulty throwing a ball at a target. The Task for Spatial Representation of Self requires a child to physically portray the view of another. A child who has difficulty performing this task may have problems with activities requiring lateral knowledge, such as the Hokey Pokey and Looby Lou.

Relay races and timed competitive games do not belong in a curriculum for young children. Tasks in the area of temporal relations indicate that it is not until most children are about eight years old that they understand the interrelationship of time, distance, and speed. In a race children start and stop at the same time. They may think, however, that the classmate who gets to the finish line first has moved for a longer period of time, since he or she has traveled the greatest distance. Children think that the hands of a clock move faster when they (the children) move faster and slower when they themselves move slower. A boring ride in a car to a nearby town is considered a much longer period of time than an entire afternoon spent with a favorite friend.

Piagetian tasks that help teachers to understand children's thinking will be discussed briefly in each chapter. The book *Cognitive Tasks: An Approach for Early Childhood Education* by Janie and Keith Osborn (1974) tells the teacher how to administer the tasks and how to apply the results to the teaching of young children. This is an excellent, easy-to-understand book that all teachers of young children will find useful.

3
children are full of pleasure

learning through play

Children are fascinated by their world from the moment they enter it. They immediately begin to explore their surroundings through play. All infants and young children continue to play provided they find themselves in an environment that makes it possible. Play is possible when adults in a child's world know and understand its value.

It has been said that play is the young child's work. One thing is clear: to the child play is purposeful. Gallahue says, "To children play is serious business and it is this awareness of purpose that gives it its value" (1976, p. 114).

What is play, and why do children play? These questions have been asked for hundreds of years, with no completely satisfying answers. Many definitions for play have been offered:

Isaacs: "Play is indeed the child's work, and the means whereby he grows and develops. Active play can be looked upon as a sign of mental health; and its absence, either of some inborn defect, or of mental illness" (1968, p. 9).

Dewey: "Children do not normally play for the sake of amusement, any more than for the sake of any end beyond the action itself. They live in their actions, and these actions are called play because of certain qualities which they exhibit" (1913, p. 276).

Dictionary of Education: "Play: any pleasurable activity carried on for its own sake, without reference to ulterior purpose or future satisfactions" (Good, 1973, p. 426).

Mitchell and Mason: "People generally come to agree, when they think it through, that when any activity is itself attractive enough to make one do it, it is play" (1948, p. 111).

44

Caplan: "Play, which is a pursuit self-chosen by the child [and adult], requires an environment that makes play possible" (1973, p. 183).

Piaget: "It [play] is therefore almost pure assimilation, i.e., thought polarized by preoccupation with individual satisfaction" (1962, p. 89).

Definitions of play have certain elements in common: Play is active, self-initiated, and pleasurable. When the activity is satisfying, it is play. If, however, the activity ceases to be enjoyable, it is no longer play. In this chapter play is defined as any self-chosen activity engaged in for enjoyment. Play may be a child rocking a doll, three children playing a game of Hide and Seek, two children pouring water from one container into another, or a child making an airplane at the workbench.

There have been many theories of children's play. Spodek (1972) refers to the classical theories, which attempt to explain why children play, and the dynamic theories, which concern themselves with the content of play (p. 202). The most familiar of the classical theories are the preexercise and the recapitulation theories. In the preexercise theory, play is preparation for future work: the child practices the roles that will be assumed as a mature adult. According to the recapitulation theory, a child undergoes, in play, the stages man has undergone in the development of the race. Children climb because primitive man lived in trees; go barefoot because early man had no shoes; identify with animals because early man was close to nature, etc. Play rids a child of primitive impulses and allows him or her to mature and become an adult (Mitchell and Mason, 1948, pp. 71–77).

The dynamic theories of play accept the fact that children play, and focus on its content. Freud saw play as a way in which children worked out their real-life problems in fantasy. Through play a child reenacts painful situations until the boy or girl comes to grips with them. Play therefore becomes a cathartic activity, allowing a child to master difficult situations. From observations of play teachers can better understand a child's emotional life. Behavior that deviates from normal can be detected and the child guided toward more acceptable behavior (Holme and Massie, 1970, p. 35).

Piaget believes play is important to intellectual development. He sees it as the bridge between sensorimotor development and symbolic thought. A stick becomes a gun, a leaf a dish, a rope a snake, and a blanket a doll. This "make-believe" play stimulates thought about objects that are not present but are represented by symbols. In fact, Piaget suggests that the development of language is dependent on play. First comes experience with the object or action, then the make-believe, symbolic representation of the experience, and then the words to represent the whole experience verbally (Pulaski, 1971, pp. 96–97).

Piaget speaks of the twin processes of assimilation and accommodation. To Piaget play is pure assimilation whereas imitation is accommodation. Children assimilate new knowledge into already existing mental structures and, in so doing, distort reality to suit themselves. Play is fun; it is playful. Whenever it ceases to be playful it is no longer assimilation but accommodation. The child is now serious and attempts to adjust to the realities of the environment. This happens through imitation, which occurs whenever a child mimics or imitates anything in the environment. A boy who sees his mother dust and later picks up a rag to rub the window is imitating. Of these two processes imitation seems to come first, although play may be combined with imitation and vice versa. When Piaget speaks of play (assimilation) he is talking about make-believe play.

What happens to make-believe as children grow up? Piaget feels that some of it is internalized in the form of day dreaming. He suggests that the imagination needed for make-believe is used by the adult in the forms of creativity, originality, and flexibility. Play, therefore, is necessary not only to the intellectual development of children but also to their creative development (Pulaski, 1972, p. 116).

The power of play cannot be ignored. It serves the total development of a child. It encourages interpersonal relations, stimulates creativity and joy in living, enhances physical development, and advances learning. Miller (1972) says:

Play fosters and maximizes children's growth and development. It is necessary for the maturation of children. Play is a great natural urge of children from infancy to adulthood through which they gain significant learnings in the cognitive, affective, and psychomotor domains. Play for children *is* simultaneously a cognitive, psychomotor, and affective experience. (p. 5)

The teacher's role in play ranges from passive observer to active play partner. Research has indicated that when children do not play, it is possible through teacher interaction to help them become active participants and to improve the quality of their play.

Smilansky (1968) found that disadvantaged children did not engage in high levels of symbolic play and that non-symbolic-playing children failed to do well in formal schooling and to acquire such basic skills as reading and writing. She also found that a combination of concrete, real-life experiences and planned teacher intervention was more effective in enriching the sociodramatic play of disadvantaged children than either method alone. Some successful techniques of planned teacher intervention were found to be asking questions, making suggestions, and actively entering into the child's play.

Whiren (1975) discusses four kinds of teacher-child interactions that lead a child to learning basic concepts through the use of play materials. The first phase is exploration. During this phase the teacher provides space and a comfortable working area, protects the child from interruptions, and gives *time* to complete explorations. The second phase is expansion. This is when the teacher describes what the child has done, "You have put all the pegs in the peg holes," or comments on the way the child is experimenting, "You are looking for a block to finish the roof of your building." Expansion is used to provide words for the child in a meaningful context. This method is particularly effective in working with disadvantaged children who may be nonverbal. The third phase is teacher-initiated activity. The teacher may invite the child to explore a material or suggest a more complex level of exploration: "What would happen if you added blue food coloring?" This type of guidance is not the same as the fourth phase, teacher-directed behavior that is expected to carry out an activity: "It's time to go outside now," or "In this game you take a card from the top of the pile," or "Put the puzzle back into the puzzle rack." Teacher-directed behavior should be used sparingly if children are to become self-directed and independent (pp. 418 – 419).

In a study reported by Wolfgang (1976) the role of the teacher in dramatic play is described on a continuum from structured to open. Wolfgang suggests that, in working with nonplayers, a teacher first establish a child's trust through physical contact—taking the child's hand, holding the child on the teacher's lap, etc. Second, a teacher should help the child to imitate and become aware of body parts: "Show me your mouth, nose," or "Do what I do." Third, a teacher helps a child learn that he or she can cause something to happen to objects. A teacher may demonstrate finger painting, easel painting, water play. Next the child is encouraged to repeat the teacher's actions. Fourth, the child plays out symbolically a simple dramatic theme. The teacher exhibits a simple action that has a beginning, a middle, and an ending; for example, the teacher dresses a doll and asks the child to repeat the actions. The teacher supports the child's play and gradually becomes an onlooker. Fifth, the teacher helps the child acquire the ability to play with others to produce sociodramatic play. This may be done by bringing together two players and one nonplayer. The teacher may join in their play while the nonplayer watches and then ask the nonplayer to take over the teacher's role. The teacher continues to support the nonplayer through questions and suggestions. The child should gradually become an active social player. Ultimately the teacher becomes an onlooker. Wolfgang cautions teachers against using these steps as a recipe, rather they should feel free to experiment, alter, and enrich the activities to fit the situation (p. 126).

The importance of stimulating environments for spontaneous play experiences is discussed by Anker, et al. (1974). They point out that children have a strong desire to investigate their environment and to make sense out of their world. Learning opportunities through play occur in *all* centers of interest as children interact with materials. Sund and Bybee (1973) state, "Piaget believes play is food for the young child's mind. . . . Many elementary school children may be suffering from malnutrition or are starving cognitively. The learning environment should be rich in materials and time for children to interact with them" (p. 23). As children explore, a teacher can expose them to a number of concepts by a question, a word, a comment, or momentary interactions (pp. 103–213).

There are many and varied forms of play (Hartley, 1952; Herron and Sutton-Smith, 1971; Spodek, 1972) that support the development of young children. Play has been delineated into manipulative, dramatic, imaginative, spontaneous, games with rules, etc. In this chapter play will be discussed under the headings dramatic play (make-believe), free spontaneous play (release of energy), manipulative play (exploration of objects), games with rules (organized games chosen by the child), and constructive play (self-chosen activities that result in a product).

play characteristics of young children

Listed in table 3–1 are play characteristics of young children from three to six years old. They represent general characteristics of children and *do not* represent the characteristics of any one child. Each child has an individual built-in rate of growth.

table 3–1
representative play characteristics of young children

From About 3 Years	to About 6 Years of Age
1. Confuses fantasy and what is real	1. Understands the difference between reality and fantasy
2. Play has high degree of fantasy	2. Play comes closer and closer to reality
3. Cooperative play beginning	3. Cooperative play prevails
4. Frequent physical aggression	4. More verbal aggression, less physical aggression
5. Is egocentric or self-centered	5. Begins to consider the viewpoint of other children and adults
6. Play groups shift constantly	6. Establishes more stable play groups
7. Play simple and unstructured	7. Play groups more complex and more structured
8. Conflicts over playthings	8. More willingness to share toys
9. Imaginary playmates may appear	9. Imaginary playmates usually disappear
10. Language beginning to accompany symbolic play	10. More words used to represent objects and situations
11. Practice games (stringing beads, walking on balance beam, piling up blocks)	11. Emergence of games with rules
12. Humor takes the form of gestures	12. Gestures and language jokes

goals for development through play

The following goals for development through play have been chosen as realistic ones for a teacher to select since they can be achieved by the majority of children from ages three to six. Since play affects the development of the whole child, objectives are written in the cognitive, affective, social, and psychomotor domains. It is important to remember that not all the objectives will be reached by the time a child is five or six. The objectives are listed as a guide for a teacher in planning and as one source for evaluating play behaviors.

COGNITIVE DOMAIN.   A child:

1.   Uses various processes (classifying, seriating, observing, predicting) in play to solve problems
2.   Combines materials, words, and/or symbols in a unique way during the play experience
3.   Shows through dramatic play an interest and knowledge gained through experience
4.   Assumes a role and expresses it through make-believe play
5.   Substitutes movements or verbal actions for real objects and situations
6.   Plays in a way that becomes more realistic and structured (five to six years)

AFFECTIVE DOMAIN.   A child:

1.   Assumes roles in order to dramatize situations with which he or she must cope
2.   Shows by actions and words that he or she is open to the ideas and suggestions of other children
3.   Shows through actions and words (smiling, laughing, jumping with joy, "I like this," "It's fun!" "Let's do it again.") that he or she enjoys play experiences

SOCIAL DOMAIN.   A child:

1.   Shares playthings with other children
2.   Solves conflicts with other children through verbalization rather than physical aggression
3.   Persists in a play episode with other children for at least 10 to 15 minutes (five to six years), 5 to 10 minutes (three to five years)

PSYCHOMOTOR DOMAIN.   A child:

1.   Develops eye-hand coordination by stacking blocks, painting pictures, setting the table, putting together construction toys and puzzles, putting on and taking off doll clothes
2.   Develops large and small muscles by running, walking a beam, climbing, throwing
3.   Develops eye-foot coordination by climbing, jumping, kicking

indoor learning centers

environment

Play may be defined as any activity chosen by a child for enjoyment. According to this definition children play in *all* learning centers, however, certain conditions encourage play. First, children must have the freedom to choose the center in which they want to play, and second, they must be able to explore materials freely as long as they do not interfere with the rights of others. A kindergarten teacher was overheard saying to a child, "You can't play with blocks today. You have played with them for two days." The child looked ashamed and walked away. It is hoped that he did not have feelings of guilt and would return to the blocks another day. Another incident was observed in a nursery school. A four-year-old girl and boy were playing with puppets in the homemaking center and decided to take the puppets for a walk. As they left the center with the puppets the teacher intervened and told them to keep the puppets in the center. She asked the children what kind of puppet each had. Bill replied, "Spider Man," and Joan, "the Tooth Fairy." The teacher refused to accept either name and continued to question the children. Perplexed, they repeated what they had said previously. The teacher, in desperation, said, "This is a boy puppet and this is a girl puppet." The children dutifully repeated the "correct" names for the teacher. As she left the center Bill threw his puppet into the refrigerator and slammed the door. Joan put her puppet under the plastic sink. The puppets had become a source of guilt and frustration to the children. Their play had ended.

This same nursery school group was observed over a period of three months. Gradually dramatic play and most other forms of play ceased. The children became regimented, principally concerned with pleasing the teacher. There was less laughter and less conversation. In almost every center the children were encouraged to listen to the teacher, please her, and not interrupt when she was talking. "Miss J. is talking and wants you to listen," was often heard. One child, after interrupting a story to ask about Easter, was told, "Keep quiet." Later Jim was told that the children would dye Easter eggs at Easter. Jim's reply was, "Oh, I don't think I'll be here then. I think I'll be in Heaven. I have lots of friends there." This seemed to be Jim's way of telling the teacher that school really didn't matter. The further away from school he was the better. When asked what his teacher liked best he replied, "quiet," and when asked what she didn't like he replied, "noise." This teacher had a master's degree in early childhood education, but one wonders where she developed her understanding of children and the preschool curriculum.

In a classroom where play is valued there will be laughter, smiling faces, and lots of activity as children pursue their interests. Manipulative play may occur at the science center as children explore equipment. Two little girls were observed playing with magnets. They were having a race to find out which magnet would pick up the most paper clips. The music center is often the scene of dramatic play as children pretend to be animals or objects while they move their bodies to music. The manipulative center encourages constructive play as children make constructions and play airport, zoo, and spaceship. There is no center that is not permeated with the play of children.

choice of play centers

Teachers sometimes become concerned when children play in the same center for several days. One of the best ways to motivate children to explore many centers is to capitalize on their interests. Block lovers can be persuaded to spend time in other centers by careful questions and thoughtful comments: "Would you like to write a sign for your building? Why don't you go to the writing table?" or "There are some books on the library table about buildings. Choose one you would like me to read." Again, "Your building is interesting. Would you like to paint a picture of it to take home?" One teacher complained that three little boys never went to the art center. When another teacher met the children he said, "You have pretty valentines in your room. I would like to have some to decorate my apartment. Could you make some for me?" All three children hurried to the art center to make valentines. Their teacher took a Polaroid picture of them in the art center. The boys were very proud of their picture and put it on the bulletin board. After this experience they began to come to the art center more often. Apparently they did not know how much they had been missing before. This activity was not play since the children were asked to make valentines; however, the visitor's suggestion led to the self-selection of other centers.

Under certain circumstances a particular center may be closed for a week or for several weeks. This may be done to encourage children to explore a variety of centers. Centers may sometimes be closed temporarily for other reasons also. The woodworking center may not be available until more wood arrives or the block center may be closed since, "We are having a party and won't have time to put the blocks away." A skillful teacher can think of many ways to expand children's interests. Some centers can be removed and new ones introduced. A homemaking center may be replaced by nesting chair blocks that give children an opportunity to make their own constructions.

influence of tv

Play that becomes too aggressive, or too loud or interferes with the rights of other children should be discouraged. Since children act out the heroes and heroines they see on TV, their dramatic play has become increasingly aggressive. The teacher is often helpless to direct children from destructive to more constructive play. One way to combat the effect of TV on play is to encourage parents to control their children's TV watching. Often parents are not aware of the effects TV can have on their children. Parent meetings about TV watching and articles and lists of suggested readings placed on the parents' bulletin board are helpful. One of the best ways to encourage constructive dramatic play is to give children a common experience (going to the grocery store, a restaurant, a turkey farm) to which they all can relate in their play.

dramatic-play center

The dramatic-play center (family living, housekeeping center) has been a part of the kindergarten curriculum since the turn of the century. It is felt that this center represents a common denominator for all children. Cooking, sleeping, dish washing, and caring for the young are considered a part of every home. This concept of the home is partially true, but family living patterns vary.

In dramatic play children reflect the culture in which they live. Two little girls were observed playing "pregnant" by stuffing doll clothes inside their pants. They talked about wanting a baby boy. These sisters came from a disadvantaged family where five girls were crowded into one bedroom. Their mother was pregnant and had expressed a desire for a boy. The girls were pretending to be grownup ladies like their mother.

A teacher can tell a great deal about the everyday life of children by listening to their conversations in their dramatic play. In one nursery school a boy and girl discussed their make-believe plans for the afternoon. The father said, "Keep the children quiet. I am working on my dissertation." The mother, carrying a doll in her arms, replied, "Don't worry, dear. I'll take the children to the playground." These children lived in a housing development on a university campus. A large part of their dramatic play centered around Daddy's schoolwork.

It seems to be a temptation for teachers to set up an elaborate dramatic-play center, often taking up the space needed for two centers. Perhaps this is because too much emphasis has been placed on a stereotyped center or because most teachers of young children are women. They may think of the center as "cute" or "fun" for girls to play in. Often boys do not participate because they are made to feel, directly or indirectly, that this is not a place for them.

One five-year-old boy told his mother he did not like school. When asked why, he replied, "The housekeeping center is babyish. There is nothing but old dishes and dolls. It's just babyish." The center in question had no boy dolls or boys' clothes, no dress-up clothes for boys, and no equipment to use for building additional structures. It is important to remember that the homemaking center is for girls and boys.

LOCATION.   The dramatic-play center is relatively noisy. An ideal location is next to the block area. Play begun in the dramatic-play center spills over into the block center and vice versa. A group of children were acting out their trip to the local nature museum. They had arranged the dramatic-play center to resemble the foyer of the museum. The puppet stage was used as a counter where tickets were purchased. The sink, cupboard, and stove, with their doors open, were used to display items for sale, such as miniature animals, cars, toys, and books. After rearranging the center and playing there for several days, the children felt they did not have enough room for the mounted animals (stuffed animals they had brought from home). They asked the children playing in the block center if they could use the blocks to build display cases. An agreement was reached, and the animals were placed in display cases built with the blocks.

There were eight children involved in dramatic play in the make-believe museum. One child sold tickets, another sold gifts, and a third was the museum guide for five children. This dramatic play continued for approximately 2 weeks and involved 15 different children.

EQUIPMENT AND SUPPLIES.   A teacher should choose a few standard pieces of equipment supplemented by items that children can use to build whatever is necessary for their play. It is unwise to buy complex equipment such as a washing machine, dryer, and electric mixer. This equipment takes up space needed for other centers and does little to enhance dramatic play.

Large equipment for the dramatic-play center may include: (all items must be child-size)

Stove.
Sink, refrigerator, and cupboard.
Table and chairs.
Ironing board and iron.
Standing shatterproof mirror.
Doll bed(s).
Doll carriage.
Rocking chair, large pillow or bean bag.
Chest of drawers for doll clothes.
Nesting chair blocks. (Ten to 20 blocks are adequate to build a stove, sink, refrigerator, tables, chairs, beds, store.)
Two telephones.
Stuffed animals.
Cash register and play money.
Plastic play food. (Not necessary unless budget permits. Children can use play dough or earth clay to make food.)

Other equipment and supplies to include are:

Black male and female dolls.
White male and female dolls.
Oriental male and female dolls.   ⎫ If children of these groups are in
Spanish American male and female dolls. ⎭ the class.
Girl and boy doll clothes (bought or made).
Set of cooking utensils.
Tea set.
Flatwear.
Screen to divide kitchen and bedroom.
Boy and girl dress-up clothes. (These may be teacher-made. It is best to make skirts and blouses, shirts, and pants child size so that children will not trip over clothes that are too long. Homemade clothes that can be easily put on and taken off are better than discarded grown-up clothes that are difficult for young children to wear. High heels may be unsafe and are not necessary.)
Boy and girl dress-up hats.

TEACHER'S ROLE.   It is not always easy for a teacher to know what role to take in dramatic play. There are times when this role is primarily one of setting the stage for play and other times when the role is more direct. A teacher may look on, ask questions, make comments, offer suggestions, or assume a role for the children to imitate.

In every group there are children who are highly imaginative and engage easily in sociodramatic play. There are also children who are imaginative and want to play but are left out because they hang back or are not popular with the other children. They may be shy, aggressive, physically unattractive, or physically handicapped. Then there are those who can be called "nonplayers," children who do not know how to play. They may be from disadvantaged homes or from highly educated middle-class homes. How a teacher handles each type of child will either encourage or discourage sociodramatic play. The skilled child with the ability to initiate roles, to make believe with objects, and to interact with other children needs only the teacher's support in play. A teacher must assume a more directive role to help the child who is left out and the nonplayer.

One five-year-old who had difficulty "learning to play" came from a highly educated, upper-middle-class home. He was born when his parents were in their early forties and had lost all hope of having a child. Don grew up overprotected, isolated from other children, and discouraged from dramatic play. He was taken out of nursery school because the teacher had allowed him to "sit on the floor in a public place." The situation was so critical that Don was not admitted to kindergarten until his parents had promised not to interfere with the program. During the first few weeks of school Don, in disbelief, stood watching the children play and made no attempt to approach. He was able to engage in constructive and manipulative play: working puzzles, painting, and experimenting with magnets. He was very bright and could read and comprehend at sixth-grade level. Socially, physically, and emotionally, however, his behavior was that of a three-year-old child. His only means of communicating with the children was to say, "How do you do?" and to cry if they laughed at him or if he did not get his way.

The teacher introduced Don to make-believe by joining the children in their play. Don was very surprised and asked her why she played with the children. She replied, "It's fun to pretend" and "I'm interested in knowing what the children are playing." Neither answer satisfied him. Her next step was to try to engage him in dramatic play. She chose the outdoor sand center. One day she filled a pie pan with sand and gave it to him. He imitated her and handed her a pan, saying, "Here." She said, "Oh, it's delicious. I like cherry pie." Don was confused and with a look that said, "Teacher, you're crazy," said, "It's only sand." He continued to take the same attitude toward play but gradually began to stand outside play groups watching and laughing, apparently enjoying what the children were doing. Attempts by the children to include him in their play were rejected.

One day the children and teacher observed a pipeline being laid to a new building across the street. Don was fascinated. He ran to the sandpile, dug a hole, and placed a stick horizontally across the bottom of the hole. He called to the teacher, pointed to the hole, and said, "Look, that's my pipeline. I'm pretending."

After this incident Don began to engage in "pretend" play. However, he seldom engaged in sociodramatic play. It is difficult to know how much permanent emotional and social damage had been done to this child. We do know that he was not able to live his kindergarten year to its fullest. This illustration, although extreme, shows how difficult it can be to help a child learn to play when he or she has never played before.

The teacher may have to be as directive with the left-out and/or aggressive child as with the nonplayer. Kindergarten children began to play "restaurant" in the dramatic-play center. They were motivated by their trips with parents to places like Hardee's, McDonald's, and Dairy Queen. Their play continued for several days, which indicated a sustained interest in the topic. Notes were taken of the children's conversations as they acted out various roles. From their notes the teacher and aide found that the children had little information about restaurants and the roles of people who worked there. It was decided to visit a McDonald's restaurant in order to give the children a common experience. The teacher and aide made a visit to McDonald's and arranged for the children to eat lunch on consecutive days in groups of 10. They discussed the things they wanted the manager to tell the children. In addition the teacher and aide agreed to discuss good table manners during their lunch at McDonald's. They had observed the children's disregard for manners in their dramatic play and during snack time.

During the tour the manager pointed out the importance of keeping meat cold, ordering food in large quantities, wearing hats while cooking, and having different people to handle food and money. After a tour the children were allowed to fix their own drinks before they were served hamburgers. While they ate, table manners were discussed, such as using a napkin to wipe the mouth, staying at the table until everyone finished eating, talking in a moderate voice, and putting cartons, cups, and napkins in the waste basket.

After the trip the children's dramatic play became more realistic. The puppet stage became the food-order counter. Pencils and pads were used to write the customer's orders. The refrigerator was turned on its side with the door open and it became the meat counter for make-believe hamburgers. The teacher entered into the play whenever she felt suggestions were needed. The children made hamburgers from brown construction paper, and the paper tore in a short time. The teacher asked, "What else could you use to make your hamburgers? Can you think of something that will not tear? What can you use for french fries?" It was decided to use play dough for meat and styrofoam chips for french fries. The next day the teacher ordered food. She asked, "How will you remember my order if you don't write it down? [Most will scribble.] Where will I sit to eat my food?" Until the teacher asked to eat in the restaurant, the children had not arranged an area for eating. They immediately removed some furniture from the dramatic-play center and replaced it with large nesting blocks that they used to make tables and chairs.

As the teacher and aide took part in the play, they made comments to support the children in their dramatic play. "I see that you remembered to wear your hats while fixing the food" or "It's a good idea to write down each order. This way you can check to see that each customer gets what was ordered." Again, "The kitchen looks neat and clean. You remembered to throw your cartons and papers away." The children's play became more structured, less chaotic, and more realistic.

The more aggressive children assumed the role of manager over the protests of the other children. On a few occasions the teacher asked to be the manager. She gave orders in a pleasant voice, and gradually the more aggressive children began to model their behavior after hers. The teacher made a list of the children's names and asked them to check off their names after they had had a turn as manager. This idea worked well; the more aggressive children gave up their role as manager after one turn and either left the center or were satisfied to assume other roles.

One very shy child brought her doll with her to the restaurant. She stood on the fringes of the center but would not enter. The teacher invited Joan to have lunch with her, and Joan quickly accepted. Joan ordered the food and brought it to the table, where she and the teacher ate and talked. Joan said she wanted to be a cook. When it was the teacher's turn to be the manager she hired Joan as a cook. Gradually Joan felt more at ease and assumed several roles. With the teacher's help Joan's play had developed into true sociodramatic play.

A teacher's role as an observer is crucial if children are to engage in sociodramatic play. On one occasion a four-year-old group was talking about summer fun. This topic led to a discussion of what their fathers and mothers did in the summer. Since the nursery school was on a university campus, most of the children said that their parents went to school or taught school. The children were invited to visit the university elementary school where one of the mothers taught.

After their visit the nursery school teacher set up areas of the room to resemble elementary school classrooms. Three centers were arranged with a small chalkboard, chalk, books, pictures, and chairs. The children were delighted with the centers and began to play immediately. Their play continued for 30 minutes. The teacher then called the children together. She assigned a role to each child and discussed the role with the child. The children went back to their areas and began to play. Dissatisfaction was shown immediately over the assigned roles with comments such as "I don't want to be the teacher," "I don't want to write on the board," "Change places with me," and "I'm not playing any more." The play stopped in less than 10 minutes. The teacher had lost sight of the definition of play. She had forced children into roles they did not want or were not ready to assume. She saw her mistake and said, "The children were playing fine before I interrupted." Then she allowed the children to play in their own way. She intervened only when she felt that the children would benefit from her comments or suggestions.

block center

LOCATION.   An ideal location for this center is next to the dramatic-play center for reasons discussed in the previous section. The center should be carpeted and be approximately 20 feet by 15 feet (6.1 meters by 4.6 meters). When space permits it is desirable to have two separate block areas. Different kinds of unit blocks and accessories may be placed in each center or hollow blocks in one center and unit blocks in the other.

Unit blocks may have as many as 13 shapes based on a unit, with a variety of sizes in multiples of this unit. While they do not permit large constructions that children can enter, they can be used to build complicated structures for extensive dramatic play.

Many teachers will have space for only one block center. Unit blocks and hollow blocks may be combined or unit blocks used exclusively. They are more versatile, take up less space, and meet the needs of a wider age range.

There are too many people in the garage.

EQUIPMENT AND SUPPLIES.   There are many types of blocks on the market. Some have cleated ends, some have hand grips, and others are designed with nuts and bolts. Some are made of heavy cardboard. The cardboard blocks are suitable for three-year-olds, whose block structures are not as stable as those of older children, however, three-year-olds should be introduced gradually to the large hollow and smaller unit blocks. Although plastic and vinyl blocks are also available, it is best to purchase the fine-grained wooden blocks. The natural color and fine grain provide simplicity that allows for many and varied constructions.

Blocks should be arranged on wide, open shelves so that children can see at a glance the block they want to use. Many teachers mark the shelves with the outlines of the blocks to help children in finding and putting them away. If possible two shelves should be used with the same kinds of blocks on each shelf. This arrangement avoids having too many children in one area and assists a child in finding choices quickly. From time to time the blocks may be rearranged for interest and to enhance visual discrimination.

Accessories, such as small transportation toys, people, and animals, sometimes distract children from building with blocks. Therefore it is usually better to wait until a few weeks after school begins to put out the accessories. On the other hand, accessories sometimes encourage play with blocks. A teacher should observe the children and then decide when it is best to introduce accessories.

A bulletin board in the block area has many advantages. A teacher can display drawings, paintings, and magazine pictures of buildings, photographs of constructions, and any photographs taken of children playing with blocks. One group of graduate students made a variety of small, three-dimensional blocks out of cardboard. Small tacks were taped on one side of the cardboard blocks so that children could attach them to a bulletin board. Playing with the cardboard models encouraged play with real blocks. Sometimes children used the real blocks to copy what they had arranged on the bulletin board. At other times they used the paper blocks to copy the constructions built with the real blocks.

Equipment for the block center may include:

Small, colored blocks in a variety of shapes
Unit blocks—approximately 200 to 400 of various shapes
Large, hollow blocks—open- or closed-sided, about 20 to 40
Cardboard blocks for younger children
Small trucks and cars
Construction workers, both black and white—wooden or rubber
Families, both black and white—wooden or rubber
Zoo and farm animals—wooden or rubber
Dinosaurs—wooden or rubber
Miniature traffic signs

TEACHER'S ROLE.   In the section on dramatic-play centers techniques were given for stimulating and sustaining children's dramatic play. The teacher's role in block play is similar to the role in any other form of sociodramatic play. A kindergarten group visited a turkey farm before Thanksgiving. The next day they drew free-hand drawings of the turkeys, cut them out, and put them on the bulletin board inside a large paper fence made by the teacher. This activity started an interest in building fences, farmyards, and farmhouses. The teacher added small people and turkeys to the other block accessories. The children used these with unit blocks to build turkey farms and extended their play to the large, hollow blocks outside. They built large pens and pretended to be turkeys or farmers. Outdoor play continued until other animals were included and it was necessary to build more fences and eventually a house for the farmer and his children.

One Halloween a kindergarten teacher put up a child-teacher bulletin board in the block area. She made a haunted house with windows and doors that opened. The children made ghosts and goblins for the house. To the teacher's surprise the children's interest in the bulletin board carried over to the block center. The children built a block house, set up housekeeping, and pretended to be all kinds of spooky creatures. The family of spooks changed in composition but the idea of the haunted house remained. Children visited the house and were welcomed by the friendly spooks. Later the children used the haunted house as a home they visited for "Trick or Treat."

outdoor dramatic-play centers

LOCATION. Dramatic play occurs in any center outdoors just as it does indoors. Most of the outdoor equipment discussed in chapter 2 encourages dramatic play. Dramatic-play centers include some type of large equipment designed to stimulate a child's imagination. Children often arrange their own play areas; for example, boards with cleats and sawhorses may be placed together to make any conceivable structure from a house to the bridge of the "Three Billy Goats Gruff."

When space permits, an outdoor block center should be set up near the storage area so that blocks can easily be moved back and forth. An outdoor porch or covered area is ideal for block play. When limited space prohibits block play, a variety of large and small boxes may be used. They will not be permanent but can be replaced readily with other boxes.

EQUIPMENT AND SUPPLIES. Equipment for the outdoor dramatic-play area may include:

Log cabin
Boards with cleats, fences, sawhorses, ladders, and bridges
Tent
Low tree house
Loft—high enough to sit under and climb on
Wooden house—may be bought commercially or made from lumber

Equipment that may be used in the outdoor block area includes:

Large, hollow blocks—20 to 40
Large, open blocks—5 to 10—may be used with closed blocks for doors and
    windows
Platform cart to move blocks
Accessories—assorted hats for firefighter, police officer, farmer
Large block of wood with wheel—may be purchased commercially or made
    with old car wheel
Wheelbarrow
Added accessories when needed—piece of hose for firefighter; large piece of
    cloth for tent, roof, or house
Empty food cartons—grocery store

TEACHER'S ROLE. Dramatic play when it occurs outdoors may be an extension of indoor play. A group of four-year-olds listened to the familiar story of the "Three Billy Goats Gruff." Outdoors they used a board and two sawhorses for a bridge. This was all the equipment they needed to dramatize the story. The teacher became part of the audience. She observed that too many children wanted the same parts. She did not intervene until she realized that the play was disintegrating. Then she asked, "Could there be more than one troll? More than one Billy Goat Gruff?" The children agreed that there could be more than one. The dramatization continued with three trolls, two big Billy Goats Gruff, one middle-sized Billy Goat Gruff, and five small Billy Goats Gruff. This dramatic play continued for several days without further teacher intervention. Acting out this story is an example of dramatic play since the children chose the activity and roles they wanted to play. In creative dramatics, discussed in chapter 7, a teacher would discuss the plot and each role with the children. Roles would be assigned, and each character would attempt to show the feelings and actions of the character as defined by the story.

free, spontaneous play

Free, spontaneous play occurs when children seem to have no purpose in mind other than letting off energy and enjoying the use of their muscles. They run back and forth across the play yard, climb up the jungle gym, shinny down a pole, slide down the sliding board, and climb in and out of barrels. Space and equipment are provided by the teacher, but unless the play becomes unsafe, the teacher does not intervene. Free, spontaneous play occurs more frequently outdoors because of the lack of space indoors.

manipulative play

indoor manipulative play

LOCATION.   Manipulative play occurs whenever a child chooses to experiment with objects. Children are constantly exploring objects both indoors and outdoors. This is the way they learn—through acting on objects. They may be seen testing various brushes in the art center. Which one should be chosen to paint the features of the face? Which one should be used for the body?

In the science center children handle insulated wires, flashlight batteries, and 3-volt bulbs. "Can I make the light burn? If more than one battery is used, what will happen?" Children continue to manipulate the equipment until the bulb burns more brightly. A music center may be the setting for experimentation with rhythm instruments. Which ones make low sounds? High sounds? In how many ways can the instrument be held to make a sound? Does the sound change? In the manipulative center children work puzzles, string beads, put together pieces of construction toys, and work on the buttoning and tying frame. Even in the dramatic-play center children are manipulating. Doll clothes are taken on and off, buttoned and unbuttoned; dishes and flatwear are put on the table and in the cupboards. There is no center where manipulation does not take place.

TEACHER'S ROLE.   The teacher's role in helping to develop concepts through experimentation with objects will be discussed in detail in chapter 5. Encouraging children to learn through the manipulation of objects is congruent with the newer methods of teaching science and mathematics. Teachers must understand that children learn through "hands-on" experience; they learn little from lengthy verbal explanations. Teachers must provide the materials and equipment through which children learn and must know when to ask questions and make comments that will lead to further exploration and learning.

outdoor manipulative play

LOCATION. Although manipulative play occurs in every outdoor center, there are two centers that lend themselves particularly to this type of play—the sand center and the water center. Both centers should be placed in a shady area whenever possible. A sandbox should have a cover to prevent animals from using it. It may be constructed like a wooden box with low sides or with concrete curbing blocks. Water and sand tables may be purchased from commercial companies, or, when budgets are limited, large plastic tubs may be used. Commercial sand and water tables are often on legs and require children to stand. When this type of stand-up table is used, a large container filled with water or sand should be placed on the ground. This gives the children the option of sitting or standing as they play.

EQUIPMENT AND SUPPLIES. Equipment for the sand center may include:

Metal or plastic sand table with cover
Combination sand and water table—with divisions through the center to manage sand play on one side and water play on the other
Plastic tubs and/or containers
Buckets, shovels, rakes, scoops, pails, sifters, funnels
Sand molds—letters, houses, animals
Sand wheel
Beam balance—plastic
Capacity-measuring containers—to discover how many containers of one size are needed to fill a given container
Measuring spoons and cups
Discarded pots and pans—free from sharp edges and rust

Equipment and materials for the water center may include:

Plastic water table
Water play trough
Combination sand and water table
Boats—objects that float or sink (objects must be safe)
Capacity measurers—to discover how many containers of one size are needed to fill a given container
Measuring cups and spoons
Water wheel
Funnels, sifters, sprinklers
Assorted plastic containers
Small pieces of plastic hose—can be used as siphons
Assorted cans and other containers—free from sharp edges and rust
Assorted paintbrushes

TEACHER'S ROLE. The teacher's role in sand and water play is far from passive. Teachers must know when to provide children with equipment, ask pertinent questions, and make significant comments. For many teachers the

The children made wooden boats with sails.

most difficult aspect of facilitating learning is to know when to intervene in children's play. There is always the danger of giving them too much information at a verbal level before they have had experiences at the concrete level. A group of nursery school children were "painting" the brick wall of the school building with water and large paintbrushes. After observing them for a while the teacher asked, "Where does the water go?" Answers were given such as: "Into the brick," "God takes it away," "It dries up," and "It evaporated." The teacher asked, "What happens when water evaporates?" A child replied, "I don't know. My daddy told me that." The teacher did not press for answers or give any explanation for evaporation. She knew that verbalization was useless since the children had had no first-hand experience with evaporation.

One summer, while four- and five-year-olds were playing with water, a child screamed, "Teacher, the tires are on fire!" The teacher looked in the child's direction and saw that the children were "painting" the tire with water. The tire was so hot that the water was evaporating and condensing in the air. All the children came to look at the "tire on fire." The teacher talked with them about the "smoke." "How did it start? What were you doing before you saw the smoke? Could it be anything besides smoke? Is there water on the tire?" She suggested that the children put water on some of the other tires, the sliding board, and the jungle gym. As they experimented the teacher asked, "Does the same thing happen?" This was a *first-hand* experience with evaporation. Of course, the children would be older before they would fully understand evaporation, but this experience was a part of the foundation on which they could build further understanding. This teacher did not let an opportunity for learning through play pass but capitalized on the "teachable moment."

games with rules

TEACHER'S ROLE. According to the definition given in this chapter, organized games are not thought of as play activities unless children enter and leave the games when they choose. One of the best ways to begin outdoor games is to say, "Would anyone like to play a game?" Children who are interested will begin the game, and other children will join in when they become interested. If children are allowed to enter and leave as they wish, "spoiling the game" is seldom a problem. When they know they can leave a game, they are less hesitant to join in. As they mature and become more familiar with games, they will remain until a game is finished.

Choose games that require some form of participation from all children. Familiar games, such as "Here We Go 'round the Mulberry Bush," London Bridge, Looby Lou, and Hot Ball, have simple rules and require children to be active. Children often select their own games, such as the all-time favorites Drop the Handkerchief and Duck and Goose. These games, however, involve less participation and require children to wait for a turn.

Hickety Pickety.

There are many excellent commercial games on the market. One that may be introduced to three-year-olds is *Hickety Pickety,* a color game. Other games suitable for older three's and younger four's are lotto games, *The Balloon Game,* and *Hi-Ho-Cherry-O.* Some good games for the older four's and five's are *Chutes and Ladders, Candy Land,* and *Winnie-the-Pooh.* Teachers should play games before introducing them to children. They must not only understand the rules but also know what skills are required.

Games are excellent sources for teaching enumeration, colors, recognition of numerals, classification, visual discrimination. Some children will profit more from one kind of game than from another. A disadvantaged five-year-old black child knew none of her colors and could not recognize herself in a photograph. After several photographs were taken and compared with her image in the mirror, she began to understand the meaning of the word "color." She was able to match colors of the same hue, but still could not name the colors. In order to help her learn color names the teacher played the game *Hickety Pickety* with her. She quickly learned four color names and was able to name objects of the same hue found in the room. Other color games were played to help her learn all the primary and secondary colors.

Teachers often ask, "What do I do when a child wants to quit because he isn't winning or seems bored with a game?" There are various reasons why a child wants to quit a game. The most obvious reason is that the game is not appropriate for the child—too easy or too hard. As children become more familiar with games they begin to choose ones that meet their needs. Children should be encouraged but not made to finish a game. When they want to leave a commercial game, they can ask other children to take their places. This is usually a satisfactory method.

It is often difficult for young children to lose. Whenever possible a game should be played until everyone has had a chance to finish it. Children may say, "I won, didn't I?" The teacher can reply, "Yes, you were the first person to finish. Let's play until everyone has finished."

The first child to start a game should not be determined by the teacher but by the rules of the game or by chance. One technique is to write a numeral from 1 to 5 or draw a colored circle on a piece of paper. Ask the children the numeral or the color. When the children have made their guesses, show them the paper with the numeral or color. The child who guessed correctly goes first. Young children accept taking turns better when their turn is determined by chance and not by the teacher or another child.

EQUIPMENT AND SUPPLIES FOR GAMES WITH RULES. There are many excellent commercial games on the market, including:

Alphabet Bingo—letter recognition
Balloon Game—color recognition
Candy Land—color recognition and enumeration
Checkers—problem solving—appropriate for older fives and six-year-olds
Chutes and Ladders—number recognition and enumeration
Color and Shape Bingo—color and shape recognition
Hi-Ho-Cherry-O—color recognition, enumeration, subtraction and addition

Hickety Pickety—color recognition, one-to-one correspondence
Perfection—visual discrimination, eye-hand coordination
Picture Dominos—visual discrimination
Swiss Cheese—color and shape recognition
Ting-a-ling-Bingo—visual discrimination of objects
What's Missing? Lotto—establish relationships
Winnie-the-Pooh—color recognition and enumeration

Equipment and supplies for outdoor games may include:

Rubber horseshoe sets—eye-hand coordination
Hopscotch—eye-foot coordination
Bean bag games—eye-hand coordination
Suction dart games—eye-hand coordination
Ring toss—eye-hand coordination

constructive play

TEACHER'S ROLE.   Constructive play is defined in this chapter as any activity chosen by the child that results in an end product. The product may be a block construction, a painting, a clay object, a story, a Lego construction, or an airplane made at the workbench. In constructive play a child usually has a purpose in mind before beginning. He or she goes to the easel to paint, uses blocks to build a spaceship, dictates a story about a drawing, or uses constructive toys to make an airplane.

A teacher's role in constructive play is primarily that of observer. The teacher tries to understand the child's purpose and gives as much support as needed to carry out the child's intentions. A kindergarten teacher observed a child mixing paints. Jane used a large brush and covered a sheet of manila drawing paper with pink paint, wrote her name on the paper, and walked away. The teacher removed the wet paper and placed it on a drying rack. Jane asked the teacher why her picture had been moved. When the teacher said she thought Jane had finished, Jane said, "You didn't ask me if I was finished. I'm not. I have a lot to do yet." The teacher put Jane's painting back on the table. Jane touched the paint several times at intervals. When she was satisfied it was dry she painted a wide black band across the bottom of the paper. When the black paint was dry she took a small brush, dipped it into white paint, and shook the brush slowly and gently over the black band. The result was a beautiful abstraction that was almost spoiled when Jane's play was interrupted.

Children are usually eager to show the things they make to their teachers and friends. A bulletin board for paintings and a low table for three-dimensional objects are needed to display children's work. Praise as well as recognition is needed.

A word of caution about praise: It is good when it is sincere and is given when children have accomplished something unique for them. Praising everything children do may defeat them; they know everything they do is not wonderful. Children may begin to question the teacher's judgment or may feel that they have failed if each object does not receive the expected praise. Children some-

They made planes for the airport they had built with blocks.

times put pressure on themselves to excel in everything, which is obviously impossible. These are children who work to please the teacher or parents and feel a loss of prestige when they fail to achieve what they feel is expected of them. One child, in desperation, said to his mother, "Please don't tell Ms. B. that I like mountains. I'll have to study about them and I don't want to."

There are always a few children who are not satisfied with their efforts. One five-year-old boy whose motor coordination was poor threw his pictures away. One day the teacher saw Pete throw his picture behind the bushes outside. She said, "If you don't want your picture, I'd like to have it. We don't have any pictures on the bulletin board." Pete looked surprised and retrieved his picture. Next day he checked the bulletin board to make sure it was there. Then he chose different children and took them to see his picture, saying, "That's my picture. Ms. J. put it on the bulletin board. She liked it." He began to accept his limitations, and instead of hiding his paintings, he proudly put them on the bulletin board. Gradually his artwork changed, as his motor coordination improved.

EQUIPMENT AND SUPPLIES.   Equipment and supplies for art and woodworking will be discussed in chapter 4. Manipulative equipment is listed in chapter 2.

scheduling

Play activities cannot be fitted into neat timeslots. Some form of play (self-directed activities) should make up at least 80 to 90 percent of the school day.

The form play takes will vary with the age of the children and the time of year. Older children (five to six years) usually engage in more constructive play and games with rules, whereas younger children (three to five) engage in more dramatic and manipulative play. The preferred types of play vary with the group of children, however.

It is very difficult for three- and four-year-olds to continue a project over a period of time. A child from five to six may look forward to the prospects of working on a project and may take as long as a week to complete it.

grouping

grouping indoors

Play groups form naturally during learning activity time. When a Choice Board (discussed in chapter 1) is used, play groups are somewhat limited. If a child wants to play with friends in a center and it is filled, another center must be chosen.

It is common for young children (especially three's and four's) to form friendships that fluctuate. Sara may be Joan's best friend today and Mary's tomorrow. Most children form many friendships; a few do not. Sometimes children, even as young as three, form lasting, close friendships. These relationships are most often but not always between members of the same sex. One close friendship between a four-year-old boy and girl continued throughout nursery school and kindergarten. Close friendships are not unhealthy as long as the children do not become totally dependent on each other or consistently refuse to allow a third child to play. When this happens it is a teacher's responsibility to help children form additional friendships. There are many things teachers can do, such as assigning children to separate cars on field trips, inviting different children to help each other with projects, and encouraging parents to invite different children to the home to play.

One year two five-year-old boys became close friends, so close that it seemed to the teacher that there were "the two of them and the rest of us." Eventually one of the boys took his friend's name and even wrote it on his own picture. The teacher consulted the school psychologist, who said that the boy's behavior was not abnormal. The teacher was still concerned and felt that the boys should become part of the kindergarten group. She talked with the parents of both boys. One family was indifferent but the other was concerned and helpful. They insisted that their son have different children to play at his home each week. Gradually this child began to play with more children at school. The teacher concentrated on building up the confidence of both boys. By midyear they readily accepted a third child. In most cases in which children are dependent on each other, one or both lack confidence in themselves.

grouping outdoors

Children form play groups naturally outdoors just as they do indoors. They are often attracted to each other when they have the same interests and skills.

Children who are skilled in throwing and catching balls may form a play group while children who enjoy water play may join each other at the water table.

Teachers must be aware of children's physical development in order to provide opportunities for practice skills. They may encourage or invite children to join group games that develop certain skills, such as throwing, running, hopping, and/or balancing.

Sometimes children who are not interested in an indoor center will choose a similar center outdoors. A child who shows little interest in building with blocks indoors may play in the outdoor block center or a child who seldom paints may paint at the outdoor easel. Selection of a few outdoor centers with activities similar to those of indoor centers gives children another opportunity to select from a variety of play materials.

first day of school

dramatic play indoors

The dramatic-play center should be inviting. Colorful placemats and a small plant help attract attention to this center. All equipment, including dolls, doll clothes, and dress-up clothes, should be clean and in good repair. Everything should be in its place: the dishes in the cupboard, the pots and pans below the sink, and the ice trays in the refrigerator. A pegboard between the kitchen and the bedroom may be used to hang up kitchen utensils on one side and dress-up clothes or doll clothes on the other. The outlines or silhouettes of the kitchen utensils may be drawn on the pegboard to show children where to place them.

There should be a special place for every item. Putting equipment away encourages a sense of order and improves classification skills: the food belongs in the refrigerator, the doll clothes in the drawer, the dishes in the cupboard, the utensils on the pegboard. It is desirable to place only large and small equipment—for example, large and small spoons, dolls, dishes, and cooking equipment—in the center on the first day. Later equipment somewhere in between large and small may be added. This method of introducing equipment is particularly desirable with younger and disadvantaged children. They learn to make comparisons and later to order items from smallest to largest and largest to smallest.

The block center should be in order, with the unit blocks placed neatly on wide, open shelves. Accessories can be added slowly during the first week after the children have had an opportunity to explore block building. A few pictures of buildings placed at eye level on the bulletin board may stimulate block play. If children do not use the blocks, a teacher may want to begin a block structure and leave it up for the children to find the next day. Children can use these blocks as a framework for whatever they want to build.

games with rules

A few commercial games may be put in the mathematics or manipulative center. These should be games with simple rules that can be played quickly. *Hi-Ho-*

Cherry-O and *Hickety Pickety* are good examples of this kind of game. If most of the children are disadvantaged or younger (three to four years) the teacher should wait until the abilities of the children are known before introducing games. When teachers are confronted with children who have already played games in school, the teacher should choose some games the children know and a few new and challenging ones. Outdoor games should not be played until later in the year or until children initiate them.

manipulative play indoors

A great deal of manipulative play will occur in all centers during the first days of school as children explore the room. A minimum of manipulative equipment should be placed in each center. Bombarding children with too much equipment is one sure way to "turn them off." A wise teacher selects some equipment with which children are familiar and a few new and challenging pieces. If possible, the teacher has found out something about each child before school begins and uses this information in setting up the room. If it is known that a certain child enjoys puzzles, a few more difficult ones can be placed in the manipulative center.

The kind and amount of material a teacher selects will depend on the composition of the children in the room. One teacher who taught in a Head Start program for the first time had read about culturally deprived children but had not worked with them. She put out very little equipment and chose a few centers for the first day. Two days later she realized that there was still too much equipment. The children were confused and darted from one center to another. The teacher took out approximately half the equipment and one of the centers. Gradually the children began to use the remaining equipment. Approximately five weeks later the teacher was able to introduce new pieces.

constructive play indoors

A few children will spend most of their time during the first days of school in some form of constructive play. The block and art centers are very popular. Crayons (with paper removed), tempera paints (red, yellow, and blue), manila drawing paper, easel paper, and play dough (any color; it can be dyed with food coloring) are good selections for the art center. The woodworking center may be introduced later in the year unless children have had experience with woodworking. The teacher must be careful to select activities for the centers which require little supervision. The main job on the first day of school is to get to know the children and to observe them in their play.

dramatic play outdoors

The dramatic-play area and block area should contain only the essential equipment suggested for these centers. Accessories may be added as the children's dramatic play demands.

Making interesting constructions at the workbench.

free, spontaneous play

A great deal of this type of play will occur during the first week of school as children become familiar with the outdoor equipment. A teacher's main role is to provide space for exploration and make certain that the playground is free from safety hazards.

manipulative play outdoors

It is not necessary to put out any sand toys on the first day of school. If children have had preschool experience, however, a few pails, sifters, and scoops may be placed near the sandpile. Water play is usually introduced later in the year. Again, this depends on the children and the climate.

constructive play outdoors

Woodworking, whether indoors or outdoors, needs supervision. Woodworking may be introduced when children have become familiar with the centers and are able to use equipment more independently.

play through the year

The play of the children and of each individual child will change as the year progresses. Play becomes more structured, more realistic, and more complex. When a child's play remains the same or becomes stagnant, that child may have a serious problem. A four-year-old continued to dress and undress dolls, fill boxes with objects and empty them, and look at the same books over and over. The teacher suspected mental retardation rather than immaturity. During a conference the child's parents became aware of the problem. They took her to several clinics, and it was discovered that she had an incurable brain disease.

The play of a few children may change very slowly over a period of time, with no obvious spurts in development. These children should be referred for testing and the classroom teacher informed of the results. Often these children do not have learning problems but are developmentally slow. In another year they will function at a higher level of maturity.

Some educators do not believe in holding immature children back in nursery school or kindergarten. Others feel that this is the time when children should be retained. When six-year-olds function as five-year-olds or younger, first-grade work may become a formidable task. When work is too difficult children often fail. It seems best, in order to avoid frustration, failure, and a loss of self-respect, for children to stay with the age group they most closely resemble developmentally.

The role of teachers as observers of children's play cannot be emphasized enough. They must constantly evaluate and reevaluate play.

meeting goals

The scheme described in chapter 2 for evaluating movement education can be applied to play. A checklist based upon the behavioral objectives for play may be kept for each child. Methods previously described for collecting data are all applicable to play situations. When videotapes are used, several learning activities may be taped at the same time and analyzed. Observing tapes will give teachers an overall picture of how learning centers are being used—which centers are being used most, least, and possibly why. Teachers should ask themselves questions such as: Can the centers be made more attractive to children? Is there a constant flow of traffic? Are there children who need more guidance? Do children appear busy? Do any activities seem chaotic? Why? Videotapes also may be made of separate play groups, such as dramatic-play episodes. An analysis of this kind of tape will help teachers better understand the play of children. They can judge more accurately when it is appropriate to intervene in the children's play.

Examples of children's constructive play can be kept in folders. Samples should include paintings; drawings; picture collages; dictated stories; original poems; and photographs of block constructions, clay models, objects made of wood, and three-dimensional structures made from constructive toys.

Piagetian tasks relating to moral development and judgment are discussed in chapter 4. The results of these tasks will help the teacher better understand a child's ability to share and to participate in games with rules.

4
children
are social

social studies for young children

Children need other people; they cannot live in a vacuum. They constantly seek interaction with others. As children grow, other people become increasingly important to them. The significant others in their lives gradually help them to form a view of themselves; thus *self* is formed.

Self-concept is a part of a broad area called the "social studies." During the preschool years much of what happens in the classroom revolves around the development of a child's positive self-concept and ability to relate effectively to others. Satisfaction with self and others is perhaps the most crucial area of social studies for young children. Seefeldt's (1977) definition of social studies reveals the importance of social skills to the young child as well as other topics of concern to the classroom teacher. She states:

Concerned with the study of people and their interactions with others and the total environment, social studies transmit a way of life while, at the same time, building the skills, knowledge, attitudes, and values needed to change and improve that way of life.

Social studies embrace all disciplines from the social science field. . . . History, geography, economics, political science, international education, ecology, career education, and current events are all social science disciplines found within the enormous social studies field. (p. 3)

The field of social studies is very broad; only those areas more appropriate for young children are discussed in this chapter.

ourselves

Social studies should be introduced with a topic of tremendous importance to children—ourselves. Piaget feels that children can move away from egocentric

VERNON REGIONAL

thought only if they interact with other children and experience points of view different from their own. The loss of egocentric thought then allows them to progress in their understanding of people and places (Elkind, 1976, p. 104).

self-concept

How crucial is the development of the self-concept to an understanding of self and others? Research suggests that the more adequate children feel, the more confident they are about learning and relating to others. Seefeldt (1977) states that "the child's self-concept has long been believed to be the foundation on which all future relationships with others and the entire world will be built" (p. 209). The emergence of a positive self-concept depends upon the ways in which children feel the significant others in their lives view them. If they feel they are viewed negatively by others they begin to doubt themselves. Self-doubt leads to despondency and despair. Teachers must help children feel positive about themselves (Hammer, 1976, p. 50). They can begin by creating a nurturing, supporting environment in which children feel wanted, secure, and safe.

experiencing different viewpoints

RACIAL PREJUDICE. It is difficult for children who are from a minority race to feel good about themselves when the message they get from others is, "You're different. You don't belong with us." Research reveals that racial prejudice begins as early as three or four years of age. On the whole, black children have poorer self-esteem than white children, as found by research. They prefer white dolls and white photographs to black ones (Greenwald and Oppenheim, 1968; Porter, 1971). Moore (1976) found that more male than female black children perceived a black model as negative. Rohrer (1977) found that black children tended to prefer their own race more often in integrated than in segregated classrooms, whereas the opposite was true for whites (pp. 28–31). Integration should be a step in the direction of helping children in minority groups overcome feelings of inadequacy.

Teachers must provide environments that promote self-respect, tolerance, and mutual regard for *all* children. They must never forget that children model their behavior after the teacher. When children know that a teacher likes and accepts children who are racially different, they are more likely to overlook differences and to concentrate on likenesses. Seefeldt (1977) suggests rewarding divergent behavior as one of the best ways to demonstrate the acceptance of differences: Encourage each child to create something, executing his or her own ideas. Give children specific problems to solve, such as, "Show us how *you* would do it." Talk about individual likes and dislikes. Ask different children to choose stories, songs, and games (p. 153).

HANDICAPPED CHILDREN.   Public Law 94–142 requires that all handi-capped children be placed in the "least restrictive environment" possible. This means they should be placed in a program best suited to their special needs and one that resembles as closely as possible that of normal children. Although the act does not mention mainstreaming, a tremendous amount of mainstreaming is being done because, for many children, the regular classroom is the least restrictive environment. Children who are mainstreamed into the regular class-room include those with physical handicaps, emotional problems, learning disabilities, and intellectual handicaps. Ideally mainstreaming means more individualized instruction for all children, since each child in the classroom is considered a child with special needs (Dunlop, 1977, p. 28).

Research suggests that children with special needs are happier and achieve more when they are mainstreamed than when placed in special classes. Jones (1974) found that children in special classes disliked the labeling that precedes placement. Gottlieb and Budoff (1972) found that children in special classrooms have less favorable attitudes toward school than those who have been main-streamed. Still other researchers report that exceptional children have lower standards of academic achievement in special classes than do similar children in regular classroom settings (Johnson, 1962). Not all studies have favored children who are mainstreamed, however. One of the most common negative outcomes has been peer rejection (Bryan, 1974).

The most crucial factor in the success of a mainstreamed classroom is the teacher. It is the teacher's example that sets the stage for acceptance of the handicapped child by other children. Wynne, Ulfelder, and Dakof (1975) state, "The ability and attitude of the teacher appear to be *the* most important factors in the success of an integrated program" (p. 75).

home and family

At one time the typical family consisted of a mother, a father, and their children. Today a family may be a father and daughter, a grandmother and grandchild, a daughter with her mother and her mother's boyfriend, or a boy and his aunt. The teacher must be careful in defining "family" for children. It is best to describe a family as a group in which "people live together and help each other." This definition will apply in most cases. There are, however, children who are abused by adults. They can relate to the first part of the definition but cannot think of the togetherness in their lives as "helpful."

Research has shown that children reflect in their behavior what happens to them in the home. Often behavior problems stem from some form of anxiety created by a home situation with which a child cannot cope. A teacher must make every effort to know the home background of each child in order to work effectively with the child and the significant others in the child's life (Cohen and Rudolph, 1977, p. 406).

Family relationships are difficult for children to understand. A particularly difficult concept for young children is the "brother of" and "sister of" relationship. Children may tell you that they have a brother and/or sister but that they, in fact, are not a brother and/or sister. The understanding that to have a brother or sister you must be a brother or sister has not been acquired by most four- and five-year-olds (Copeland, 1979, pp. 80–87). The difficulty lies in seeing that one and the same person can be in two relationships at the same time (Elkind, 1976, p. 186).

career education

career choices

The idea of asking young children to think of the future when they are barely able to understand the concepts of yesterday and tomorrow seems somewhat inappropriate. But the preschool is an ideal place to begin education for a career because it is during these years that attitudes, skills, and values are learned (Seefeldt, 1977, p. 187). Children can understand the meaning of work as they fulfill their jobs in the classroom and talk about the occupations of the significant others in their lives.

sex stereotyping

One of the most important concepts to explore with children is the wide range of career choices open to them. There was once a stigma attached to the selection of a career associated with the opposite sex. Women who chose to be doctors or bricklayers were frowned upon, and boys who wanted to become ballet dancers and teachers of young children were looked upon with suspicion. Although society still maintains some of its prejudices, psychologists, sociologists, and educators are recognizing the importance of each individual's right to choose the occupation for which he or she is best suited.

It is commonly believed that sex roles derive from innate differences between males and females. There may be some evidence of innate differences, but a review of the research by Birns (1976) suggests that there are none. Rather sex differential behavior is due to environmental forces, such as parental attitudes. Baby boys are handled more roughly than baby girls; baby girls are cooed to and often handled more gently. Boys are encouraged to be active and to explore and girls to be more passive and sedentary (Fagan and Osborn, 1975, p. 73; Mitchell, 1973, p. 235).

Mitchell's (1973) review of children's toys and books reveals that boys' toys appeal to power and action whereas girls' toys are essentially passive and sedentary. Picture books for preschool children show girls watching boys climb trees, bringing them tools, and generally keeping things tidy (pp. 229–230).

In recent years a number of children's books have depicted males and females in nontraditional roles. Ethnic groups and the aged have been treated more positively than in the past. Madsen and Wickersham (1980), however found, in a survey of children's books from 1976 to 1978 that realistic fiction for young children did not reflect equivalent treatment of males and females or the culturally pluralistic makeup of United States society (p. 276).

Nilsen (1977) suggests ways a teacher can provide a natural environment for children that does not push them into sexist roles.

1. Grouping: divide children into heterogenous groups where they can make friends naturally.
2. Arranging classrooms: Combine the block and homemaking centers. In this way the more active (boy-centered) and passive (girl-centered) activities will be closer together.
3. Choosing curriculum: Include stories of both males and females in discussions of history and science. Minimize the difference between males and females so that children can be free to identify with persons whom they admire of either sex.
4. Teaching about the English language: Help children understand the use of generic words. Use words such as "police officer" and "nurse" (not "male nurse") so that children will not think predominantly of males in the first case and females in the second instance.
5. Involving parents: Send notes home addressed to both parents and ask both father and mother to become involved in school projects.
6. Expressing attitudes toward aggression: Help both boys and girls to "talk out" solutions rather than use "beat the hell out of them" solutions.
7. Giving encouragement: Treat boys and girls more alike. Count how many times you compliment girls on appearance and how many times you compliment boys (pp. 55–58).

values and morality

A value may be defined as "the comparative weight, esteem, or price attached by the individual to a given idea, person, or object" (ASCD Yearbook, 1949, p. 154). Webster's (1975) defines morality as "conformity to ideas of right human conduct" (p. 748). Values affect the way people think and feel about something. Values determine how people act in a given situation (morality).

Children learn values from the significant people in their lives—primarily parents and teachers. The more attached children are to older people the more they emulate their behavior and attitudes. This is particularly true of young children (Elkind, 1976, p. 157).

In teaching values the teacher should consider those values that are held by a democratic society. Seefeldt (1977) lists values that are consistent with living in a democracy:

1.   Valuing the dignity of each individual
2.   Universal participating in rule setting and rule establishing
3.   Permitting each person freedom of speech, opportunities to express ideas and feelings
4.   Reinforcing the rights of each individual for protection and happiness
5.   Seeing that everyone has a part in the school society and that everyone has some responsibility to others (p. 259)

Piaget has identified stages in the development of morality which are helpful in dealing with characteristic behaviors of young children. Children from three to six base their moral judgment on the outcome of the deed rather than on the intention of the deed. In other words, it is more serious to steal five cookies than one, more damaging to spill a bottle of ink than a little ink, not as serious to cross the street if you don't get hurt than if you do. Around the age of seven or eight children begin to think of the intent of the deed. Was it accidental, with no intent to disobey? Was it carelessness? Was it good intentions gone wrong? Was it a conscious effort to disobey? (Evans and McCandless, 1978, p. 411).

Young children take a hard-and-fast attitude toward justice in the class-room. They see behavior as either right or wrong and fail to see any shades of gray. The standard for right is the authority figure (teacher, parent, or police officer.) Teachers are the authority figures in classrooms, and children strive to please them. Children feel guilty when teachers disapprove of their actions, and they blame themselves even when they do not understand what it is that they have done.

Young children think of rules as unchangeable even though they often break them. They expect others to follow the rules and become very upset when they don't. They often "tattle" on other children who have broken the same rule they have broken. Their egocentricity justifies what they did (they forgot or don't know why), but they can't put themselves in the place of the other child (Sayre and Ankney, 1976, p. 239).

Moralizing and lecturing young children about right and wrong is futile. A better means of teaching children desirable behavior is to provide experiences with real people and actual events.

death and religion

In the past the subject of death was taboo; today it is openly discussed. As Wren-Lewis (1975) observed, "Death has moved from the status of a taboo, a subject not discussed before children, to a major topic of psychological and sociological study" (p. 14). Young children as early as two years of age are aware of death. They are incapable of abstract thinking about death until five or six years of age, however, and cannot grasp religious or philosophical explanations until nine or ten (Furman, 1978, p. 27; Crase and Crase, 1976, p. 22).

Whenever persons very close to children die, they may grieve outwardly or inwardly. Teachers should not ignore death with the hope of making a loss easier for children. One teacher did not mention a parent's death, but ignored it hoping the child would forget. Later the child said, "You never told me you were sorry my mother died." Sometimes a teacher must take the first step by mentioning the loss to the child and expressing sympathy in a way that implies, "This will be with us for a long time. I hope you will feel free to come to me, talk with me, or feel with me about it" (Furman, 1978, p. 29).

Differences in religious beliefs are always present in a classroom. Teachers have their beliefs, which may or may not coincide with the beliefs of parents. Whenever possible the teacher should tell parents the questions their children ask and the unbiased answers they have given. Crase and Crase (1976) state, "Parents deserve the opportunity to share their personal beliefs with children; they will appreciate being alerted to the possibility of such a discussion and the events which stimulated a child's interest" (p. 23).

the aging process

Twenty, even 10, years ago young children came into contact with elderly people; learned to respect, love, and above all to enjoy them. The mobility of families, increasing financial burdens, women working full time jobs, divorce, and the availability of nursing homes have changed the profile of the "typical family." Grandparents often do not see their grandchildren for long periods of time, and those with divorced children may seldom or never see their grandchildren. Some children therefore grow up with little or no contact with the elderly. Nearly 90 percent of children interviewed in a study of attitudes toward the elderly responded negatively when asked how they would feel about being old. To the children the elderly were seen as sick, passive, feeble, sad, taking medicine, and having heart attacks. The activities the children thought they could do with the elderly were to play cards, go to church, and sit and rock. This research typifies the immobile and quiet life children assign to the elderly (Jantz and Fulda, 1975, pp. 24–28).

A study of books for children ages three through nine reveals the following facts: the omission of older characters in over 80 percent of the books, more elderly male than female characters, more white elderly characters than black or minority groups, elderly characters pictured alone, and personality descriptors of the elderly as old, sad, wise, and feeble (Ansello, 1975, pp. 120–122). Teachers should be selective in choosing books for children. Stories depicting warm, loving, and humorous relationships between the young and old are not numerous, but they are available. Seefeldt, et al. (1978) and Storey (1977) list and describe books that portray older people in a diversity of roles leading active and interesting lives.

Children who have contact with the elderly have more positive attitudes toward them. However, the "kind of situation in which the contact takes place and the physical condition of the elderly persons involved may influence the attitude of the young people as much as the contact itself" (John, 1977, p. 524). Providing models of elderly who are satisfied and enjoy life is crucial. Volunteers from the community can make significant contributions. Canady and Darnley (1977) describe the contributions of a 91-year-old man, a naturalized American citizen from Italy, who volunteered to help a three-year-old Italian boy with

English. Not only did Mr. A. (as the children called him) aid the boy's integration into the nursery school, but he also gave the children an elderly male model—an active, vital person.

The old have much to contribute to the young and vice versa. John (1977) states, "To be young is to reach for the future; to be old is to possess the past. Old and young meet in the present and hold the key to the betterment of humanity. Surely a mutual understanding is needed if this is to be accomplished" (p. 527).

history

History has been defined as a time-oriented study that refers to what we know about the past (Seefeldt, 1977, p. 106). Children enjoy hearing and talking about the past, especially their *own* past. Their egocentric point of view enables them to become interested in what they were like when they were little. From children's point of view, the existence of others begins in their own memory. Others did not exist until they were born (Pulaski, 1971, p. 168). This self-centered point of view limits their ability to go backward in thought. They are unable to coordinate the happenings of the past with those of the present. Elkind (1976) states, "Only after the age of nine or ten do the children deal with topics which are both spatially and temporally distant from them" (p. 214).

Young children may use transductive reasoning (thinking from one particular to another) to explain a sequence of events or the relationship of events. A child may say, "I haven't had my snack so I can't eat lunch" or "We are going swimming this afternoon because Daddy stayed home from work." In the latter statement the child draws conclusions about the present from previous experience. He or she thinks that what happened under certain circumstances in the past will happen again under similar circumstances. They went swimming last week when Daddy was home, therefore the child concludes that it is time to go swimming again. It is possible for children to arrive at the correct conclusion but not necessarily for the right reason (Rosen, 1977, p. 15; Copeland, 1979, pp. 229–230).

This does not mean that young children should never be exposed to the past. It does mean that they should not be expected to acquire knowledge and meaning through reading and listening to others. Wadsworth (1978) states, "Experience—actual learning—remains crucial. . . . Younger children can comprehend only those readings and talks that closely relate to knowledge they have constructed through active learning" (p. 184). Children must have the opportunity to see first hand and, whenever possible, to touch. Experiences should be concrete and pertain as directly as possible to their interests.

field trips

For most children ages three to six, field trips to local or nearby places offer direct contact with the physical world. Hymes (1968) states:

The *field trip* is clearly the best way of providing this added stimulus. Young children cannot read but they can see. They cannot read but they can touch and hear and smell. They cannot read but they can ask questions. A field experience is the prize stimulus for learning at any age. . . . We can almost thank God for the young child's illiteracy. It forces us to do the very best thing, to take him to first hand sources. (p. 89)

Trips should be planned with care. A teacher must visit the site ahead of the children. Too many field trips are as undesirable as too few. A teacher must ask, "Why am I taking these children on this trip? What will they learn from the experience?" Split-group trips are more desirable since children do not have to wait as long for a turn and there is more opportunity for conversation. Often children gain from visiting the same place again. They can visit for a different purpose, learning something from each trip. The wise teacher plans few, well-selected trips with specific purposes in mind (Seefeldt, 1977, pp. 316–322).

holidays

Holiday celebrations with young children can be fun and at the same time impart knowledge about the past and current customs associated with the holidays. On the other hand, celebrating holidays can become meaningless and chaotic. Seefeldt (1977) suggests the following:

The routines of the regular school day are preserved . . . the children are fully involved in planning the celebration . . . the activities are kept simple and low key . . . parents and other resource persons are involved in the celebration . . . and a few key concepts are selected for development. (pp. 115–116)

The true meaning of the holiday rather than the history and traditional customs should be taught. Key concepts appropriate for holidays are: Halloween—reality versus fantasy; Thanksgiving—thankfulness; Christmas—giving; Hanukkah—friends and family; Valentine's Day—friendship; Easter—renewal of life; and birthdays—growing up (Seefeldt, 1977, pp. 116–117).

In an article entitled "Classroom Holidaze" (Timberlake, 1978) the frustrations surrounding the celebration of too many inappropriate holidays are discussed. Timberlake says:

In making a decision we must recognize that young children have more years of school ahead. If they do not celebrate St. Patrick's Day this year, you may be sure that they will for many years to come. . . . Time is not running out. It is just beginning for young children; we must not feel compelled to stuff them. (p. 129)

international understanding

Some teachers use a globe to help children locate their own and other countries in an effort to bring about international understanding. Concepts about countries, oceans, and land masses are far too abstract for young children to grasp. A child does not yet have the mental structures to permit the recording of such information; therefore the knowledge is not retained (Elkind, 1976, p. 213).

There are teachers who try with little success to teach children the relationship of their city, state, and country. Children cannot understand the part-whole relationship, which Piaget calls "class inclusion." They cannot think of the whole (America) and its parts (city and state) at the same time. It is not until children are seven to eight that they can move back and forth between the parts and the whole in their thinking and understand that the whole is greater than its parts (Pulaski, 1971, pp. 60–61). A similar phenomenon is found in the child's thinking about family members, discussed under Home and Family in this chapter. Teachers who attempt to teach children the relationship of their city to their county and the relationship of their country to the world are wasting their time.

The most important aspect of international understanding for young children is learning to like and respect children with different ethnic heritages. Since children learn best from direct experiences, the teacher must capitalize on the interactions of children within the classroom. Seefeldt (1977) states, "The most effective resource to help children develop an understanding of cultural pluralism is the children. . . . Teachers, with the children and their parents, can explore the ethnic heritage of the children within the class" (p. 156).

current events

Children gather information about current affairs from TV, radio, newspapers, magazine pictures, and adult conversations. The range of topics that children talk about is surprisingly broad, but the range of information about any one topic is likely to be narrow. Often children have difficulty sorting out information so that it is meaningful to them. Concepts formed are sometimes inaccurate and confusing to a child. The teacher's role can be one of accurately informing and educating young children about current events.

The inclusion of current topics in the social studies curriculum means that the curriculum must be adjusted from time to time to include topics of current interest to young children. Generally the topics discussed will arise from their immediate concerns. Seefeldt (1977) states, "Children may first become interested in current events by making news themselves." (p. 182). The news may be a lost tooth, a new baby in the family, a visit from a relative, a trip to the beach, or a new pet.

As children begin to gather information it becomes increasingly important for teachers to include items they feel affect the children's lives; for example, the current energy crisis: why the principal asked us to turn off some of our lights; a local accident in which several people are killed: why some people died and others lived, and what caused the accident. Seefeldt (1977) states, "Early education must make children not only aware of, but also knowledgeable about, the events that occur around them" (p. 173).

geography

An understanding of the earth as the home of mankind begins early in children's lives. Nearly all their experiences involve concepts from geography. Digging in the sand, exploring places around them, playing in water, making mud pies, and climbing on rocks are adventures children love. Seefeldt (1977) states:

The study of geography becomes an important integrating element in the curriculum, serving to connect different content areas. Measuring distance and time means children draw upon and use mathematical concepts, and the study of the earth requires the methods of the scientist. Learning to locate self in space develops psychomotor skills, and learning to read a map, by gaining meaning from symbols, is actually a reading readiness activity. It could be concluded that geography, an integral part of all the social sciences, is also an integral part of all other areas of the curriculum—science, mathematics, language, reading, and physical development. (pp. 77–78)

the earth

Basic to understanding the concept that the Earth is a place where people live is an understanding of what constitutes life. Young children view the world at their own level of thinking, not at the adult level. Their egotism leads them to believe they can control the Earth. The sun and the moon follow them wherever they walk, and they can make the rain go away by saying rhymes such as "Rain, rain, go away. Come again another day."

Another characteristic of egocentric thought is animism, the belief that the world of nature is alive and endowed with purpose. The moon shines "to watch over us," the "clouds move when I walk and stop when I stop," and the chair is bad because "it bumped into me." Closely akin to animism is artificialism, the belief that human beings created natural phenomena such as the moon and the stars. Often the child attributes the creation of natural phenomena to an authority such as "my father" or "God" (Pulaski, 1971, pp. 42–45, Elkind, 1976, pp. 102–103).

An accurate understanding of the revolution of the Earth around the sun is not possible for young children. Experiences that focus attention on the effects of the Earth's revolution are possible. Observing the effects of weather conditions and changing seasons is a first step in understanding the revolution of the Earth (Seefeldt, 1977, pp. 82–84).

It is difficult to convey the idea that the Earth is made up of both land and water unless children have actually seen an ocean, a lake, or a pond. Photographs and pictures are helpful, but they cannot replace the real thing. Sometimes pictures are misleading. Elkind (1976) urges teachers to expose children to pictures that relate to their lives. He states:

It is rather amusing, in a way, that these graphics take for granted that children can deal with the near-far symbolism. . . . But the near-far issue is not the problem with the photographs. To really relate to them children need to tie them to their own experience. How much more meaningful and exciting the photographs would be if they were of the child's city, the child's street, or the child's school. (p. 214)

direction

It is through movement in space that children learn directionality. They become aware of their bodies and what they can do with them. Directional terms, such as "up" and "down," "right" and "left," "beside," "front" and "back," and "in back of," are learned as children explore space. The importance of movement in children's awareness of space is discussed in chapter 2.

location, distance, and measurement

Concepts of location include an understanding of direction and distance. Children gradually learn to locate objects in front of, behind, beside, and to the left or to the right. A full understanding of directionality, however, will not be completed until adolescence (Seefeldt, 1977, p. 85). In order to determine the distance between objects children must understand conservation of distance and of length (Copeland, 1979, p. 299). To understand children's ability to conserve distance a simple Piagetian task is given. Model trees are placed 50 centimeters apart, and children asked whether they are near or far apart. Then a cardboard screen is placed between the trees and the question asked again. Children less than four to five years old report that the distance is now less. These children consider two intervals instead of one. The four- or five-year-old child sees the overall distance but thinks the screen takes up space and the distance is less. The older child from six to seven understands that the distance between the two trees does not change.

Conservation of length is not understood until the child is about seven to eight years old. Young children do not understand that the length of one object does not change when it is moved along another object being measured. In a simple Piagetian task children are given two sticks of the same length and asked to place them parallel to each other. The children agree that the sticks are the same length, but when one stick is moved forward, away from the other stick, they think the stick that has been moved is longer. They do not realize that the length of the stick is constant (Copeland, 1979, p. 303).

Experience with distance and measurement for children who cannot conserve must be informal. The objective of the teacher is to help them refine the meanings of words that express distance. Children's attention in play situations may be called to the nearest house, the farthest tree, the doll close to the chain, and the plant beside the road and close to the barn.

Arbitrary measures, such as hands, feet, string, ribbon, cord, and paper strips, can be used by the children to measure. Primary rulers and yardsticks may be available at the workbench or mathematics center, but not as actual measuring tools (Seefeldt, 1977, p. 90).

map making

Copeland (1979) outlines the stages of development in children's ability to make maps. Map making involves the ability to understand topological relationships, see a layout from different points of view, use imaginary horizontal and vertical axes to locate objects, and understand perspective.

Young children do not view shape as a rigid thing. Their first understanding of shape is topological in nature. In the mathematics of topology, figures are not considered fixed or rigid. Simple closed figures, such as squares, circles, and triangles, are equivalent topologically because they may be pulled or squeezed to form each other. Children's understanding of topology explains why at three or four years old they may draw a circle when they have been given a square to copy.

The first elementary topological spatial relation is that of proximity, or the nearness of objects; the second is the separation of objects from other objects or the parts of an object from the object; the third is order; and the fourth is enclosure. "Order" may refer to the order of the features of a face or the order of a car slowing down, stopping, and a figure getting out. "Enclosure" refers to the surrounding of objects; for example, the eyes are enclosed by a face, a door is enclosed by a wall, and the car is "in" the street and the dog is "in" the yard. Children proceed from simple topological ideas to those involving projection and the Euclidean concepts necessary for reproducing a simple map.

To analyze children's ability to reproduce two-dimensional maps, a layout on a piece of paper is presented to a child. The child is asked to reproduce the same layout on an identical piece of paper using objects like those seen in the first layout. In stage 1 the child cannot reproduce the layout except for the use of the topological knowledge of proximity. Objects seen near one another are placed in close proximity. In stage 2 a child picks out objects that correspond to those in the layout and tries to locate them in similar positions, but fails because he or she has no system of reference that would allow correct placement of the objects. The child is unable to use the edges of the model or paper as a frame of reference. The edge of the paper is used as a reference axis only for objects near the edge of the model. At stage 3A, age seven to eight, a child can coordinate all objects into a simple whole but cannot preserve the correct distances. At stage 3B, age nine to eleven, a child establishes correct intervals of distance between objects by measurement. He or she is now able to coordinate imaginary vertical and horizontal axes to locate objects (Copeland, 1979, pp. 328–333).

Also necessary to making maps is perspective, a most difficult concept for young children. In a Piagetian task a cardboard range of mountains is set on a table in front of a child. The child is asked to walk around the mountains viewing them from all sides. Several drawings are given to the child, who is asked to select the one that shows his or her point of view. Then a doll is moved from one point to another around the table. The child is asked to pick the picture showing the doll's point of view. It is not until the age of seven or eight that the doll's angle of view is correctly identified (Pulaski, 1971, p. 143).

Map making thus should not be taught until the sixth or seventh grade. Instead young children should be exposed to the ideas of proximity, separation, order, and enclosure (Copeland, 1979, pp. 271–272).

characteristics of young children related to social studies

Listed in table 4–1 are characteristics of young children related to social studies. They represent general characteristics of children and *do not* represent the characteristics of any one child. Each child has an individual built-in rate of growth.

goals for development through social studies

The following goals for development through social studies have been chosen as realistic ones for the teacher to select since they can be achieved by the majority

table 4-1
representative characteristics of young children related to social studies

From About 3 Years	to About 6 Years of Age
1. Is self-centered—sees things from own point of view	1. Begins to consider viewpoints other than own—may not reach until seven or eight years
2. Parallel and associative play prevail	2. Cooperative play prevails
3. Perception dominates reasoning—seeing is believing	3. Perception continues to dominate thinking
4. Is unable to construct knowledge from abstract materials	4. Source of knowledge and meaning is largely confined to concrete materials
5. Shows anger and frustration through physical aggression	5. Verbal aggression gradually replaces physical aggression
6. Is anxious to win the approval of adults	6. Is still anxious for adult approval; peer approval is becoming important
7. Play groups are small, two to three children	7. Play groups are larger, five to seven or more children
8. Finds sharing difficult—believes possessions are symbols of self	8. Is more willing to share; understands that possessions and self are separate entities
9. Finds difficulty in learning rules—becomes confused when some aspects of a new situation are the same and others are different	9. Finds rules easier to understand—is beginning to recognize similarities in situations in spite of differences
10. Has difficulty in thinking of self as a member of a group	10. Thinks of self as a separate entity at the same time as a member of a group
11. Identifies own sex and that of others	11. Is aware of own sex and differences in sex roles
12. Is conscious of racial prejudice	12. Racial prejudices may develop depending on the environment
13. Judges people by acts, not intentions	13. Begins to consider motives that prompted actions
14. Understands the here and now	14. Understands today, yesterday, and tomorrow
15. Believes in artificialism—that human beings create natural phenomena	15. Artificialism is still present; begins to seek logical explanations for natural phenomena
16. Believes in animism—that inanimate objects are alive and have human characteristics	16. Animism is still present; begins to differentiate between animate and inanimate objects
17. Does not conserve length and distance	17. Does not conserve; a few may conserve length and distance
18. Sorts objects according to likenesses—simple form of classification	18. Uses multiple classification; a few may understand class inclusion
19. Begins to understand topological relationships—proximity, enclosure, order, and separation	19. Understands most topological relationships; begins to view objects as rigid in shape (Euclidean geometry)
20. Views positions of objects from own point of view independent of perspective	20. Begins to view objects in relationship to other objects
21. Cannot use an imaginary or concrete set of axes as reference systems to position objects	21. Cannot establish a reference system to compare distances and positions simultaneously

of children from ages three to six. Since social studies affects the development of the whole child, objectives are written in the cognitive, affective, social, and psychomotor domains. It is important to remember that not all the objectives will be reached by a child by five or six. The objectives are listed as guides for teachers in planning and as one source for evaluating social behavior.

COGNITIVE DOMAIN.   The child:

1. Uses multiple classification—considers more than one classification property of an object
2. Knows the names of the seasons and can describe their characteristics
3. Identifies morning, afternoon, and night
4. Describes changes in the earth due to weather
5. Acts out such ideas as up, down, over, around, through, under, left, right, stop, go, like, different
6. Locates familiar indoor and outdoor areas from classroom photographs
7. Arranges pictures in sequential order
8. Uses the rise and fall of a thermometer to describe changes in temperature
9. Describes a family as people who live together and do things for each other
10. Recognizes himself or herself in a photograph
11. Names and describes a variety of occupations
12. Discusses various career choices open to him or her when grown up
13. Compares living and nonliving things
14. Describes death as a state from which animals and plants cannot return as they formerly existed on earth
15. Describes physical changes that come about with aging
16. Describes himself or herself as growing from babyhood to present age
17. Compares the characteristics of babies and toddlers with those of four- and five-year-olds
18. Uses time words, such as "minute," "hour," "day," "night," "yesterday," "tomorrow," and "today"
19. Recognizes instruments that measure time, such as a clock and a calendar
20. Names and describes activities associated with Christmas, Thanksgiving, Valentine's Day, Halloween, and Easter
21. Gives the date of his or her birth and his or her age
22. Describes the surface of the earth as land and water
23. Builds block constructions that represent things he or she has seen and/or heard

AFFECTIVE DOMAIN.   The child:

1. Tells whether he or she is a boy or a girl
2. Accepts own physical makeup and compares it with that of others
3. Does many things independently and shows a recognition of own abilities
4. Asks for help when necessary
5. Shows by words and actions that his or her limitations are accepted
6. Completes a task once it is begun

7. Shows through dramatic play interest and knowledge gained through experience

SOCIAL DOMAIN. The child:

1. Shares equipment and materials
2. Contributes ideas and feelings while interacting with others
3. Shows by words or physical actions an absence of prejudice against another child in the group because of any differences from himself or herself or from the majority of the group
4. Willingly takes turns with other children
5. Listens to other children's ideas
6. Uses words instead of physical actions to release emotions
7. Willingly follows directions
8. Cares for the room by putting toys and materials away
9. Cares for plants and/or pets found in the room
10. Contributes to and follows class rules
11. Asks questions and makes comments about classroom activities
12. Shows through actions and words a concern for children who are hurt or handicapped
13. Shows by actions and words that he or she is beginning to move away from an egocentric view of self

PHYSICAL DOMAIN. The child:

1. Manipulates small blocks in order to build a construction
2. Manipulates large blocks in order to build a construction

indoor and outdoor learning centers and social studies

Activity in the area of social studies can occur in any learning center throughout the year. Holidays are times for social studies activity. At Halloween, pumpkins, pumpkin seeds, and pumpkin plants may be seen in the science center. On the Fourth of July, the music center may contain patriotic songs, such as *My Country 'Tis of Thee* and *It's a Grand Old Flag.* At Thanksgiving, the dramatic-play center may contain Indian headdresses, long skirts, and knee breeches for dress-up. Children can be observed outside digging in the soft soil after a rain. Every center reflects the holiday or current topic under discussion.

A news board may be kept in one of the centers. Children can bring in clippings or any form of newsworthy item to place on the bulletin board. Recent photographs taken at home, at school, and/or on a trip can be included. Local news items may involve the children's parents or friends.

center arrangement

Indoor centers should be spaced far enough apart to avoid congestion. Open spaces between centers are created when shelves, used as dividers, are moved away from the walls. This arrangement allows children to enter and leave centers from either end. Teachers should periodically evaluate the flow of traffic in the room. It may be necessary to relocate or rearrange a center. When centers are small, large furniture should be removed and replaced by smaller but equally effective equipment. Large pillows take up less room than and are as attractive and as useful in a library center as tables and chairs. One double easel instead of two single easels may be all that is necessary to accommodate a group of 20 to 25 children.

teacher's attitude

Children take their cues from the environment. What the teacher values, they learn to value. What happens in learning centers reflects the teacher's beliefs about what is important. When one center is emphasized over another, children soon learn that "this is the most important center to the teacher." When freedom of choice is restricted, children learn that "My ideas are not good. The teacher makes choices for me." When learning centers are crowded and poorly planned, children learn, "I have to push to find room for me." When rules are not set, children learn, "It's O.K. for me to hit. I can do anything I want to do here." When centers are well planned, freedom of choice is allowed, and guidance is given, children learn, "My ideas are acceptable. I can do many things. I cannot do anything that will hurt someone else. I can go to my teacher for help."

equipment and supplies

Some pieces of equipment teach children directly about their bodies. A full-length mirror, several small hand mirrors, a scale, and a device for measuring height are a must. Other types of equipment that may be added or borrowed throughout the year are a microscope to look at hair and blood samples, a stethoscope to listen to heartbeat, and a plastic skeleton to "see what our bones look like."

Concepts about various occupations and holidays may be developed in the dramatic-play or in the block center. Children can improvise when they need additional furniture or equipment for their dramatic play. The following accessories may be added to both indoor and outdoor centers for dramatic play related to occupations and holidays.

Restaurant:

Aprons
Trays
Pad and pencils or crayons
Cash register and play money
Pocketbooks and wallets
Play dough
Artificial flowers and containers
Plastic place mats
Nesting chair blocks

Hairdresser:

Wigs
Brushes and combs for wigs
Hair dryer (never attached to an outlet)
Magazines and books
Rollers for wigs
Assorted empty plastic bottles
Hand mirrors
Nesting chair blocks

Hospital:

Child-size cot
Stethoscope
Empty plastic bottles
Doctor's and nurse's caps
Trays and pitchers
Plastic bowls
Suitcase
Doctor's bag
Artificial flowers and containers
Magazines

Grocery Store:

Empty cans (edges smoothed) and food boxes
Cash register and play money
Pocketbooks and wallets
Plastic fruits and vegetables
Play dough
Aprons
Pushcart for groceries
Nesting chair blocks

Schoolroom:

Chalk and chalkboard
Books
Flannel board and figures
Magnetic board and letters
Games
Nesting chair blocks

Halloween:

Pumpkins
Clay pots and dirt

Pumpkin seeds
Spring scales
Equal-arm balance

Valentine's Day:

Satchel for letter carrier
Canceled envelopes

Fourth of July:

Large American flag
Model of the Liberty Bell
Old-fashioned dress-up clothes
Wigs
Pictures of the current United States president, Washington, and Lincoln
Records of patriotic music

Christmas:

Records of Christmas music
Rhythm instruments, especially bells
Small Christmas tree to decorate
Large box to make chimney for dramatic-play area
Art media, collage materials, and wood for making Christmas gifts and tree
    decorations

Easter:

Baskets
Plastic eggs to hide outdoors
Real eggs to dye with food coloring
Stuffed animals—rabbits, chicks, lambs

Our Own History:

Baby and preschool pictures
Toys played with as baby
Baby clothes
Large calendar with each child's birthday marked
Long strips of paper to measure height

teacher's role in social studies

The teacher's role in social studies will be described below for the various topics.

ourselves

DEVELOPING A POSITIVE SELF-CONCEPT.   Before children can become interested in others they must first find out about themselves. A teacher can capitalize upon this natural interest in self to help each child feel special. There are no two children exactly alike. As one child expressed it, "Twins look alike, but they *are* different."

Teachers take it for granted that children are familiar with their physical appearance. Surprisingly, children often do not know their eye and hair coloring, and a few do not recognize themselves in photographs. One five-year-old girl did not recognize herself in a photograph taken with a Polaroid camera. Her teacher suggested she look in a full-length mirror and then at her picture. The teacher carefully pointed out that Jane was wearing the same clothes as those in the photograph. Jane only shook her head and looked puzzled. The teacher realized that Jane did not know color names. Her descripton of Jane's red, blue, and yellow dress meant nothing to Jane. After several days spent examining photographs of herself and comparing them with her image in the mirror, Jane began to realize that the photographs were pictures of herself. It was a memorable day when Jane touched herself and then pointed to her photograph and said, "That's me."

Four- and five-year-olds may tell you that their hair and eyes are one color when in reality they are a different color. More sophisticated children will say that their hair is strawberry blond or auburn and their eyes are violet or hazel. At the beginning of the year hand mirrors may be placed in each center and children encouraged to look at themselves. One little boy asked, "What are those spots on my nose?" He had never before noticed his freckles.

Children's names are very precious to them. On the first day of school a teacher called a four-year-old by his name. He jumped up from his chair saying, "Me! I go first. You knew my name!" When there are two or more children in the class with the same first name, a teacher should write both first and last names on their name cards, lockers, paintings, etc. A child can lose his or her identity if known only as John T. or Jane W. A five-year-old girl became very upset when she learned that there would be two Alices in the room. Her mother said that Alice had been called Alice P. all through nursery school and refused to come to kindergarten if the teacher was going to call her Alice P. The letter "P" had unpleasant connotations for her.

Children who are considered normal may feel different from their classmates. Noticeably smaller, taller, or heavier children in the group are particularly conscious of their size. A four-year-old girl stood beside a measuring tape every day and said, "I'm bigger today, aren't I?" The undersized boy, however, is often more disturbed than the small girl. A five-year-old boy who was very short and small-boned was helped to accept his physical appearance by talking with his parents and the teacher. His parents pointed out that they were both small and that he would grow but would probably never be a very tall man. He was a well-coordinated child and the teacher helped him capitalize on his physical skills, which gave him the confidence he needed to accept himself.

Children who wear glasses are often self-conscious. They may lower their heads, hide their faces, and shy away from other children. One way to help children accept glasses is to admire their appearance. Glasses can be attractive, pretty, and becoming. When teachers show acceptance of children's appearance they accept themselves more willingly.

One way to help children overcome feelings of being different is to stress the ways they are like other children. Teachers can focus on the interests children have in common by taking pictures of various learning centers. Children will discover that their play is similar to that of other children. They may not play with all the same things but they do have similar interests. They also have similar feelings: No one likes to be hit or called names. Everyone likes to laugh, but sometimes cries if hurt.

EXPERIENCING DIFFERENT VIEWPOINTS.

Overcoming Prejudice.   Racial prejudice is present in almost any mixed racial group. It stems from the attitudes of parents and those of society. The teacher's acceptance of racial differences is the most crucial factor in children's attitudes toward racial groups in the classroom.

Jimmy was the only black child in a class. He was playing at a table with play dough. One child said, "Don't give the white clay to Jimmy. Give him the green clay. He's black." When the teacher heard the remarks, she moved to the table and began to manipulate the clay. As she handled the clay she gave different colors to Jimmy and the other children. A child asked, "Have you ever heard black people called niggers?" She replied, "Yes, I have, but I don't like it. No one likes to be called names." Later the same child asked, "Do you go to church?" She said yes and the matter was dropped. The teacher wondered if this child associated kind treatment with church doctrine rather than with feelings for others. It is very difficult for young children to put themselves in another's place. This is one reason why lecturing them on how they should feel toward other children is a waste of time.

Sometimes children can be helped by pointing out contradictions in their thinking. A teacher was standing next to a jungle gym where three boys were playing. They were admiring a motorcycle parked nearby. When a black man came out of the building and got on the motorcycle, one child said, "Oh, he's black. I don't like that motorcycle!" Other children joined in, "We don't either." The teacher said, "Miss C., one of your teachers, is black. You told me yesterday that you liked her. Why don't you like the black man's motorcycle? Is it because he's black?" The boys thought about this and one said, "I guess black people are alright." He was not convinced but had begun to think about what he felt.

Children are aware of the variations in skin color within the same racial group. One black teacher's class called her the "beige teacher." She was not offended and pointed out that the skin coloring of blacks is not always the same. In spite of her efforts to explain that she was black, the black children insisted that she was white, the Chinese children that she was Chinese, and the white children that she was black. Since she was "beige" she belonged to each race in a special way. This incident emphasizes the importance of comparing skin colors and of showing that white people also have different shades of skin color.

Children with Special Needs.   Children who are different in some way or are mainstreamed into the classroom may have difficulty forming a positive self-concept. Jennifer was of normal intelligence but could not walk because of heavy leg braces. The teacher was unable to lift her from place to place, and she decided to discuss the problem with the children. They were asked to think of some ways to help Jennifer. Finally it was decided to move her in a wagon. Each day two children assumed the responsibility of pulling the wagon. In turn Jennifer helped the other children. One day, for example, there were many puzzle pieces left to put together; Jennifer volunteered. The teacher's concern and caring attitude toward Jennifer was reflected in the children's treatment of her and her treatment of the other children.

Children with physical handicaps are easier for other children to accept than children who are retarded or emotionally unstable. When children with special needs behave in ways that are strange and even frightening, the group should be given an explanation for the behavior. A retarded child with a progressive brain disease exhibited behavior that was occasionally bizarre and puzzling to the children. Krissey would take off her pants and hide them when no one was looking. The children found this behavior disturbing rather than funny. The teacher talked about Krissey's behavior while she was in the resource room. The teacher asked them why the children thought Krissey behaved as she did. Answers ranged from "she's bad!" to "she doesn't like to wear pants." The teacher explained that Krissey's brain had been injured at birth, and therefore she was not able to think as they did. She told the children that she would talk to Krissey about her behavior, and that if Krissey understood, the behavior might stop. It did, but Krissey continued to disrupt in other ways. The children never fully accepted her behavior, but they were tolerant and kind to her.

Children often show genuine concern, thoughtfulness, and kindness toward each other. These qualities must be reinforced by teachers. An unusually thoughtful six-year-old boy showed kindness toward children and adults. His comments, such as "That's O.K. He didn't mean it" or "That was nice of you" or "I'm sorry you're hurt," were reinforced by the teacher with honest replies such as, "You're thoughtful to remember Tom's feelings," "I was happy to do it for you," and "What you said may help Mary feel better."

home and family

A family may be defined as "a group of people who live together and help each other" and a home as "the place where the family lives." Sometimes children of divorce talk about two homes. One child spent a week each month with her father and three weeks with her mother. She spoke of "my two homes." Three-year-old Susie, whose parents were divorced and whose mother had deserted her, lived with one set of grandparents one week and the other the next week. She was a much loved child, but the necessity of moving from home to home brought her to the verge of a breakdown. The school psychologist suggested that she stay with her father, who lived in another town. A year with her father Susie was a stable, happy child. She remained with and continued to develop satisfactorily.

Teachers must be aware of changing family patterns and the crises that face many children. One little boy said, "My mother cries every time I go to my daddy's house; she doesn't want me to see him." A little girl said tearfully, "My mother can't live with my daddy. He bloodies her up." It was difficult for the teacher to know what to say to these children. In the first case she suggested, "Tell your mother you will be back soon. Mothers miss children when they are away." In the second case she told the child that sometimes her parents were unable to get along together and that it might be better for them to live apart. Teachers cannot solve problems for children, but they can listen and give them as much emotional support as possible.

One of the most effective ways to talk with children about their families is to relate what they do at home to the activities they enjoy at school. Pictures taken in school with a Polaroid camera may be placed on the bulletin board and changed regularly. In small groups questions can be asked such as "What are you doing in this picture?" "Do you hang up your coat at home?" "Do you put your toys away?" and "What else do you do to help at home?" Children may be encouraged to bring pictures of family members to school. This activity must be voluntary and informal, since not all children have photographs of themselves and/or family members. The pictures can be used to relate what happens in school to what happens at home. They can also be used to discuss different kinds of families.

Teachers should refrain from asking children to draw themselves or family members. Most four- and five-year-olds have not reached the schematic stage of art and do not make recognizable drawings of people. Children have been known to groan, "I can't draw people," "I don't want to," "I don't know how to draw my mother," and "I can't draw me!"

Encouraging children to tell something about themselves and/or their families at the beginning of the year can be just as frustrating. They may not be able to think of anything to say or, being very literal-minded, take the attitude, "Well, here I am! Can't you see me!" This request also can encourage children to make up things about themselves. A five-year-old boy wanted a baby brother very badly. When asked to tell something about himself, he announced, "My mother is going to have a baby, a baby boy." The other children in the room became excited over what was wishful thinking on the part of the boy. Another child reported that she always ate peanuts for breakfast, adding, "That's something different about me." Teachers must guard against saying, "You're making that up." Instead they must try to find out the facts. The teacher learned later that Alice did indeed eat peanuts for breakfast.

It is difficult for children to understand the relationships of family members. A five-year-old and his teacher were discussing his cousin Sara. When the teacher said that his mother was Sara's aunt, he yelled, "My mother is not an aunt, she is my mother." Some children will insist that they are older than their big brothers and sisters because they are taller. "The bigger, the better" is the rule with most three's, four's, and five's. A four-year-old who had two teachers insisted that Ms. Smith was older than Ms. Jones because she was bigger. Actually Ms. Jones had gray hair and was old enough to be Ms. Smith's mother. The child ignored the gray hair and wrinkles and concentrated on size.

Young children often refer to a teacher's husband as her father or grandfather. It is just as difficult for them to understand the single teacher who does not

Big brothers can help too.

have a husband and/or children. Comments like these are often heard: "You're not married! Why not? You can marry me when I grow up." and "Why don't you have children? Are they dead?" If it is impossible for children to visit their teacher's home, photographs of family members are the best substitute. One teacher made a book about herself and each year added a new page. The book told her story in photographs from the time she was a baby to the present.

A teacher should not be alarmed if children say, "I wish you were my father/mother." This is the same as saying, "I like you so much that I wouldn't mind if you were my father/mother." Occasionally children do prefer their teacher to their parents. These usually are children who have very poor relations with one or both parents. One five-year-old said that she was coming home with the teacher and putting her clothes in the closet. This child really meant what she said. Jane's behavior was hostile toward a younger sister who was made the center of attention in the home. It was hard for Jane to understand that no one was sure that her sister, who had suffered a birth injury, would grow up to be normal. Jane retaliated against the extra attention shown her sister by becoming a behavior problem at home. After several parent-teacher conferences the parents began to understand Jane's problem. By the end of the year mother and daughter achieved a satisfactory relationship. Unfortunately the conflict between them began again in the first grade, and Jane ran away from home twice as a teenager. She remained hostile toward her mother into adulthood. Teachers cannot always change the home situation for a child, but they may be able to ease and/or alleviate some of the problems.

One overprotected four-year-old's behavior was like that of a three-year-old. Steve reverted to baby talk at school, told the teacher, "I'm tired," when he did not want to do something, and said, "My daddy will fix it," whenever he did not have his way. Steve did not know how to relate to other children; he chose one child as his buddy and followed him everywhere. Everything was fine until his buddy began to play with other children. Fortunately Steve's father realized what was happening to his child. At the end of one conference he said, "It's my fault; he will never change until I do." Steve's father stopped doing everything for his son and encouraged him to start doing things for himself. Within a few weeks there was a noticeable change in the child's behavior.

All preschool teachers can relate experiences similar to those described above. The important thing is to continue to try to help children with family problems no matter how hopeless the situation may seem. A teacher who suspects child abuse should notify the principal or the proper authorities at once. Some states have child-abuse telephone numbers one can call and remain anonymous.

career education

CAREER CHOICES. A kindergarten teacher began career education by talking about the classroom. "Who takes care of it? Do you? Do I? Does anyone else?" The biggest surprise for the children was to learn that the teacher prepared the materials and ordered their equipment. She also studied, read books, and went to school to learn more about children. After school another teacher took pictures of the classroom teacher as she worked. The next day these pictures were discussed in small groups and a list made of all the things teachers do to prepare for school.

The children took turns being teacher for the day for one day each month. With the teacher's guidance the child whose turn it was planned for the school day, including materials, snack, and stories. The day before, the prospective teacher for the day helped the teacher get materials and the room ready for the next day. One child commented, "I know my teacher works hard. I was teacher for a day."

Teachers should acquaint themselves with the various occupations of the children's parents. They can help children understand about the work of their parent(s). Two boys were asked what their fathers did and the first replied, "Works in an office," whereas the second said, "I don't know, but he comes home sweaty and dirty." The first child's father was an executive with a telephone company and the second child's father was a veterinarian. Neither child had visited his father's place of business.

Whenever possible parents (both mothers and fathers) should take their children to see where they work and observe what they do there. A four-year-old was asked what her mother did at work. She replied, "She's a secretary and she cooks and makes beds." These were things she had seen her mother do at home; she had no idea of what a secretary did.

Not all mothers work; some are housewives and spend much of their time at home. A teacher asked, "Do your mothers work?" If the mothers were housewives, the replies were similar, "No, she stays home," or "No, she takes care of the baby," or "No, she cooks." One mother was invited to tell the children about her work. She brought a younger boy to school with her. She described how she cared for her home and family. While she talked different children were asked to watch the two-year-old. They soon learned that they had an important and difficult job. One little boy said, "That's too much work. He moves fast."

SEX STEREOTYPING.   Attitudes toward careers are often affected by the child's sex. As one child said on observing a woman bricklayer, "Why are you doing that?" The woman answered, "I like doing it. I've done it most of my life." The shocked child replied, "But ladies aren't bricklayers!" In the minds of many children there are specific occupations for men and for women: a nurse is a woman, a doctor a man, a hairdresser a woman, a plumber a man, a secretary a woman, a police officer a man.

The best way to counteract these stereotyped images of male and female roles is to introduce children to men and women who have been successful in more unorthodox occupations. A kindergarten teacher placed several wigs in the dramatic-play center. After much combing the wigs began to look shabby. One day the teacher wore a wig to school, took it off, and explained that she had it combed by her hairdresser, who was a man. The children laughed at the idea of a man being a hairdresser. A visit from the male hairdresser was arranged. He brought the children a wig, showed them how to comb it, and talked with them about washing and caring for their hair. The children visited the beauty shop and watched Mr. J. at work. He showed them pictures of his wife and children. Gradually the children's attitude began to change toward the role of men in what they had thought was a woman's occupation. They set up a beauty parlor in the dramatic-play center. Boys as well as girls were observed playing hairdresser.

In one community preschool groups were invited to visit the local hospital each spring. Their experience was followed by a visit from a male nurse who talked to them about his work. He left several nurse's and doctor's hats, an empty syringe (without needle), and a stethoscope. A play hospital was set up in the dramatic-play area. Although most girls chose the nurse's hats and boys the doctor's, a few boys willingly took the role of nurse.

A policewoman visited one kindergarten classroom. She showed the children her police car, allowed them to talk on the radio and listen to the siren. The girls were excited about the possibility of becoming a policewoman when they grew up. They had not known that a woman could be a police officer.

A noted artist spoke to a group of kindergarten children about his work. He was especially interesting to the children because he was the creator of Snap, Crackle, and Pop, figures used by the Kellogg Company to advertise one of its cereals. He told them about his boyhood, the years he spent living in poverty, and the various jobs he had before becoming a successful artist. In this way the children learned that training and effort are a necessary part of preparation for a career.

Teachers must remember that children will change their minds many times about their professions. They are not ready to decide what they will be when they grow up. Instead of asking, "What do you want to be when you grow up?" talk with children about the many things they can do when they grow up.

values and morality

Children's sense of right and wrong comes from the authority figures in their lives. They are told what is expected of them, and in order to please and avoid unpleasant consequences, they comply with adults' wishes. Teachers' expectations of children must therefore be reasonable and realistic. It is reasonable to expect a few blocks to be put away, but it is unreasonable to expect a child to put away all the blocks. It is reasonable to expect a child to sit quietly for 5 to 10 minutes but unreasonable to expect a child to sit still for 30 to 40 minutes.

Children become confused and insecure when teachers are inconsistent and when they don't know what teachers expect of them. When teachers say, "It's time to ——" or "You can't ——," they must be certain they can carry out what is said. A nursery school teacher told a child he would have to taste everything on his plate before he could get up from the table. The teacher and the child sat until 2:00 P.M., when the child finally gave in. It is best for teachers to avoid statements that involve threats. It is better to say, "Try to taste a little of each kind of food before you go outside," than to say, "You must taste each food before you go outside."

Often teachers create problems because they are unsure of themselves and/or afraid they will offend children. This is surprising since children know when they are liked and what is fair. When children ask to do something they cannot do at the moment or perhaps at any other time, they should be told firmly and pleasantly, "You can't do that because ——. You may do —— instead." Teachers should find alternatives for children whenever possible. In the summer many children ask to take off their shoes on the playground. When there is clover and bees are plentiful, this is not advisable. Children can be told, "You must keep your shoes on or the bees might sting you." If a child continues to insist on taking off his or her shoes, the teacher can say, "You may keep your shoes on or stay indoors." A child continued to take off her shoes when she had been asked to keep them on. She was stung by a bee, which ended the shoe episode. When the teacher pulled the stinger out of her foot, the child said, "I guess you were right. Children need to keep their shoes on."

Never give children a choice that is not a *real* choice. Questions like, "Would you like to go outside now?" or "Would you like to hear a story?" deserve a "no" answer. When it is time to go outside the teacher can say, "It's time to go outside now," or "We're going outside." So often teachers say, "I'm sorry, but ——." If they are sorry, they should not expect the behavior from the children.

Extreme behavior problems must be dealt with differently. If children are interfering with the rights of other children, they must be stopped. Most children understand "I can't let anyone hurt you and I can't let you hurt anyone. I'm a teacher, and it's my job to keep children from getting hurt." There are children who get into the habit of certain kinds of behavior, and they need to find out what it feels like to behave differently. One little girl who persisted in hitting was isolated from the group (in a part of the room where the teacher could see her and she could see the teacher). This child began to hit herself whenever she was tempted to hit someone. She verbalized what she was doing by saying, "I won't hit! I won't hit!" Eventually the hitting stopped.

Sometimes immature children take things home from school. They are not thieves and should not be treated as if they are. Children may take things because they want to bring something home from school or because they find an object attractive. When teachers see children put things in their pockets, they can wait and later say, "I can't find the blue truck. Look around and see if you can find it. I want to put it on the shelf so it won't get lost." Children usually respond to this strategy. One little boy said, "I can't find the fire truck anywhere." The teacher said, "Before we go outside we'll have to find it." The boy reached inside his sock and said laughingly, "Oh! I found it in my sock." He had saved face with his teacher and returned the truck.

Teachers sometimes say to children, "You need to do ——" This seems illogical when children probably do not feel they *need* to do it. Another remark that seems illogical is, "We don't hit here. We are all friends." This may be hypocritical because most children like some children better than others and may not consider everyone their friend.

There are teachers who tell children to say "I'm sorry" when they are probably not sorry at all. Insisting on "I'm sorry" may lead to feelings of insincerity and resentment. It is better to talk about how both children feel rather than to insist on an apology. Saying to children, "What do you say?" when you want them to say "please" or "thank you" may be just as undesirable. Children learn best by modeling the behavior of adults who say "thank you" or "I'm sorry" or "excuse me."

A teacher must decide which behaviors are inappropriate in a democratic classroom. Any behavior that interferes with the rights of others cannot be allowed. Certainly, throwing equipment and biting are inappropriate behaviors. Expected behaviors may vary from one situation to another. One school had a river running directly behind the playground. It was important to tell children on the first day of school that they must stay within the fence and never walk along the river.

On the whole, rules should be made as situations arise. One day a new loft was moved into a classroom. The teacher observed children as they played on the loft. They did the natural things children do—jumped off and threw things from above. The teacher asked the children to stop playing and come together in a group. She talked with them about what was happening on the loft. The children described their own behavior and decided it wasn't safe. They dictated those things they wanted to remember while playing on the loft. The children had made their own rules, which were read when needed.

DEATH AND RELIGION.   Children come in contact with death most frequently through the death of an animal. If teachers do not like animals and/or cannot make provisions for them during summers and weekends, they should not have a

We take good care of our guinea pig.

pet in the classroom. Children become indifferent to animals teachers ignore. They learn that the life of an animal is not important and it doesn't matter how they are treated. Since children identify closely with animals, they relate what they have learned about animals to people. They may become insensitive to people and mistreat them as they have seen animals mistreated.

Occasionally a well-cared-for pet becomes sick and dies. When an animal dies of natural causes children should be allowed to touch it. An elderly gerbil died at the age of five. She had outlived her normal life span by two years. The teacher talked with the children about their dead pet and how much they had liked her. They discussed the funeral and where Queenie should be buried. The teacher did not allow the children to see Queenie, who was in a small box with a closed lid. She said, "You don't want to look at her; it will make you sad." These children had only the teacher's word that their gerbil was even in the box. They had the right to see her and touch her. Only through concrete examples of death can they form concepts about the nature of death. They must understand the finality of death. There is no more movement, no more eating or drinking, no more normal sleeping and waking up.

Children may suggest having a funeral for a dead pet. They should be encouraged to plan and execute the funeral. One year chickens were hatched in an incubator. One of the chicks was born with a stomach that was not fully formed. The children talked about the chick and wondered if it was in pain. There was no way to make it well, and it died. The teacher put it into a small box. Each child asked to touch it and say goodbye. The chick was buried with great ceremony. Its grave was marked with stones and flowers. One child drew a picture of it (alive) to put on the grave. The teacher did not suggest a prayer, but several children asked to pray. One child prayed, "Dear God, if you want to, take this bird to heaven." Another child remarked, "This is just like Winston-Salem (a Moravian cemetery) in the graveyard." These children learned respect for dead things, an important concept to learn in order to respect life.

When children ask questions about religious beliefs a teacher can explain that different points of view exist. One child asked, "Isn't there an animal heaven?" The teacher replied, "Some people believe that animals go to a special place when they die; no one is sure. Perhaps you may want to ask your mother and daddy about this." Whenever possible tell the parent(s) the questions children ask and the answers you gave them.

The question is sometimes asked, "If an animal seems to be in pain should it be put to sleep?" The answer probably depends on the circumstances and the attitudes of children. One summer a group of 13 five- and six-year-olds collected insects for six weeks. The teacher carried a jar in which to kill the insects immediately after they were caught. He explained that it was very cruel to stick live insects with pins or leave them in a jar until they died. By the end of the six-week period each child had a box filled with mounted and identified insects. In this case killing the insects was a humane act and a good learning experience for the children.

When a parent or sibling dies the teacher has the responsibility of explaining the circumstances to the other children in the class. In one kindergarten a child's father died. Mr. B. had spent a great deal of time in the kindergarten room helping the children build a bird feeder, set up an aquarium, and fly kites. He was loved by all the children. They became very quiet and listened as the teacher told them about their friend's death. She told them that a blood vessel had burst in Mr. B.'s head and that there had been nothing the doctors could do to mend it. One little boy would not accept the explanation. He said, "They took him to the wrong hospital. If they had taken him to the convalescent home he would have gotten well. Orpha went there and she got well." This child reasoned from one particular incident to another. Even after an explanation from the teacher and his mother, Jim was not convinced. A child who had been mainstreamed due to mental retardation walked around the room saying loudly, "This is terrible, just terrible." The aide asked Sara if she wanted to sit with her. She pulled her chair next to the aide and continued to mutter, "It's terrible." Teachers should remember that children react differently to death, just as adults do.

Sometimes children continue to talk about a death for a long time after it occurs. One five-year-old girl felt her daddy who had died the year before was with her at all times. She made comments such as "I am going to swing high and touch my daddy" or "My daddy watches me at school" or "I'm making this picture for daddy." During a parent conference Kate's mother told the teacher that she did not want Kate to forget her father and that she was reminded every day to think of him. Kate continued to talk about her father and at Christmas made a present for him. The teacher suggested that she give the present to someone who could use it since her father would not be able to receive her present. Kate decided to give it to a male friend in her neighborhood. She changed the name on the card and seemed satisfied.

Unsure of her decision, the teacher talked with the school psychologist, who told her he thought she had done the right thing. The teacher had a conference with Kate's mother to explain what she had told Kate about the Christmas present. The mother was not convinced that the teacher had made the right decision but fortunately was not angry about the incident. Later, when the class buried a dead animal on the playground, Kate said, "I'm glad my daddy isn't buried. He isn't under the ground." The teacher talked again with the mother, who told her that Kate had not gone to her father's funeral and did not know he was buried. The teacher uged her to show Kate her father's grave. The teacher realized why Kate was so convinced that "Daddy is watching me." Kate's mother took her to the cemetery and showed her where her father was buried. She also told Kate not to worry anymore about forgetting her father. From then on Kate mentioned her father occasionally but she never again referred to his watching her.

Often children are concerned about what would happen to them if their parents died. A five-year-old asked the teacher if she would adopt him if his parents died. He did not want his godparents to adopt him. During a parent conference the teacher learned that Jim's parents were the godparents of a little girl, but the girl's parents were not Jim's godparents. After assurance that "Mr. and Mrs. D. are not your godparents; you have no godparents," Jim relaxed. Children who are disturbed about what is going to happen to them at their parent's death need reassurance that they will be cared for by loving relatives or friends.

THE AGING PROCESS.   Young children should learn not only to respect older people but also to appreciate them. An 83-year-old man talked with a kindergarten group about his past and present life. He brought an old gas lamp with him; the shades were drawn and, to the delight of the children, the lamp was lit. Mr. H. talked about the one-room, gas-lit schoolhouse he had once walked two miles to attend. He told them that he was no longer able to walk two miles but that he enjoyed working in his flower garden. The children visited Mr. H.'s garden, which was close to the school, and observed him at work there. They were amazed at what he could do sitting on the ground digging in the soil. Mr. H. gave them flowers for the classroom. He was invited to come to visit at any time and became a frequent visitor and a vital part of the group.

A well-known, elderly artist living in a community was invited to talk to a group of four- and five-year-olds. He described his life as an artist, drew pictures, and told the children about his present work. They were able to visit his home and see his previous paintings as well as the work on his easel. Mr. V. was known by both the children's parents and their grandparents. From this experience the children gained a feeling for the continuity of life.

A child suggested that the class invite their grandparents to school. The children made invitations that were sent to their grandparents and in some cases great grandparents. If a child did not have grandparents living in the community, he or she invited an older friend. The children had a typical school day; the elderly people entered into their activities. Through these experiences the children began to talk about the elderly very differently from the way they had before.

I invited my grandmother for lunch.

Not all elderly people are reasonably well and alert. A teacher took a group of children to a nursing home to sing Christmas songs. She was stunned when the elderly people were unaware of the children. The children were confused, and some were afraid. This situation should never have happened. The teacher had not visited the home ahead of time nor had the children been prepared for the visit.

A 5-year-old asked his 43-year-old father if he was getting old. The father asked, "Do you think I am getting older?" The child answered, "Yes, because you have a wrinkle on your forehead and gray hairs." The father replied, "Yes, I am getting older every day just as you are getting older."

Children need concrete experiences to help them understand that they, too, are aging. A mother and father brought their two-week-old twins to kindergarten. The children talked about how small the babies were and how they could not take care of themselves. Several children were surprised that the babies were so small and said that they had never been "little like that." The teacher encouraged them to bring their baby pictures to school. They took turns guessing, "Who's the baby in this picture?" They laughed when one of the pictures turned out to be the teacher. "You didn't look like that, did you?" they asked. The teacher showed them other pictures of himself at different ages. They noticed that as the child in the pictures grew older he more closely resembled their teacher. They decided that the most recent picture looked more like him than any of the others.

Polaroid pictures of the class were taken and compared with the children's baby pictures. If a child did not have a baby picture, the Polaroid picture was compared with a picture taken at the beginning of the school year. The children realized that they had changed and would continue to change as they grew older.

history

Children's comments about the past, present, and future reveal their limited knowledge of time, which is closely related to the study of history. A six-and-a-half-year-old boy said, "I'm going to spend two weeks with my grandmother, maybe even one week." The teacher asked, "Which is longer, one or two weeks?" He thoughtfully replied, "I guess two weeks." She asked, "How many days in a week?" He replied by naming the days of the week. She asked, "How many days did you name?" He answered, "That's about seven hours, I think." This conversation reflects the young child's confusion over days, weeks, and hours. The same child said he knew everything that had ever happened in the world. When asked how he knew, he replied with complete confidence, "Oh, I just knew before I was born." Other familiar comments made by children are "Is today tomorrow?" "I stayed up late last night, I think to about six o'clock," "I am going to the beach today [meaning tomorrow]," and "I won't be in school anymore. I'm going away for the weekend."

It is difficult to teach children about last week and almost impossible to teach them meaningfully about the past. Their natural egocentricity, however, motivates them to have a natural interest in their own past. Looking at pictures of themselves when they were younger is especially interesting. The use of baby pictures in studying the past was discussed under The Aging Process.

If possible allow children to bring a baby toy and an article of baby clothing to school. A teacher brought toys she had had as a baby and little girl. It was very interesting to the children that anyone "so tall" could fit into the "little shoes and dresses." Even more interesting were the toys. Their form and use have changed very little but the materials from which they are made are very different.

The most effective way to help children understand time concepts is through daily routines. Although the schedule is flexible, there are regular routines such as, "after playing outside we have a short rest," "after learning-center time we go outside," and "before snack we wash our hands."

A teacher took pictures of children throughout the day. She showed individual children three pictures and asked them to describe each. She asked the children what they did when they came to school, in the middle of the day, and before they went home. Then the children were asked to put the pictures in order. The teacher was amazed that so few five-year-olds could seriate the pictures, whereas the six-year-olds had no difficulty and some of them could seriate as many as six pictures. She showed commercial pictures depicting a child's foot, a foot with a sock, and a foot with a sock and a shoe. She found that older children could seriate the pictures but the older four's and younger five's were unable to put the pictures in order. She asked the children who were having difficulty to take off their socks, look at their bare feet in the mirror, and then look in the mirror and put on their socks and shoes. Now the children were able to put the pictures in order.

Children often become confused about time if the sequence of events is changed. One summer a group of children four and a half to six and a half years old visited a nature museum. They prepared their snack at school the day before. On the day of the trip they talked about each thing they would do in sequential order. The teacher emphasized that the snack would be eaten at the museum. When the children returned to school several said, "We haven't had our snack so we can't go home." These children used transductive thinking as they reasoned from one particular to another.

Children should know ahead of time what is going to happen, because any sudden change in routine may make them feel insecure. A teacher forgot to tell the class that she would not be at school the next day. Two children became very upset and refused to accept the substitute's explanation that their teacher would be back the next day. They fretted most of the morning and told their parents that Miss M. had gone and they had a new teacher.

Occasionally emergencies arise and changes in schedule are necessary. In one school a bomb scare occurred. The children moved outside quickly since the teacher had prepared them ahead of time for possible emergencies. She had told them that if something happened that was a real emergency, they must not be frightened but do exactly as she told them. The children did not panic but quickly followed her instructions. During the Cuban missile crisis the situation became so serious that, in one school, parents helped gather blankets and food in case the children would not be able to leave the school building. The teacher was uneasy, but she had to remain calm at all times. She reassured the children that, no matter what happened, they would be taken care of, something she was not at all sure of herself.

HOLIDAYS. Teachers must guard against presenting stereotypes to children. The Indians who helped the Pilgrims did not live in teepees, and the story about George Washington and the cherry tree is a legend. The history of a holiday is not as important as the customs of the local community. In some parts of the country children go for "Trick or Treat," but in other areas this custom is not practiced. Memorial Day is observed in the North, but only mentioned in passing in the South. Saint Patrick's Day is not an appropriate holiday for most preschool children, but a few communities celebrate this holiday. "Know your local customs" is a must for teachers.

There are holidays that are celebrated in all parts of the country. Those appropriate for preschool children are Thanksgiving, Christmas, Valentine's Day, and Easter. In one kindergarten the teacher stressed friendship during the month of February. She began with activities stressing the "self" and "others." Then children talked about the things they could do to show they liked someone. Many ideas were discussed, such as "tell them you like them," "buy them a present," "send them a letter," and "make them something." Children were encouraged to carry out their own ideas. Some children used art media to make things for the principal, the teacher, the custodian, their parents, and in some instances, other children in the room. These activities led to a discussion of "What is a friend?" and "How do you know when someone is your friend?" Since it was close to Valentine's Day the children made valentines for each other and for their other friends. The traditional exchange of valentines was carried out; however, the main focus was on friendship.

Most five-year-old children are capable of planning their own activities to celebrate a holiday. The teacher must accept children's suggestions unless it is impossible to carry them out. One little girl wanted to roast hot dogs over a fire at Easter. Her idea was discussed with the children, who decided that it would be dangerous to build a fire in the building. Another child wanted to bob for apples on a string for Valentine's Day. The suggestion surprised the teacher, who said, "We did that for Halloween." The child replied, "Why can't we do it again? Apples are red, aren't they?" This class is probably the only kindergarten group in the United States that bobbed for apples on Valentine's Day.

During the Christmas season emphasis should be placed on making and giving things to others. Make available all kinds of art media, including earth clay and wood. When children decide what they want to make, the teacher can write it on a piece of paper so they won't forget. They may make as few or as many gifts as they like. Children should be encouraged to use their imaginations and should never be given patterns to copy. A child's painting mounted on construction paper makes a lovely present.

During a religious holiday, such as Christmas or Easter, teachers should follow the children's lead. If they talk about Jesus' birth or his death, the teacher can ask them to tell what they know about the event. One child said, "You forgot the baby Jesus." When asked to tell what she knew about Jesus, Jane said that people celebrate Christmas because Jesus was born. The teacher explained that many religions celebrate Christmas, whereas others celebrate Hanukkah or do not consider Christmas a religious holiday. One year a Jewish boy and his mother told a class how Hanukkah is celebrated. Dick brought the gifts he received for Hanukkah to school each day. The children decided that it was much better to be Jewish than Christian—"You get more presents!"

Some children's parents are atheists, Unitarians, or Christian Scientists or belong to some other religious group. Teachers should find out as much as possible about the parents' religious beliefs, often reflected in children's attitudes. One child refused to drink Coca Cola. He told his teacher that his religion said it was wrong. When the teacher talked with the mother she learned that the child was correct. His religion forbade the drinking of any carbonated beverage. It is important to point out to children that people have different beliefs but that all religions stress caring about and doing things for other people.

FIELD TRIPS.   It is best to take children on field trips in small rather than large groups. A kindergarten group was invited to an ice cream parlor owned by a parent. The children visited in four groups of six on two successive days. When small groups cannot be arranged it may be better to omit a trip unless children can be active and outdoors. A group of 25 children with 3 adults can visit a turkey farm and look at the turkeys or a pumpkin patch and look at the pumpkins. When children are taken indoors and asked to sit or stand quietly, listen and ask questions, however, they should be in small groups.

One child came back from a trip to the post office with his kindergarten class of 25 and asked, "Where were the letters?" There had been too many children to see what was happening. Many of them became bored and wandered about the post office. For most of these children the trip was a waste of time.

They're buying stamps for their valentines.

Children can help make their own rules before going on trips. They can be divided into small groups with each group making its own rules. Since teachers are a part of the group, they can add any rules they think are necessary. Each time children go on a different trip they can discuss previous rules and add any new ones they need. This procedure does not mean that the same children always go together on a trip. Instead groups can share each other's rules, which are usually similar.

international understanding

The key to helping children learn about the customs and language of other countries is to provide concrete learning experiences. Exposing children to pictures, books, and verbal information without first-hand experiences is futile. One teacher attempted to teach Hawaii to kindergarten children in an eastern state. There were no experiences provided with real objects and people. The children's comments and answers to questions showed that their learning was very superficial. One child said, "Hawaii is right up the street." Another said, "Everyone in Hawaii wears sarongs and dances all day."

It is very easy for teachers to teach stereotyped concepts of peoples of other countries. They must learn the most current information about a foreign country or faraway places. One group of kindergarten children made igloos out of plastic bowls, marshmallows, and glue. Not only was the concept that all Eskimos live in igloos incorrect, but the marshmallows impressed on young, literal minds the idea that igloos are made either of marshmallows or of ice resembling marshmallows.

Most young children do not understand the concept of class inclusion. An attempt to explain city, state, and country is met with little success. A foreign language teacher who had never worked with young children asked a group of four-year-olds where they lived. The replies ranged from "at my house" to "Rock Hill." The teacher repeated, "Where do you live?" One child in desperation yelled "in South Carolina." the frustrated teacher in a loud voice said, "No! No! Where do *all* of you live?" Seeing the bewildered faces of the children she said, "You all live in America! Say together, 'We live in America.'" The children replied in unison, and then many of them still insisted that they lived in Rock Hill. These four-year-olds could not understand that they could live at home, in Rock Hill, in South Carolina, and in America all at the same time.

A teacher of five-year-olds was overheard attempting to teach that a school is a part of a city, a city is a part of a state, and a state is a part of a country. She was using nesting blocks, carefully fitting one inside the other—the blue box was the school, the red box the city, the orange box the state, and the purple box the country. Although the teacher used concrete objects, it is doubtful that the children were able to relate to them. They referred to the colored boxes by name but made no attempt to put them together. They gave little indication that they had learned more than new names for the colored boxes.

A group of children had a student teacher from India. The teacher prepared the children for this experience by attempting to explain the differences between an American Indian and someone from the country of India. The children were fascinated by Ms. M. She wore a sari, pulled her hair back, and had a red circle on her forehead. At first the children perceived her clothing and physical countenance as strange and perhaps something to be feared. One child referred to the red spot on her forehead as "the devil's spot"; others as "the clown's spot," "funny spot," "red dot," and "silly red spot."

The most meaningful experience for the children was the day Ms. M. brought pictures of her husband and little boy, who still lived in India. She had pictures of her child at various ages, and the children were able to order the pictures according to his age. Comments were made such as "he wore diapers," "he learned to walk," and "he grew until he was a big boy like us." Ms. M. became a real person to the children. They learned to respect her and were pleased when she allowed them to dress up in her sari. She also taught them a few Indian words, songs, and games. Although the children could not understand the location or significance of the country of India, they learned to value and respect someone from that country.

When children from other countries and/or backgrounds are in the classroom, the opportunities for intellectual understanding are greatest. One year two Oriental children from Hong Kong entered a kindergarten class. The other children were fascinated by the two little girls. Although they dressed like American children, their physical appearance was different. They talked about a Chinese person's skin, hair, and eyes.

The girls' mother visited and talked about children in Hong Kong—their dress, toys, games, and family life. She spoke with broken English and explained that she and her family were learning to speak English. The kindergarten children were encouraged to help the girls learn English, and in turn they learned to pronounce a few Chinese words. The characters of the Chinese language were fascinating, and the children enjoyed trying to copy them on paper. They decided that English was easier to write than Chinese.

The children's grandmother came from Hong Kong to visit. She did not understand or speak English. She smiled at the children and spoke to them in Chinese. What impressed them most was that she smiled and patted them on the shoulder. They concluded that she was happy and liked them because she smiled and touched them. These children learned that spoken language is not the only means of communication.

The class was invited by the girls' father to his Chinese restaurant for lunch. Special menus were made for the children, listing only those foods they would be served. At the restaurant the children were given chopsticks. They were more interested in the strange names of the foods than in the chopsticks. They asked about the Chinese writing on the walls of the restaurant and were told that the words meant, "health, wealth, and happiness." Chinese fortune cookies were a big hit. The children interpreted their fortunes in their own way, distorting them to fit their level of understanding. One little boy's fortune said, "Be wise and you will inherit great wealth." After the fortune was read he said, "Oh boy! I'm going to be a rich man."

Children are interested in young people from other countries even when they are of the same race and speak the same language. A four-year-old girl moved to the United States from Australia. Although Susan looked like the other children and spoke their language, she spoke with a British accent. The children liked to hear her talk and would ask her to repeat certain words. Susan enjoyed the attention, and whenever possible she would bring a toy from Australia. Her mother was a nurse, and the teacher asked her to talk with the children about good health. She pointed out the importance of caring for the body no matter where you live. The similarities between good health habits in Australia and in America were stressed.

After a trip to Africa a teacher was asked to talk to the kindergarten children. She brought in some things she had collected in Africa. The use of some objects (animal bookends) was more obvious than the use of others (animal napkin rings). Hints were sometimes helpful, but no one guessed how the wooden elephant with the hole in its back was used—to hold butter. By using concrete objects the children could see and touch they could relate to the animals and to a few African customs.

The next week she talked with the children about the Masai people of Africa. She showed beaded jewelry that the women make and told the class how the young children take care of the cattle. They saw slides of the Masai homes, dances, cattle, and jewelry. The work of the children in Masai tribes impressed them the most. Later the children built a safari car in the block center. The dramatic-play center was used as a gift store where "Masai jewelry" (beaded jewelry collected by the teachers and parents) was sold.

current events

The egocentricity of children is shown by the importance they attach to everything that happens to them. Losing a tooth and having a new baby in the family may be of equal importance. One child brought a flyer to school publicizing his father's candicacy for the schoolboard. He wanted all the children to vote for his father.

In order to help the children better understand the voting process, a teacher asked a sociologist to talk to them. Mr. W. began by relating voting to the learning centers in the room. He told the children that each morning they had a choice to make. There were several centers to choose from, and they went to the center of their choice. This was a form of voting. Mr. W. showed paper ice cream cones filled with colored crepe paper. He asked the children to pretend they had to make a choice between eating strawberry or chocolate ice cream. Each child chose a flavor. Then they counted the number of children who had chosen strawberry and the number who had chosen chocolate. More children chose chocolate than strawberry. This meant that chocolate was preferred over strawberry and had won the majority vote.

When teachers encourage children to express their current interests, they must be prepared for those that are stimulated by their home life. Once a Head Start child told his teacher that his father had been arrested for drunkenness. This was not in the papers, but the child was very excited about the arrest. He said, "They found my daddy asleep. He didn't wreck no car. It's better to sleep when you drunk than have an accident." The teacher agreed that this was true and made no further comment about the incident. Of course, children who are not disadvantaged may also have unhappy homes. A little girl from a privileged home came to school in a taxi. She reported, "My mother is so drunk she can't stand up. She couldn't drive me to school."

Birthdays are current and of immense importance to children. Often teachers invite parents to visit school on their child's birthday. This is a worthwhile practice as long as all children have the same opportunity. In most heterogenous classes a large majority of mothers and fathers work and many cannot leave their jobs. Then it may be best to have a class party. A special snack can be made for the occasion. Collage materials may be used to make a special birthday hat. An artificial birthday cake with real candles makes it a festive occasion. Children can take the candles home after they burn.

One teacher encourages the children in the group to think of a happy wish for the birthday child. In addition the child dictates a story about himself or herself. It is written on a large chart and read to the other children. The birthday child takes the story home.

geography

THE EARTH.   A five-year-old asked his teacher if she had ever seen a broken moon. She said no. He said, "The moon was broken last night, but don't worry, God will find the pieces and glue them back together." Richard revealed his belief in animism and artificialism, which are characteristic of young children. They believe that objects that move spontaneously are alive and that God or some authority made them. Moving away from these beliefs is primarily a matter of maturation.

Teachers can help children understand the differences between living and nonliving things. A close inspection of the immediate environment can lead to a discussion of the things that are found on the Earth: rocks, insects, people, grasses, trees, other animals, and water. "What does it mean to be alive? Are rocks alive? How do you know? Do they change? Get bigger, smaller, taller, get new parts? Do they grow? Can a rock change? How?" A group of children became interested in planting seeds. One little girl decided that she would plant a rock instead. When the rock didn't grow the children wondered if a different kind of rock would grow. They planted rocks, bits of green leaves, dead leaves, sticks, and other parts of plants. The classroom became cluttered with labeled jars. Some parts of plants grew but no nonliving objects grew. Later the children discussed what it meant to be alive—movement, increase in size, reproduction, etc. Objects in the room and on the playground were found which were living and nonliving.

In order to better understand the Earth on which they live, children can explore different land surfaces. What do you find on the surface of the playground? On the surface of the sidewalks? Of the driveway? Some surfaces occur naturally; others are man-made. A field trip to watch workers laying pipes in the ground helps children understand how the surface of the earth can be changed by man. They can change its surface themselves by digging holes, wetting the ground, moving rocks, or planting a garden.

Change is an important element in children's lives. One thing is certain—things will change. Teachers should help children accept change in their lives and in natural phenomena. Careful observation of familiar areas can be made. "Look at the playground. Do you remember how it looked yesterday? How does it look today? How does it look different? Will it change again?" One group of children was divided into three small groups. Each group chose a small area of the playground to observe. Areas were marked off with different colored strings. Every day the children observed their patch of land. Soil samples were collected and analyzed. They were sifted through various sifters, heated in the oven, mixed with water, dried in the sun, or observed for forms of life. The children learned that soil changes over a period of time and that both man and nature can change it.

Although children do not understand the revolution of the Earth, they can understand its effects, such as weather and seasonal changes. Children comment on weather changes: "It's raining and I wore my raincoat," "The weatherman said it would snow," "It's hot outside," "Do you think it will thunder and lightning?" Observing changes throughout the morning and afternoon helps children understand that the weather does not stay the same. One group of children observed the weather at 9:00 A.M. and 11:00 A.M. They drew pictures and dictated a word or sentence to describe their observations. At the end of the month they had a weather record. They could not only observe weather changes over a period of time, but they could also see graphically the number of days in a month.

Children enjoy dressing dolls for weather changes. Suitable doll clothing—sweaters, jackets, raincoats and rainhats, snowsuits, sundresses, caps, shorts and long pants—can be provided so that children can dress dolls appropriately. Paper dolls may be used in place of or in addition to real dolls. "What is the weather today? Is it sunny? Is it raining? What kinds of clothes should the dolls wear outside?"

Thermometers should be placed in the room and some taken outside. Although not all children can read the markings on a thermometer, they can tell whether the line is up or down. Readings indoors and outdoors may be compared. "Is the line on the thermometer higher on the inside thermometer or on the outside thermometer?"

A thermometer may be placed outside in a shady place close to a window. The teacher and children can observe the thermometer and decide which wraps, if any, should be worn outside. An indoor thermometer may be placed at the children's shoulder level so that the teacher can regulate the room temperature as needed. Inexpensive thermometers can be placed in different areas of the room and the readings compared. Why is it cooler in the middle of the room? Warmer near radiators? Outdoor thermometers may be buried in the sand, placed in the shade, buried under wood chips, left in the sun (may burst if they get too hot), and hidden in grass. Children will find that readings vary according to the placement of the thermometers. Readings also vary before a storm, after a storm, on a sunny day, in a snowstorm, and on a sunny morning. Allow children to hold thermometers and move from one area of the playground to another. Changes in temperature will be noted.

Seasonal changes are more obvious in some localities than in others. In warmer climates jack-o'-lanterns may be cut outside in October and art activities continued outside throughout the year. There are some noticeable changes in seasons, but these changes are not as obvious as those in states further north. It is unfortunate when teachers introduce changes in leaf color in October when the leaves children see are still green on the trees. It is important to wait until real changes occur which children can observe first hand. Talking about a cold, snowy winter has little meaning to children who have never experienced one.

LOCATION.   Whenever possible children should experience different types of land formations: hills, mountains, sand dunes, and massive rocks. The locality in which the children live determines to a large extent the types of formations they can see. Trips with parents provide another way to experience land formations. Children may bring postcards or photographs of places they have been. These pictures may be difficult for other children to understand; however, they do provide children with the knowledge that not all places are the same as their immediate surroundings.

After a field trip one teacher placed a series of pictures of different views of a mountain on the bulletin board. He waited for the children to notice the pictures. One child asked him where he had gotten the pictures of "all those big hills." The children were unable to relate the pictures to their recent experience or to understand that all the pictures were views of the same mountain.

It is best to first introduce children to different views of familiar surroundings. Take pictures of different areas of the playground while children are playing. Even when children are in the picture they may have difficulty finding the location shown in the picture. Teachers can point out significant landmarks before they take pictures and then, if possible, take the pictures with a Polaroid camera. Most children can find the location of a picture that has just been taken. Gradually, with more experience, children learn to find locations of pictures taken at a previous time. Very few children can locate the place where the photographer stood when he or she took the picture. Teachers can allow children to take their own pictures, examine them, locate the area shown, and stand where they think they stood to take the picture.

DISTANCE AND MEASUREMENT.   Two boys playing with blocks were planning to build roads. David said to John, "You make yours as long as mine." John said "OK", and the boys built roads beside each other which were approximately the same length. The teacher overheard their conversation and asked, "Are your roads the same length?" John said no. Removing a block from his road he said, "Now they are the same." Since the roads began and ended at the same place the boys agreed that they were the same length. The teacher asked, "If you drive your cars down the two roads, will they travel the same distance?" Both boys said yes. In order to make room to sit beside his road, John pushed it forward. David said, "Oh boy! I'll beat you now. My road isn't as long as yours." John immediately pushed his road back to its original position. "Now they are the same," he said. John's road had seemed longer since it extended beyond David's road. Both boys had been fooled by perception.

There were two box turtles in a science center. Several children wanted to have a turtle race. They placed two pieces of masking tape of exactly the same length on the floor and decided that the turtle who got to the end first was the winner. The teacher asked if both turtles had the same distance to travel and the children agreed that they did. They had something concrete to consider—two pieces of tape which they could see were exactly parallel to each other and the same length. Had one piece of tape been moved ahead of the other, most of the children would have insisted that one turtle had further to travel than the other. They, too, would have been fooled by perception.

Children also can be encouraged to use arbitrary units of measurement, such as hands, feet, a length of string, or a stick. At Christmas teachers in a school were asked, over a weekend, to choose a Christmas tree from among many trees brought to the school. The teacher asked the children how tall a tree they wanted. They gave various answers and showed her with their arms and hands how tall the tree should be. She asked, "How will I remember how tall a tree you want?" One child said, "It should be as tall as you are." She said, "I'm five feet, eight inches. I can remember my height, but what will I use to measure the tree?" She expected them to tell her to stand in front of the tree, but no one thought of this. Instead she was asked to lie down on the floor while they measured her with a long roll of paper. One child held the roll at her feet while another child cut the paper off at her head. They triumphantly handed her the strip of paper she was to use to measure the tree.

Children should be encouraged to measure with parts of their bodies. Several children got into an argument about the length of a Mickey Mouse Game rug. They decided to measure by walking across the rug and counting their footsteps. Each child got a different answer. They repeated the process several times, but still could not agree on the length of the rug. The teacher encouraged them to think about the problem by asking such questions as "Did you start at the same place? Did you stop at the same place? Why do you suppose you got different answers? Do you wear the same size shoes?" The children took off their shoes and placed them side by side. They soon realized why they had been getting different answers and agreed that they were all correct. They could communicate by saying, "It's 20 feet long and 30 feet wide by John's shoes, but 22 feet long and 32 feet wide by Peter's shoes."

MAP MAKING.   The elementary idea of a map is shown as children work with blocks—building airports, runways for planes, expressways, and shopping centers. Blocks give children a semiconcrete experience in constructing three-dimensional maps and help them understand that block constructions can represent something.

Children may be encouraged through photographs to make a layout of a first-hand experience. A group of five-year-olds visited a turkey farm before Thanksgiving. Photographs of the farmer's house and barns were taken from different perspectives—the bottom of the hill, the fence in front of the house, and the side and back of the house. Pictures of the turkeys were taken from the fence, the farmhouse, and the barn. Later the pictures were discussed with small groups of children. The location of the farmhouse with reference to the barn was noted—the farmhouse and the barn were next to each other and close together. The fence did not enclose the house and the barn, but it did enclose the yard filled with turkeys. There were no trees in the enclosed area with the turkeys, but there were three oak trees near the house and barn: two in front of the house and one in front of the barn. The photographs were placed on the bulletin board in the block center. Additional accessories were added to the block center— miniature wooden trees, turkeys, and small colored blocks. The children lost no time in reproducing the turkey farm they had seen. Questions were asked such as "Is the barn close to the house?" "Does the fence go all around the turkey yard?" and "Look at the photographs. Were all of the trees together, or were some further apart than others?" The children made a fairly accurate map (reproduction) of what they had seen. Their powers of observation, accuracy of location, sense of perspective, and knowledge of proximity, enclosure, and separation improved with similar experiences.

Children often rearrange furniture in their play. They can be encouraged to talk about these arrangements and consider other possible ones. Teachers and children can make a simple picture map by arranging pieces of construction paper on a large sheet. Then they can refer to the map as they arrange the furniture. A small arrow may be drawn to locate the front of the map. Children can choose colors for the various pieces of furniture. Not all children will participate in such an activity, but those who do will be able to relate the drawing to the arrangement of the learning center.

Children's drawings are simple forms of maps since they are reproductions of their interpretations of what they see. Children in the schematic stage draw houses, flowers, and trees coming out of the ground and people standing on the ground. They use their knowledge of proximity, enclosure, separation, and order to place objects in their pictures. Is the bird flying in the sky? Are people standing on the ground or in the air? Do houses have doors and windows? Are trees close to the house or dangling in the air? Children's artwork should be studied for these characteristics.

scheduling and grouping

Activities in social studies occur spontaneously throughout the day just as they do in other content areas; however, the teacher plans for stories, filmstrips, movies, field trips, and discussion groups. These activities should be planned for small groups of children. Carrying out small-group activities during learning time eliminates large-group instruction, which often involves waiting, sitting too long, restlessness, and inattention. A group of children returned from a trip to a turkey farm which took most of the morning. The next day the teacher outlined a bulletin board with a paper fence. The teacher invited several children to look at the bulletin board with her. In small groups of three to seven the previous day's trip was discussed: "Where were the turkeys kept? What color(s) were they? What kind of sound did they make? How did the farmer take care of the turkeys? Where did he and his wife live?" After a brief discussion the teacher encouraged the children to draw and cut out turkeys for the bulletin board. This activity continued for four days with a few children joining the group each day. Some children participated in the group discussion but did not draw turkeys. A few children did not join any of the groups. This did not disturb the teacher, who knew that the children would enter into group discussions when they were more mature and/or the topic was of more interest to them.

first day of school

Centers may be set up as described in chapter 1 under "first day of school." Every effort must be made to make each child feel important. Assigning individual lockers (discussed in chapter 1) gives each child the feeling, "That's mine." A well-planned room with appropriate centers requiring a minimum of supervision leaves the teacher and aide free to interact with the children.

Nothing is more precious to children than their names. If possible, children should be called by their names on the first day of school. A teacher can memorize the children's first and last name before school begins and when he or she meets a child put the name with the face. This method is sometimes as effective as wearing name tags.

If possible some type of questionnaire should be filled out by the parents before school begins. Vital information such as age, sex, name called, siblings, allergies, physical limitations, and parents' occupation(s) can be learned ahead of time and other information absorbed as teachers become acquainted with children.

It is important to show children that you know something personal about them, such as "How is your new baby brother?" "You just had a birthday, didn't you?" "Your mother teaches second grade in this school." "Where do your older brothers go to school?" Personal interest taken in children gives them security and the desire to come back the next day. "I like my teacher" is a feeling children should take home with them.

Parents may be allowed to stay with children on the first day. The children are usually ready to give up their parent(s) by the second or third day. Occasionally there is a severe problem, most often the result of overprotectiveness and/or the parent's unwillingness to give up the child. A teacher can ask such parents to leave the room for short periods. The children can be told their parents are leaving for 5, 10, or 15 minutes and can be shown on the clock when they will return. At the given time the parents should return to reassure the children. Eventually the children should be able to remain at school without their parent(s).

Sometimes a child transfers a dependency on the parent to the teacher or aide. This is probably a good sign since the behavior indicates that the child can be content without the parent. Sometimes children become upset if the teacher moves out of their line of vision. In one kindergarten there was a little boy who shrieked until the teacher came into sight and then became quiet. This behavior continued for several weeks, until the teacher thought of a game to play with him. She asked him to play a game called "I Can't See You." She would move out of sight while he counted to 5 or more (no more than 10). If he didn't cry, he won the game; but if he cried, she won. He laughed and said, "I can stand it without you." Sometimes teachers must try things that make sense to them even when they have not read the technique in a book or used it successfully before. Children let teachers know immediately when something they do seems foolish to them. Perceptive teachers recognize this.

When children persist in having problems in adjusting to school, and parent conferences have not solved the problem, a teacher should consult a school psychologist or other professional. A little girl cried whenever a child looked at her or brushed against her accidentally. The teacher was confused by the child's behavior and sought help from the parents, a former nursery school teacher, the principal, and the school psychologist. She was told that Jean had had a traumatic experience at the age of two, had a heart murmur, and must be handled with great care. It wasn't until the teacher consulted the child's pediatrician that she got any concrete advice. The pediatrician assured her that the child's heart murmur was slight and was not the cause of her behavior. He also felt that Jean was spoiled and got attention by her crying spells. The teacher had used every technique except firmness. She decided to tell this child the facts: she would have to leave school if her behavior continued. She told Jean she could cry when she was physically hurt or when someone hurt her feelings, but not when someone looked at her or accidentally touched her. The teacher was delighted when Jean responded to her firmness. Jean stayed in kindergarten two years and steadily improved. Although she remains very much of an individualist, she grew into a productive and happy adult. She remembers her earlier behavior but cannot explain why she acted as she did.

Sometimes shy, withdrawn children are practical children. An invitation to feed the fish or the gerbil or water the plants gives them something useful to do. The teacher may have to find a job for them to do each day until they have adjusted to school.

Some children want to bring toys from home during the first days of school. If children are having trouble making the break from home to school, they should be allowed to bring something from home. When they are more secure the toys can be left at home. A little girl insisted on bringing her teacher a gift (hair ribbon, washcloth, button) every day for approximately a month. As she grew more secure she no longer needed this link between home and school. On the whole playthings should be left at home with the explanation that there are toys at school.

Children adjust best when they are met by a naturally warm and friendly teacher. Adults may be able to fool other adults with a facade, but seldom children. They see through superficiality. Some children are naturally affectionate and express their feelings verbally and physically. When a child shows affection through touch (putting arms around teacher, kissing teacher's cheek, sitting on teacher's lap), the teacher can respond by showing affection. Unfortunately there are teachers who push their attentions on children rather than waiting for an invitation for affection. A friendly hello on arrival at school and a "goodbye, I'll see you tomorrow" at the end of the day go a long way toward making a child feel accepted at school. In a few cases a demonstration of overt affection may be needed—when a child is hurt, sick, or extremely shy.

social studies through the year

Most of the activities and materials needed throughout the year have been covered in this chapter; however, one subject that needs careful consideration is the selection of audiovisual aids. Pictures are valuable teaching aids, but only those that are clear and concise should be used. The best picture is one that speaks in the child's own language. A teacher must choose between two pictures to use in a follow-up after a visit to a restaurant. The first picture depicts a woman, a man, and two children sitting at a table holding menus. The second picture shows several tables with people eating a variety of foods, two waiters carrying trays, and the hostess seating a couple. Which picture should the teacher choose? Which is less complex? Which contains fewer details? Which one is more open-ended? Which one will stimulate more thinking? The picture that is less complex, lends itself to divergent thinking, and therefore stimulates more thinking is the first picture. "Is this a family? Why do you think so? How old are the children? Why are they eating in a restaurant instead of at home? What kind of restaurant is it? Does the picture tell us? What kinds of foods do you think are offered on the menu? Can the children read the menu? What do you think the children will order? Why?"

Sometimes pictures are inappropriate for the age level of the child. Pictures of hurricanes and volcanos are most often inappropriate because it is difficult for children to understand what they have not experienced. This does not mean that pictures outside of the child's realm of experience should never be used. Rather children must have a knowledge of or an interest in the topic. Pictures depicting peoples of other countries must be up to date. Stereotypes such as Japanese wearing kimonos, children in Dutch shoes, Africans in loincloths should be avoided since only a minority of these groups dress in this fashion.

Pictures should depict children of all races engaged in activities. No one race should be favored over another. Although there may be no Oriental children in a classroom, pictures of these children should be included. Sex stereotyping should be avoided. There are many good commercial pictures that show both men and women in a variety of roles.

The same rules for choosing pictures are applicable to selecting filmstrips and movies. In addition, a filmstrip or movie should not last over 15 to 20 minutes. In one school 45 minutes of movies are shown each Friday. There is no preparation or follow-up for any movie. It is doubtful that children learn from these films. In order for children to have a learning experience the teacher should introduce the filmstrip or movie in a meaningful way. A filmstrip about the self-concept may be introduced by asking each child to look in a hand mirror and describe himself or herself. Follow-up should be short but meaningful. In the example above a teacher could dismiss the children by describing something about each one that makes him or her unique.

A teacher introduced a short movie about fall by showing a few colored leaves and discussing them briefly. In the follow-up the children named signs of fall they saw on their playground. This activity took 20 minutes and was carried out with small groups of children. Teachers should ask themselves the following questions before choosing a filmstrip or movie: "How long is it? What concepts does it teach? Are these appropriate? Do the activities coincide with the children's interests? Is it suitable to show in small groups? When was the last time I showed a filmstrip or movie?"

Stories with tapes should be chosen with care. They should be stories appropriate for children and books that may be handled easily. The indicator (bell, gong, rap) for turning the pages should be clear and at the end of each page. Scratched records or records with indistinct sound should not be used. Earphones, language masters, and listening centers must be in good repair.

meeting goals

The evaluation scheme described in chapter 2 may be applied to social studies. A checklist based upon the behavioral objectives should be kept for each child. The methods described for collecting data are applicable to social studies situations.

Videotapes may be made throughout the day in the various learning centers. These may be analyzed to determine where and with whom children are playing. Some children may be isolated by their own or the group's choice. Some may play with the same children all the time and ignore others. Sometimes tapes reveal that children the teacher feels relate well to others are actually dominating the situation with little protest from the others.

A sociogram is not reliable when given to small children, but it does reveal those children who are very popular or unpopular. When used it should be given several times over a long period. A wide range of questions should be asked in preparing a sociogram, such as "Who would you like to sit beside? Play with outside? Indoors? Visit you at home? Help you put toys away? Help you work a puzzle?"

Piagetian tasks relating to moral development and judgment may be given to each child. The results give the teacher a better idea of the kind of thinking the child does in relation to himself or herself and others.

Piagetian tasks that relate to logical thinking about the world may be given.

Directions for giving the tasks that relate to social studies and are described in this chapter may be found in *Cognitive Tasks: An Approach for Early Childhood Education* (1974) by Janie and Keith Osborn. These tasks are Conservation of Distance, Conservation of Length, Classification, Class Inclusion, and Spatial Representation of Self. The Assessment of an Understanding of Family Relationships may be found in *Piaget for the Classroom Teacher* by Barry Wadsworth (p. 267).

5
children
are curious

science and mathematics

All healthy children are curious. They are constantly exploring and experimenting with the objects in their world. Their thirst for knowledge is not satisfied until they have learned all there is to know about an object *to their satisfaction.* Piaget explains this intense desire to act upon the world as a self-regulatory process that he calls "equilibration" (Furth, 1969, pp. 206–207). When something in children's environment does not fit into their mental schema (mental structure) they find themselves in a state of disequilibration. They act on objects or ideas in order to return to the original state of equilibration. They may fit new information into their already existing schemata (assimilation) or, in the process of assimilation, they may alter schemata or form new ones (accommodation). It is through the processes of assimilation and accommodation that learning occurs.

Children may have a schema for "dog." Upon encountering other four-legged animals, they call them all "dogs" (assimilation) because of the similarity to their own dog. Later, through many experiences with animals other than dogs, they begin to differentiate between their dog and other four-legged animals. They form new schemata for such animals as cat, cow, or rabbit and in the process alter their schema for dog (Rosen, 1977, pp. 8–9). Hence children play an active and crucial role in understanding their world. Flavell (1963) states, "The cognizing organism is at all levels a very, very active agent who always meets the environment well over halfway, who actually *constructs* his world by assimilating it to schemas while accommodating these schemas to its constraints" (p. 71).

The theories of intellectual development presented by Piaget have affected all areas of the early childhood curriculum. Reviews of research in science and mathematics reveal, though, that his influence has been more apparent in

the "new" methods of teaching these subjects than in any other content areas (Seefeldt, Ed., 1976, chap. 5 and 6).

The movement to improve science and mathematics teaching at the elementary school level began in the 1960s. The new curricula were laboratory-centered. This trend was reflected in three of the best-known national programs: Science: a Process Approach (SAPA), Elementary School Science (EES), and Science Curriculum Improvement Study (SCIS). These programs and others were planned around children as active learners—embryonic scientists in a labora-tory (Riechard, 1973, pp. 438–440). Scientists, mathematicians, and educators embraced the ideas of Piaget and attempted to apply them to the new curricula. Piaget's theories of intellectual development stressed children as active agents in their own learning. In order *to understand,* children must first experiment for themselves, observe what happens, compare their findings on one occasion with those on another and with those of other children. Each child must ask his or her own questions and find his or her own answers.

Science was defined by some educators as *process,* a way of finding out about the environment. A person who is observing what is happening in the world and formulating the simplest set of suppositions to explain these happen-ings is doing science. Other educators viewed science as *product,* a body of useful and practical knowledge. Advocates of science as product believed science is an achievement, not a method of achieving. A middle position was taken by those who advocated a *process-product* approach: Both learning concepts and the methods by which concepts are formed are important. Propo-nents of both the process and the product methods suggested a "hands-on" approach to science teaching (Dietz and Sunal, 1976, pp. 126–130).

Science for young children may be defined mainly as a method of achieving (process), and to a much lesser degree a useful set of achievements (product) (Dietz and Sunal, 1976, p. 237). The emphasis is on how to learn and not on what to learn.

Mathematics education in the 1960s moved in a direction similar to that of science education, but with a distinct difference. Mathematics became more content-oriented. Children at an early age were exposed to sets, open structures, properties, geometry, and graphing. This increase in content resulted in less time for developmental work. When developmental activities were introduced they often disintegrated into paper-pencil discovery activites rather than exploratory experiences with real objects (Payne, Ed., 1975, pp. 23–28).

In the 1970s emphasis was again placed on the exploration and manipulations of objects. Mathematicians who viewed mathematics as the process of searching for patterns (Good, 1977a, p. 54) focused on the child's interaction with the environment. Mathematical knowledge is abstracted "by the child from the child's action on objects. . . . There is *no other way* that comprehension and meaning can be derived" (Wadsworth, 1978, p. 166). Elkind (1976) stressed the uselessness of explaining mathematics to young children at a verbal level. Verbalization does not ensure that they understand a mathematical idea; rather their actions on objects and discussions with others are the means by which they learn mathematics (pp. 203–208).

Piaget's intellectual stages reveal the relationship between physical and logico-mathematical knowledge that is basic to both science and mathematics. A child must be able to place physical objects into meaningful relationships before he or she can fully understand logico-mathematical knowledge. Kamii and DeVries (1978) say that logico-mathematical knowledge (relationships the child introduces into or among objects) cannot develop without physical knowledge (feedback from the qualities inherent in the objects themselves) (p. 16). Although there is a distinction between the source of physical knowledge and logico-mathematical knowledge, the "two are not entirely different because, in the psychological reality of the young child's experience, the two are inseparably linked" (p. 17). In essence physical experiences help the child structure his or her logico-mathematical framework, and "the better this framework is structured, the more accurately and richly the child will be able to read facts from reality" (p. 20).

The stages defined by Piaget are invariant; all children pass through the same stages at approximately the same ages, although some children move more rapidly or slowly than others.

Piaget placed children from one to seven in the preoperational stage of reasoning, which has certain characteristics that affect the way children view their world:

1. *Egocentricity.* Children are self-centered and view objects and ideas from their own point of view.
2. *Transductive reasoning.* Children's thinking proceeds from particular to particular. It is neither inductive nor deductive. Children may reason, "I haven't had my nap yet so it isn't afternoon."

3. *Centration.* Children attend to one object or event at a time (centered thinking) rather than considering two or more aspects simultaneously (decentered thinking). In the Conservation of Quantity task, two clay balls are used. Children agree that the two balls have the same amount of clay. When one ball is changed into a sausage shape, however, children say there is either more or less clay than in the unchanged ball. They center on only one variable at a time, either the width or the length of the clay, but do not consider both the length and the width at the same time.

4. *Irreversibility.* Children's thinking is irreversible. Children are unable to follow a process from beginning to end and then trace the steps back to the starting point. In the example of the ball of clay they are unable to think back to the way the clay was before its shape was changed and to compare that shape with the present shape.

5. *Static thinking.* Children's thinking is static. Children ignore transformations (changes) that occur before their eyes. Instead they focus on separate states. In the example of the clay ball children ignore the transformation that occurs when the ball changes from a round shape to a sausage shape (Rosen, 1977, pp. 12–17).

Piaget's intellectual stages suggest prerequisite understandings, derived from physical and logical knowledge, that are basic to science and mathematics. Those pertaining especially to young children are classification, seriation, one-to-one correspondence, conservation, temporal relations, and spatial relations.

classification

sorting

A simple form of classification occurs when a child places like objects in a group.

multiple classification

Multiple classification occurs when a child understands that a given object may belong to more than one group. A red, square, wooden block can at the same time belong in the subgroup of red objects, square objects, and wooden objects. Most children start to use multiple classification between the ages of six and seven.

class inclusion

Class inclusion is the ability to understand that the whole is greater than its subsets and that the subsets are less than the whole. If a set of children includes a set of boys and a set of girls there must be more children than either girls or boys and there must be fewer boys and girls than there are children. If a child is given a box of wooden beads, nine yellow beads and two white beads, he or she will insist there are more yellow beads than wooden beads. The child is able to compare only the parts (subsets). The concept of the whole (all wooden beads) is lost when the parts—yellow beads and white beads—are considered. Most children start to use class inclusion between the ages of seven and eight (Copeland, 1979, pp. 142–147). The importance of class inclusion to social studies is discussed in chapter 4.

cardinal number

Cardinal number answers the question, How many? Determining the cardinal number involves assigning a number name to each member of a set. A child, however, can find the cardinal number of a group of objects and still be unable to understand that 5 includes all the objects that came before 5—1, 2, 3, and 4. To count meaningfully a child must also understand class inclusion and seriation (Kamii and DeVries, 1976, pp. 7–8).

seriation

ordering

In order to count meaningfully the child must be able to order objects either mentally or physically (Kamii and DeVries, 1976, p. 7). The ability to seriate begins with the ordering of objects by comparing them according to some criterion, such as length, color, or size. Most children of 6 to 7 years can order 8 to 10 objects by comparing each object with the previous one and the one that follows it. Younger children use a trial-and-error approach to seriation or may line up the tops or bottoms of the objects rather than compare the objects in a logical manner (Copeland, 1979, pp. 46–52).

ordinal number

Ordinal number answers the question, Which one? Is it the first, second, or tenth object? The ability to understand ordinal number follows the ability to order objects and appears around the age of six or seven (Copeland, 1979, pp. 99–102).

one-to-one correspondence

The child is able to match objects in one group with objects in another group so that an equivalent set is formed. The child understands that there is the same number of objects in each set. When the sets are not equivalent, the child is aware that one set has more or fewer objects than the other set. The ability to count is not necessary to determine the equivalence of sets. Kamii and DeVries (1976) feel that encouraging children to count is not a good way to help begin quantifying objects. A better approach is to ask them to compare sets (pp. 11–13). Enumeration (meaningful counting) involves one-to-one correspondence since the child assigns a number name to each object in a group.

conservation

conservation of number

When a child understands that the number of objects in a group remains the same regardless of how they are arranged, he or she is said to conserve number. If a child counts six objects but thinks that there are no longer six when the physical arrangement is changed, he or she does not understand that $3 + 3 = 6, 4 + 2 = 6, 5 + 1 = 6$, etc. The child may be able to memorize these facts but does not understand the logic behind the operations (Copeland, 1979, pp. 110–112). Conservation of number appears in most children around the age of six to seven.

conservation of quantity

In order to conserve quantity a child must understand that the mass of an object remains the same no matter what shape it takes. Although the shape of a ball of clay may be altered, the amount of clay remains the same if nothing is added to or taken away from the clay ball. Most young children think that when a cookie is broken into several pieces they have more cookie. Conservation of quantity appears in most children around the ages of eight to nine (Good, 1977b, pp. 98–99).

conservation of distance and length

Conservation of distance and length is explained in chapter 4.

temporal relations

Temporal relations refers to the child's ability to understand the passage of time, measure time in units, and follow events in a sequential order. Young children feel that they control time. When they move fast time passes quickly and when they move less rapidly time passes more slowly. Since children believe that time is closely related to their activities, they are unable to comprehend a standard unit as a measurement for time. Clocks, stopwatches, hourglasses, and three-minute timers seem to move at the same rate as the child (Copeland, 1979, pp. 190–207). The relationship of temporal relations to social studies is found in chapter 4.

spatial relations

Spatial relations that relate to social studies are discussed in chapter 4. They are direction, perspective, horizontal and vertical axes, and topological relationships. These same understandings are important to both science and mathematics.

characteristics of young children related to science and mathematics

Listed in table 5–1 are characteristics of young children related to science and mathematics. They represent general characteristics of children and *do not* represent the characteristics of any one child. Each child has an individual built-in rate of growth.

table 5–1
representative characteristics of young children related to science and mathematics

From About 3 Years	to About 6 Years of Age
1. Experiments with objects, often repeating the same actions over and over.	1. Expands experimentation and exploration by creating a variety of actions on objects.
2. Believes in artificialism—that human beings create natural phenomena.	2. Artificialism is still present; is beginning to seek logical explanations for natural phenomena.
3. Believes in animism—that inanimate objects are alive and have human characteristics.	3. Animism is still present; is beginning to differentiate between animate and inanimate objects.
4. Thinking is centered—attends to one aspect of an object or event rather than considering two or more aspects simultaneously (seeing is believing).	4. Continues to center on one variable at a time; decentering varies with children and may occur earlier in some children.
5. Thinking is irreversible—is unable to follow a process from beginning to end and retrace steps back to starting point.	5. Irreversibility of thought; reversibility varies with children and may occur earlier in some.
6. Thinking is static—ignores transformations or changes and instead centers on separate states.	6. Continues to ignore transformations; dynamic thinking varies with children and may occur earlier in some.
7. Transductive reasoning prevails—reasons from one particular to another: "I haven't had my nap, so it isn't afternoon."	7. Transductive reasoning continues; inductive and deductive reasoning may occur.
8. Beginning to understand topological relationships of proximity, enclosure, order, and separation.	8. Understands most topological relationships; begins to view figures as rigid in shape (Euclidean geometry).
9. Is nonconserver of number, length, and distance.	9. Is still nonconserver; a few may conserve number, length, distance.
10. Sorts objects according to likenesses—simple form of classification.	10. Uses multiple classification; a few understand class inclusion.
11. Verbally compares two or more objects.	11. May seriate as many as 8 to 10 objects according to a given criterion, such as color, length, size.
12. Is unable to construct knowledge from verbal explanations.	12. Source of knowledge is largely confined to concrete objects.
13. May count by rote to 5, 10, 20.	13. May enumerate up to 10 or more objects.
14. Is unable to pick out relative position of objects, i.e., first, second, third.	14. Can pick out a few relative positions; some children, from first to tenth.
15. Believes own actions control time.	15. Continues to believe actions control time; most cannot use standard units to measure time.
16. Is self-centered—sees things from own point of view.	16. Begins to consider viewpoints other than own; some may not reach this point until seven or eight years of age.

A table of the relative ages at which children attain an understanding of the concepts discussed in this chapter and in chapter 4 may be found in *How Children Learn Science* (Good, 1977b, pp. 107–108).

The strengths and weaknesses in the young child's thinking described above should not form the structure for science or mathematics instruction. Instead they should be used as a guide to plan more meaningful activities. Science and mathematics can be fun and intellectually challenging if teachers remember that they must not cram facts into children's heads. Instead they should strive to understand the developmental stages in order to plan a curriculum compatible with children's thinking about their world.

goals for development through science and mathematics

The following goals for development through science and mathematics have been chosen as realistic ones for the teacher to select since they can be achieved by the majority of children from age three to six. Objectives are written in the cognitive, affective, social, and psychomotor domains. It is important to remember that not all the objectives will be reached by the time a child is five or six. The objectives are listed as a guide for the teacher in planning and as one source for evaluating scientific and mathematical understanding.

COGNITIVE DOMAIN.   The child:

1. Identifies geometric figures—squares, circles, and triangles (five years old).
2. Shows in drawings and descriptions of objects an understanding of topological relationships.
3. Selects 1 to 10 objects from a group of objects when asked.
4. Identifies numerals 1 through 5.
5. Writes a few numerals.
6. Uses ordinal numbers—first, second, third, etc.
7. Uses multiple classification: considers more than one possible classification for an object.
8. Matches one group of objects with another group of objects: one-to-one correspondence.
9. Names the number property of a set of objects—1 to 10 (cardinal numbers).
10. Compares sets of objects using such terms as "greater than," "less than," "more than," "equal to."
11. When shown a set of objects, duplicates it with another set in the same order.
12. When shown an ordered set of objects, chooses the object that comes next in the sequence.
13. Describes objects as heavy, light, short, tall, small, big, smooth, rough.
14. Uses comparative terms—"-er" and "-est"—correctly when discussing height, weight, and length.

15. Demonstrates through experimentation that a substance can be changed by factors acting on it (liquid to solid by freezing, solid to liquid by warming, dry sand to wet by watering, hard to soft by cooking).
16. Introduces words not used previously in the child's conversation.
17. Shows that a problem can be solved with the information at hand—moving heavy blocks with a cart, using a string to measure a board, identifying an insect using a book).
18. Correlates cause and effect (ice melts because it is warm; plants die because they are not watered; sand is wet because it rained).
19. Eliminates knowns to arrive at unknowns. ("The grass on the playground is wet. It did not rain last night or this morning. The rain did not make the playground wet. Only part of the playground is wet. The yard man must have sprinkled that part of the grass." or "Our plant died. Its leaves are withered. No one remembers watering the plant. It had light, warmth, and soil. It must have died because no one watered it.")
20. Uses various processes—observing, classifying, seriating, measuring, predicting—in solving problems.
21. States alternatives to problems in order to reach a final decision ("Let's make ice cream outside. The electrical cord won't reach. There is no extension cord. We can make ice cream indoors." or "We need something to make hamburger for our grocery store. We have earth clay, plasticine, and play dough. Earth clay will break; plasticine is sticky. Play dough will be best for our hamburger.")
22. Seriates six objects according to some criterion such as length, color, or size.

AFFECTIVE DOMAIN.   The child:

1. Shows through dramatic play an interest and knowledge gained through experience.
2. Returns to the same topic for additional information or reinforcement.
3. Approaches and manipulates objects in the centers.
4. Asks questions and makes comments about classroom activities.
5. Helps care for classroom plants and/or animals.

SOCIAL DOMAIN.   The child:

1. Shares equipment and materials.
2. Contributes ideas while interacting with others.
3. Is open to the ideas of others.

PSYCHOMOTOR DOMAIN.   The child:

1. Manipulates objects to improve eye-hand coordination.
2. Manipulates objects to improve eye-foot coordination

indoor learning centers

science learning center

A science learning center should contain a rectangular, triangular, or kidney-shaped table. These shapes allow children to work on all sides of the table and reach across it without difficulty. A bulletin board to display pictures and a shelf for books and permanent science equipment are desirable additions to the center. A partition may be needed to separate the center from other areas.

LOCATION.   The center should be located near running water and on a tile rather than a carpeted surface. An ideal location for the science center is near the art center since both require running water and combine elements of art, science, and mathematics (see chapter 1). When possible the science center and the mathematics center should also be close together.

EQUIPMENT AND SUPPLIES.   Permanent pieces of equipment include:

Equal-arm balance.
Spring scale.
Inexpensive thermometers—two to four.
Magnifying glasses—four to six.
Color paddles.
A glass or, preferably, plastic aquarium to house plants and/or animals.
Assortment of inexpensive science information books; set of encyclopedias
     and/or *Childcraft* (an older set may be borrowed from a parent or teacher).

     Other pieces of equipment include:

Large assortment of heavy glass and plastic containers.
Magnets—assortment of different kinds and sizes.
Prisms—two to three.
Kaleidoscope—clear.
Watering cans.
Batteries, bulbs, and insulated wire.
Parts of old toys—springs, gears, wheels.
Miniature wooden or plastic animals.
Beautiful junk of all kinds.
Animals.—Guinea pigs and/or gerbils make excellent pets. A guinea pig seldom
     bites unless mistreated. It enjoys being handled by children. It is messy, and
     its cage must be cleaned every day or at least every other day. It should be
     fed green food at least once during the weekend. Gerbils are difficult to
     handle but interesting to watch. They don't bite and have very little odor.
     Their cage requires cleaning every two weeks, and enough food and water
     can be left to feed the gerbil over the weekend. Other satisfactory pets are
     goldfish, tropical fish, parakeets, a toad (if it will eat), and *small* hermit
     crabs. Large or medium-size crabs have strong claws that pinch. Hamsters
     usually are not good pets since they frequently bite.

Plants.—Some sturdy plants are philodendron, geranium, coleus, sweet potato.

Supplies should include:

Potting soil.
Litter for animal cages.
Colored cellophane, tissue paper, and construction paper.
Paste.
String.
Masking tape.
Refrigerator tape.

TEACHER'S ROLE.   It is the teacher's responsibility not only to order materials and equipment for the centers, but also to display objects so that they arouse children's interest. Unfortunately some teachers' philosophy is, "the more things to see, the better." A child looking at his classroom science center said, "Who can find anything in that mess?" Two four-year-olds were asked, "What is the name of your pet?" Looking around the room with a puzzled expression one said, "What pet?" The other said, "Oh, she means that thing in the cage." The visitor was horrified: not only did they not know the gerbil's name, but they referred to it as a "thing." Upon closer observation she realized that the animal cage was nestled among a number of jars of dead insects. It was difficult to see the gerbil amid the clutter and through the dirty glass-walled container. No wonder the children were puzzled by the question. The animal was obviously not a pet.
   It is best to display a few well-chosen objects attractively. In a Head Start classroom an old orange crate was painted bright yellow. Each section of the crate contained a challenging object placed on a piece of colored construction paper. The objects stood out and invited hands-on experiences. There were a large and a small magnifying glass; two inexpensive thermometers; a set of color paddles; red, yellow, and blue cellophane squares; and a set of wooden animals. On top of the crate was a small fishbowl with two small hermit crabs, and a book about crabs. Children were looking at the crabs through the magnifying glasses, predicting color combinations with the color paddles, and comparing the thermometer readings. Two children were classifying the wooden animals into groups with similar characteristics.

mathematics center

The mathematics center and the manipulative center may be combined since the equipment is interrelated. Sometimes the equipment for the two centers is placed on separate shelves and the same table(s) or floor space is used for both centers. If space permits and the children are developmentally ready to explore number in depth, a separate mathematics center is desirable.

LOCATION.   The combined mathematics and manipulative center or the mathematics center should be placed next to the science center; however, the science and art centers require running water, and it may not be possible to include the mathematics center with them.

EQUIPMENT AND SUPPLIES.   Equipment should include:

Unifix blocks
Colored wooden cubes
Beads and string
Pegs and pegboards
Magnetic board, and magnetic numerals preferably all the same color
Cuisenaire rods or similar rods
Counting frame
Flannel board with felt numerals
Wooden numerals
Sandpaper and/or beaded numerals
Play clock
Timers
Inexpensive alarm clocks
Three-minute sand timers
Hourglass
Small toy plastic watches with movable hands
Match mates
Puzzles—8 to 23 pieces
Shape forms
Sequence counters
Day-by-day calendar
Shape inserts
Counting box

Supplies should include:

Scissors
Paste
Easel paper
Construction paper
"Beautiful" junk—bottle caps, popsicle sticks, small boxes, buttons, checkers, toy animals, artificial flowers
Crayons
Large and small pencils

TEACHER'S ROLE.   Materials in the mathematics center must be in clear view, with no one piece obstructing another. Equipment with several parts should be in clear plastic containers. To interest children in specific items, place them on a table. These items may be a partially worked puzzle, a few felt objects and numerals on a flannel board, a block pattern with additional blocks to complete one pattern, a collection of small toys to stimulate an interest in classification, or a real clock placed next to a toy clock with movable hands.

A teacher complained that children ignored a new, large cardboard puzzle of a boy. "I paid a lot for that puzzle. They should like it since it is as big as they are," he commented, shaking his head. The visitor asked, "Where is the puzzle?" "In the red box," he answered and pointed to a rather worn cardboard box. The visitor suggested placing the puzzle pieces in a transparent container and putting it on a table. The next day the children *discovered* the puzzle and were delighted with it.

cooking center

This center may be small and consist of a table and hot plate or, if space permits, it can be a well-equipped, permanent center used every day. The size and use of the center will depend on the space and on the number of available outlets. An often ignored center, it provides worthwhile experiences in science, mathematics, language arts, and social studies.

LOCATION. This center should be in a kitchen or near running water. Since heat is involved it may be out of the line of traffic and partitioned off from the rest of the room.

EQUIPMENT AND SUPPLIES. Equipment should include:

Stove or hot plate.
Small refrigerator or ice chest.
Small table and four chairs.
Cooking utensils—cookie sheets, cutters, rolling pin, frying pan, other pots and
    pans.
Large spoons and measuring spoons.
Dry and liquid measuring cups.
Pegboard and pegs—to display needed cooking equipment and recipe cards. A
    small shelf could be used for this purpose.

Supplies should include:

Foods for cooking.—The teacher should choose nutritious foods. Raw or cooked
    vegetables, fruits, and milk cost less than cake, cookies, HiC, KoolAid, and
    other foods high in sugar.

TEACHER'S ROLE. Cooking experiences give children the opportunity to observe physical changes. Children can help prepare the daily snack. On Thursday four children's names are placed on a chart in the cooking center. These children help plan the snacks for the next week. The children and the teacher must consider those foods already purchased as well as foods needed for the coming week, selecting foods that have no sugar except natural sugars. Ways to prepare the foods are discussed: An apple may be eaten whole, made into apple sauce, cut into pieces and spread with peanut butter, baked, or made into apple salad. On Monday any child may have a turn to make a portion of the snack. Some children participate occasionally, others every day. The children who have helped plan the snack check their names off the chart. In this way each child has a turn to help the teacher plan every five or six weeks.

Children sometimes make up their own recipes. This is a simple process for snacks such as celery sticks and apples with peanut butter, carrot strips, and apple and orange slices. When they plan to cook, however, snacks become more complicated and recipes are needed. Questions may be asked such as "How many apples do we need to make apple sauce? How long must the apples cook? How will we know when they are done? Do we need a recipe?" Children should know where recipes are found and assist as the teacher transfers them from a child's cookbook to teacher-made picture cards. (Illustrations of teacher-made recipes may be found in Kamii and DeVries, 1979, pp. 280–283.) Picture cards may be displayed on a pegboard in sequential order. Some children are able to read recipes, whereas others learn to recognize only a few words.

Children should be encouraged to predict changes in foods: "What will happen to water when it is heated? Will it boil? How do the apples look and taste now? Will cooling change them back to the way they were before cooking? Will the apples fall apart in the water?" As changes take place in the apples, remove one occasionally and allow children to taste it with a plastic fork.

After children have had opportunities to observe baking, cooking, and freezing of foods, allow them to suggest ways to prepare food. Their suggestions may be somewhat unusual but nevertheless safe and often tasty. Children may suggest coloring water with food coloring and freezing it in an ice tray. The cubes are colorful but, as children learn, add no flavor to the water. Other out-of-the-ordinary recipes have been cooked raisins with butter, cooked peaches and carrots, frozen grapes and watermelon balls, and baked tomatoes. Often ideas used in previous cooking experiences are combined with others to create new dishes. The importance of these learning experiences cannot be overemphasized. These are the children's own creations. All the foods created are eaten, although some taste better than others. When an original recipe is not tasty it can be discarded or revised by the children and tried again. Recipes may be classified into "those we like" and "those that aren't so good." Other ways in which recipes may be classified are fruits, vegetables, salads, sandwiches, and desserts (mostly fruits with little or no sugar added). Books of mimeographed pages with the recipes under appropriate headings can be made. These may be taken home to share with children's families.

outdoor learning centers

LOCATION. Outdoor learning activities should be an extension of indoor learning and vice versa. When possible, centers similar to those indoors should be extended to the playground. One summer the children made a collection of "nature," as they called it. They set up a science center outside with a board and two bricks. Nature objects were placed here, and the collection grew. The table was covered with an oilcloth after outdoor play because the children were afraid it might rain and ruin their "pretty things." Thus an outdoor science center was created.

TEACHER'S ROLE. Many activities thought of as indoor—painting, looking at books, eating snacks, building with blocks, and playing with sand and water—are just as effective outdoors. In warmer climates large- and small-group discussions can occur outside. One summer, during outdoor play a teach-

The children found objects for the outdoor science center.

er talked with children in small groups of six to eight. Each group tried to guess what was inside a large box covered with a cloth. They asked questions that could be answered by a yes or a no. When each group had had a chance to guess, the box was opened and the contents, an ice cream freezer, examined. A problem arose when the children wanted to make the ice cream outside. How could they use an electric freezer when there was no outside electrical outlet? One child suggested an extension cord and to his delight found one that reached to the outside. The next day ice cream was mixed inside and frozen and eaten outdoors.

teacher's role in science and mathematics

classification

A teacher should encourage children to look for similarities in objects and put the objects into groups that "belong together." Children should be allowed to set up *their own* criterion for grouping. Reasons given for their classifications should be accepted since their answers are correct at their stage of development.

During the first weeks of school shells may be placed on the science table next to an equal-arm balance. Children can handle the shells, noting similarities and differences, and be encouraged to put together those they think belong together. At first most children sort shells by placing those of the same kinds together. Teachers can ask questions such as "Why did you put these shells in this group?" "How are the shells alike?" "Can you find another way to group the shells?" After experimentation a child said, "I put the shells I like best together." She had two piles of shells: in one were the shells she preferred and in the other the less favored shells. Although this child had sorted objects into only two groups, favorite and nonfavorite, she had set up her own criterion.

The children in a kindergarten class collected different kinds of seeds. They brought fruits to school and removed the seeds; others were collected from some of their snacks. The teacher placed colorful boxes on the science table and asked, "Can you put the seeds that go together in the boxes?" Several children sorted seeds into various boxes. One child asked the teacher to look at his seeds. He had put brown seeds in one box and green seeds in another. Pointing to the boxes Jeff said, "I put all the brown ones in this box and all the green ones in this box. What will I do with these?" (indicating some brown and green speckled ones). Before the teacher could answer, he said, "Oh, I know, I'll put them in a box by themselves."

A class of five-year-olds was very interested in dinosaurs. As a result they brought many models to school. They enjoyed playing with the dinosaurs, and as they gained additional knowledge their play became more realistic. They used multiple classification to group the dinosaurs by color, size, texture, etc. One day they were overheard discussing them. They examined each one and discussed its eating habits. One child said, "Let's put all the meat eaters together and all the plant eaters together. The teacher moved to the science table and asked, "Why did you put these dinosaurs together?" Two children explained that

Can you find another way to group the seeds?

some dinosaurs ate plants and others meat. Then she asked, "Do you have more meat eaters (the larger of the two groups) or more dinosaurs?" Both children quickly replied that there were more meat eaters than there were dinosaurs. Although these children were able to put objects into more than one grouping using logical knowledge (multiple classification), the concept of class inclusion had not developed. The teacher did not correct the children, which would have been useless since their reasoning was correct at their stage of development. Observing and questioning gave her clues about the children's ability to classify objects, however.

cardinal number

A teacher should give children the opportunity to work with the quantitative aspect of objects. "Do you have enough cups for every child? Do you have more cups than you need? Fewer cups? How many more will you need?" Careful questioning by the teacher helps children place objects in one-in-one correspondence to determine the equivalence or nonequivalence of sets. Terms such as "more than," "less than," and "the same" are learned. When children understand the quantitative relationship of sets, they are ready to assign a number name to each object. Teachers can encourage children to order objects and count them to find how many there are. Children must be able to count by rote to know the numeral name that comes next.

Children as young as three explore mass. Older children enjoy using a standard unit (buttons, blocks, washers, paper clips) to determine the weight (mass) of an object with the equal-arm balance: "It takes 10 buttons to balance the rock and only 3 buttons to balance the sponge." "I have to add 4 buttons and 2 paper clips to the little rock to balance the big rock."

Cooking offers numerous opportunities for using cardinal number: "How many cups of milk do we need?" "The recipe says two teaspoons of salt." "We need a tablespoon of sugar." A group of five-year-olds were making ice cream and needed seven cups of milk. The teacher poured two cups into the mixture without counting and then said, "How will we know when there are seven cups in the mixture?" A little girl who had just had her sixth birthday said, "I'll keep count." She made a mark on a piece of paper each time a cupful of milk was poured. She counted the marks as she made them and told the teacher to stop when there were seven. This child used cardinal number and one-to-one correspondence.

Matching a written numeral with the idea of a cardinal number is primarily a matter of memorization. Commercial and teacher-made materials help children match numerals to the correct number in a set. Math center equipment such as match mates, sequence counters, sorting boxes, and wooden numerals helps teach cardinal number and number recognition. Many commercial games suggested in chapter 3 help with an understanding of cardinal numbers.

seriation

Seriation begins when a child first makes a comparison between two objects: "How are the objects different?" When a child compares three or more objects and orders the objects according to some relationship, true seriation occurs. A teacher must encourage children to see differences among objects and to put objects into some kind of relationship.

A group of five-year-olds were exploring changes in water due to the addition of red, blue, and yellow food coloring. After several days of exploration one child said, "Look, I put red in both jars but the color isn't the same." The teacher said, "The colors are different. You may be able to make more colors." She supplied Carrie with additional red coloring, a pitcher of water, and several baby food jars. Later she noticed that Carrie placed three jars in a row, changing their positions frequently. She moved to the science center and observed that the three jars were placed in a sequential order from the lightest to the darkest. She said, "Carrie, tell me why you put the jars in this order." Carrie quickly explained that the colors were not alike and that she placed them from the lightest to the darkest. The teacher encouraged her to make more colors using red and to fit the resulting colors into her present series. This proved a difficult task. She persevered, however, and whenever two jars were too close to determine which held the darker color, she solved the problem by adding more water to one jar. The result was five jars of colored water arranged in sequential order. Other children began to experiment in a similar fashion, but none was able to seriate more than three colors successfully.

Three children were comparing shells in the science center. The teacher sat on the rug beside them and asked, "Can you find the smallest shell? The largest shell? Which is the next-to-largest shell?" Some children were interested in seriating a few shells and repeated the actions with different sets of shells. Other children showed no interest in seriation but only in comparing the sizes of two or three shells.

Another fascinating activity is comparing the masses of different shells using the equal-arm balance. Not every child realizes that if one pan is lower than the other, the object in the lower pan is heavier. Children can be encouraged to hold one shell in each hand and predict which is heavier before placing the shells on the balance. When the weights of objects vary slightly it is difficult to predict the heavier one. Children are often surprised when their predictions are inaccurate. Although enthusiastic about using a balance, not all children attempt to seriate objects by mass. Mass (called "weight" by children) is less observable than size, color, or shape. You can't see mass, and children find it difficult to compare masses or to keep in mind comparable masses of more than two or three objects. This ability requires kinesthetic memory as well as the ability to make comparisons.

ordinal number

A knowledge of ordinal number evolves from seriation (ordering objects). The child must place objects in some kind of sequence in order to count them. As the idea of cardinal number develops, the concept of ordinal number begins: "Which object did you count first? Second?" "Show me the object you named third." "Put the objects in order from 1 to 5." "Find the fifth object, the last, the first."

Cooking involves ordering. Recipes are put together in steps—first, second, third, etc. Picture recipes may be prepared on 8- by 11-inch cards, with a step represented by a single card and a numeral. By following the cards from left to right the child knows he or she does the action on card 1 first, card 2 second, etc. Recipes should be as uncomplicated as possible. Apples with peanut butter may consist of the following steps: card 1, wash apples; card 2, cut apples in half; card 3, spread with peanut butter. All cards are later put together with masking tape accordion fashion. Children set them up on the floor to look at and may be heard repeating the steps.

A group of five-year-olds planted bean and corn seeds that grew rapidly. They become interested in how much each plant grew each day. The teacher asked, "How can we find out how much they are growing?" Several suggestions were given, such as "Look at them every day." "Measure them with our hands." "Draw pictures of the plant." "Use a ruler to measure." "Take pictures." The children were encouraged to use any method they chose. Most found they could not remember from day to day what they had learned about the plants and that growth varied from plant to plant.

One child brought a camera from home to take pictures. He chose one bean and one corn plant to study. The teacher asked "How will you remember which plants you are studying?" He thought this over and said, "I'll write my name on masking tape and put it on the plants." When he observed a change in either plant he took a picture. When the plants were "grown up," as John described them, the film was sent away to be developed. John brought the pictures to school and put the sets of six bean pictures and six corn pictures in order. He

Following the picture recipe to make a snack.

Our seeds sprouted.

numbered each set from 1 to 6. The teacher made a cardboard frame with sections into which the pictures were arranged from left to right. John referred to the first, second, or sixth picture. The pictures showed sequential order but did not reveal the time interval between them since no record had been kept of the age of the plant when a picture was taken.

Another child drew pictures of the same plants John was photographing. Each set of pictures was placed in sequential order. The pictures were placed on a chart in order from left to right, the bean pictures at the top of the chart and the corn pictures directly under them. This time the children referred to the changes during the fifth day, seventh day, or tenth day. The ages of the plants—5 days, 10 days, 12 days—had been written on the pictures. These pictures thus revealed changes during time intervals as well as sequential order.

one-to-one correspondence

One-to-one correspondence is important in determining the equivalence and nonequivalence of sets and in assigning a number to each object in a set. A meaningful situation occurred during movement education when a teacher showed a class of four-year-olds a bag of balloons. A child asked, "Are there enough balloons for everyone?" The teacher replied, "I don't know. How could we find out?" A child volunteered to count the children as a way to solve the problem. She counted 22 children but realized that the number of balloons would also have to be counted. As the teacher opened the bag to count, another child shouted, "Don't count the balloons. Give us all a balloon and see if you have enough." They found that there were more balloons than children.

A teacher hatched eggs in an incubator. The directions for operating the incubator said it would hold four dozen eggs. When the teacher asked, "How many eggs will that be?" no one answered until finally one boy said, "That's four 12s because there are 12 eggs in a dozen." This was advanced thinking for a six-year-old. The teacher asked, "Can you show us four 12s?" The boy brought all the books from the library center and started to put them in rows of 12 each. He did not have as many books as he needed. He discarded the books and got a box of colored cubes from the mathematics center saying, "I think I have enough blocks." He made four rows of 12 blocks each and then counted the blocks, finding 48.

conservation of number

The teacher should not attempt to teach conservation of number, but rather should introduce events into the children's environment that do not fit in with the concepts they have formed about number. Most five- and six-year-olds are not conservers of number; however, some children are in a transitional stage in which they fluctuate between a true understanding and a partial understanding of number conservation. A few children conserve number as early as five or six years of age.

At mealtime one day, a four-year-old counted the number of children at the table and announced that there were eight. Several children followed his example, and each found the same number. The teacher asked, "If you counted yourself first would there still be eight children?" The children in unison said "No!" Then one child reconsidered and insisted there would still be eight. He counted himself and then the other children and triumphantly announced, "It doesn't matter who you count first." The other children disagreed and began to count, each time counting eight children. They were not convinced and continued to count, beginning with a different child each time. One child commented, "I wonder why there are always eight."

Chip found seven pretty rocks on the playground. He gave them to two friends; Ben received three and Jimmy four. Then an argument began over who had the most rocks. Ben insisted that he needed only one more rock to have as many as Jimmy. Chip told Jimmy to give Ben another rock. Jimmy gave up a rock and realized that he now had fewer than Ben. He told Jimmy and Chip that he was short a rock. This did not disturb the other boys, who were satisfied with the arrangement. Jimmy began to cry, and Chip was disturbed. He said, "Both you guys give me back my rocks." Reluctantly the rocks were handed back. Realizing that the teacher had overheard the conversation, Chip confided to him, "I had seven rocks, now I only have four and three, but it's alright." The teacher suggested that Chip count all the rocks. He counted seven but was not convinced until he had counted several times. He ran back to the other boys and said, "Oh, boy! I still have seven."

A group of five-year-olds were collecting a quantity of rocks from their playground. The teacher observed for several days, listened to the children's comments, and watched what they did with the rocks. Most of the actions consisted of lifting the rocks, washing them, describing their texture, and making constructions. Some of the recorded comments were: "This rock is heavy." "Isn't this rock little? It's a baby." "These rocks are dirty. Let's wash them." "This rock isn't very heavy." "Let's use the big rocks to make a fence." During the second week of exploration the teacher noticed one child counting the rocks. He enumerated well, generally counting as far as 28 or 29. One day he took a handful of rocks, placed them in a row, and counted them. Then he placed the rocks in various arrangements, counting each time. Suddenly he ran to the teacher very excited and said, "I have eight rocks; it doesn't matter how I count them" (the physical arrangement of the rocks doesn't matter). The teacher said, "Show me what you are doing with the rocks." He began counting the rocks as they were in a circle. He then placed them in a straight line and in three small groups, each time counting eight objects—no more and no less. Through his actions he had discovered a logico-mathematical concept. The type of object (rocks) was not important. He could have used any type of object—sticks, buttons, cookies, beads. It would have been unfortunate if the teacher had intervened in any way to stop the child's own actions with the rocks.

conservation of quantity

Conservation of quantity will not be understood by most kindergarten children, but teachers can provide experiences that show children that mass does not change no matter what shape it takes. Discrepancies in their environment may cause a state of disequilibration. In turn the children will act on the information in such a way that assimilation and accommodation occur.

Knives were provided to cut apples. Several children cut their apples into two pieces, insisting they had more apple than the other children. It did not occur to any child that the apples may not have weighed the same before they were cut.

The next day apples were placed on the science table. The children enjoyed comparing the masses of the apples using the balance. When one child got the scale to balance, the teacher intervened. She asked, "Would the scale balance if one apple were cut in half?" The answer was no. The apple on one side of the balance was cut and put back on the balance. The scale was still balanced with one whole apple and one cut apple balancing each other. The children cut one apple into several more pieces, and the scale still balanced. They saw what happened, but they were never totally convinced. It was almost as if something magical had happened.

Teachers find it helpful, when children disagree about who has more clay, to suggest placing the clay balls on the equal-arm balance. Sometimes children find there is very little difference in the amounts of clay. When children argue about the amount of water or juice they have to drink, teachers can place two plastic bowls of the same size on the balance pans. Juice from one glass can be poured into one bowl and juice from the other glass into the other bowl. Children are often surprised by the results. Adults, too, can be fooled by vision: certain containers look alike but some hold more than others.

conservation of length and measurement

Activities pertaining to social studies were discussed in chapter 4. Those focusing more directly on science and mathematics are included in this chapter. The majority of children between six and seven do not understand the use of standard units for measurement. They are not conservers of length. They believe that when a standard unit is used to measure length or width, the unit changes as it is moved along the object to be measured. It is best to encourage children to use a single unit of measurement, such as a strip of paper, wool, thread, string, or ribbon.

At the beginning of the year a strip of adding machine paper may be used to measure height from the bottom of the shoe to the top of the head. Each child's height is duplicated with an identical strip that he or she takes home. Children are measured again at the end of the year and as many times during the year as they desire.

Kindergarten children became interested in finding out how much paper it took to go around their waists, wrists, chests, ankles, and upper arms. Comparisons were made of the resulting strips of paper. Some children pasted each strip on a large piece of paper to show the length and circumference of their body parts.

At the workbench children usually measure wood by placing one piece against another, drawing a line, and cutting as closely as possible to the line so that the two pieces will be the same length. Some children, however, use a unit of measurement. When a child moves any unit along an object to be measured, questions may be asked such as "How many times did you move your hand? Foot? Paper?" "Is it almost four hands long?" "Is it a little more than three hands?"

Cooking activities provide experiences with liquid and dry measurement. Children can compare standard measuring cups and spoons with drinking cups and tableware. Children discover that all cups or glasses do not hold the same amount of liquid, sand, rice, or beans. They can predict which holds more and test their predictions. These experiences often contradict what the child believes to be true, that is the bigger the better. "Does it make any difference whether a standard measuring cup is used to make a recipe, or can *any* cup serve the same purpose?"

Water and sand play give children experiences with measurement. Teachers should not expect children to form sophisticated concepts about measurement, such as two half cups equals one cup or three teaspoons equals one tablespoon. Instead they should encourage exploration with measurement by questions such as "Which container will hold more water (sand)? How can you find out?" Two children solved this problem by filling one container to the top and pouring the water into the second container, which ran over. After doing this three times they decided the second container held less water. Another group of children solved the same problem by using a cup and counting the number of cups needed to fill each container.

Questions such as "How many cans of water will you need to fill the large container? How many measuring cups? Teaspoons? Tablespoons?" stimulate problem solving. One child asked if it would take all the water in the pitcher to water the outdoor pansies. The teacher told him she didn't know and asked him how he could find out. He said, "I'll water them." When he finished he said it took three pitchers of water. Later in the week he was puzzled because he used only two pitchers. He was asked to feel the ground. He did and said triumphantly, "The ground was sort of wet. It rained last night and the flowers had water."

conservation of distance

A true understanding of distance is not possible for young children. They see and describe objects as either near or far. A few five- and six-year-olds conserve distance, understanding that the distance between objects does not change when other objects are placed between them. The relationship between speed, distance, and time is not understood, however, until children are much older. Activities to help children understand distance are included in chapter 4.

temporal relations

The conventional activity of telling time should be postponed until second grade. Children need concrete experiences to begin to have a feeling for time. Interested children should be given experiences with an hourglass, an alarm clock, a one- or 3-minute timer, and a 60-minute timer. Teachers can place several different types of timers, such as an hourglass and a 3-minute timer, in the dramatic-play and mathematics centers. The 60-minute timer can be set to go off at different intervals. These devices do not help children tell time, but they do teach the concepts that three minutes is longer than one minute and that it takes many minutes to make an hour.

Before children put toys away, set a 60-minute timer and show it to each group of children saying, "You have 5 (3 or 10) minutes to finish what you are doing. When you hear the buzzer go off it is time to put the toys away." Children respond more eagerly and rapidly to the buzzer than they do to the request "stop what you are doing: it's time to put things away." A few children become very interested in watching the arrow on the timer move. They will set the timer in another center and watch to see if both timers go off at the same time. Most classrooms have a wall clock children can watch.

A game children like is Magic. They are asked to "hold their magic" for 1 minute, 5 minutes, no longer than 10 minutes. Holding your magic means sitting still without moving or even making a sound. This game not only quiets children when they have become restless but also gives them a feeling for the passage of time.

Many adults say to children, "We'll go in a minute," "I'll be ready in five minutes," or "Just a second." Children become confused by what they are told, when the event usually happens much later. Children cannot learn to "feel" time when "5 minutes" mysteriously takes 30 minutes to an hour.

Calendars should be used with five-year-olds but in a concrete way: "How many days until Halloween? Christmas? My birthday? Let's count the days on the calendar." It is important to have three types of calendars available for children to manipulate: one on which they can put a numeral for each day of the month, take the numerals off, and put them back again; a wall calendar at their eye level which shows the days of a given month; and a calendar that opens and shows each month on a separate page. Children can leaf through this calendar to find their birthdays, which may be shown by a birthday cake and name on the designated day. It is the teacher's purpose at this time not to teach children the months or the days of the week but to familiarize them with another method of measuring time. The interest of four-year-olds in calendars is usually short.

Other activities related to temporal relationships and social studies are included in chapter 4.

spatial relations

The teacher's role in spatial understanding and activities is included in chapter 4.

It is obviously impossible to talk about one subject area without discussing another. It is true that an activity may relate more closely to one subject than another, but it is never in total isolation. Knowledgeable teachers make every effort to integrate subject matter. They know that setting aside blocks of time for separate subjects is as meaningless as trying to teach part of a child rather than the whole child.

scheduling and grouping

Scientific and mathematics activities occur spontaneously throughout the day just as do activities in other content areas. Most grow out of problems that arise during explorations with physical objects. Children form their own groups as they seek solutions to the problems. The teacher remains in the background, observing and listening, ready to help when he or she feels the time is right.

Teachers can plan small-group activities to encourage further explorations with objects. Several children planted bean seeds and watched them grow. They became interested in knowing the height of their plants. After school the teacher set up part of the mathematics center as an area for measurement. Manipulative items, such as small blocks, strips of paper of varying lengths, dowels, construction paper, scissors, paste, and a bean plant, were placed in the center. The next day, during learning-center time the teacher approached the center when a child began stacking blocks next to the bean plant. The teacher asked, "How tall is the plant?" Pete replied, "Almost five blocks high." He left the center and returned with his own plant. Pete used blocks and other manipulative materials to measure his plant. Before he left the center he said, "It took six blocks to show how tall my plant is, but only four dowels." Other children brought their plants to measure. This activity continued for several days.

first day of school

Permanent objects and a few other inviting objects, such as shells, rocks, or seeds, should be on the science table. A classroom pet should not be included unless adequate supervision is provided. A well-set-up science center is immediately popular. Here are objects to handle and act upon. The equal-arm balance is often the most interesting piece of equipment.

The mathematics center should contain familiar and unfamiliar objects and equipment. Most children have worked puzzles and strung beads. There should be puzzles with as few as 6 pieces and others with as many as 20. The teacher should choose a challenging piece of equipment, such as a sequence counter or Unifix blocks, for children who are more advanced.

The teacher's role is to observe how children use the equipment. It may be necessary to remove more difficult pieces and replace them with less complex ones or, in some cases, to add difficult items, such as match mates and/or wooden numerals.

Whether or not to include children in making snacks during the first week depends on their maturity and the available supervision. Usually it is best to wait until children are adjusted to school and can work rather independently.

science and mathematics through the year

providing materials

Teachers must be alert to the ways in which children use physical knowledge to discover relationships that lead to logico-mathematical knowledge. Whatever a teacher learns from observations is used as a guide for selecting and presenting materials. Constructions made at the workbench can lead to explorations with water. Children made boats and placed them in the water table. They wanted to know, "Will my boat stay up or will it go to the bottom?" Materals—paper, aluminum foil, cardboard, rug scraps—were added to the workbench to use as accessories in making boats. There was much enthusiasm as boats were constructed and predictions made about their launching in the water table.

Sometimes children ask for materials to mix with others. The teacher supplied a group of five-year-olds with rice and beans with the understanding that they must first find a way to separate the rice and/or beans from the sand. Several solutions were explored: picking the rice out of the sand, sifting the sand through the fingers, and using various sieves to remove the larger particles. The latter proved to be the most satisfactory.

Just as it is crucial to know when to present appropriate materials, it is important to know when to remove them. When children have explored to their satisfaction all possible ways to use batteries and bulbs, it is time to remove them and present new materials to explore. This does not mean that an interest in batteries and bulbs will not be renewed. After a visit from a senior citizen who had used kerosene lamps as a boy, one child asked, "Where are the batteries and bulbs?" The teacher told him to look in the storeroom. He returned happily with a box labeled "Electricity" and went right to work.

observation

Effective teachers know when and when not to intervene in the affairs of children. Knowing when to help, ask questions, and make comments is the most important and most difficult part of teaching. "Should I make a suggestion? Should I show him or her how to do it?" are questions constantly facing teachers. In order to know when to intervene teachers must know how children think about their world. They must listen carefully to spontaneous comments and questions.

A multiage group of four-, five-, and six-year-olds is especially interesting since the wide age span provides a great range of intellectual development. On the first day of school a teacher told the story "Yertle the Turtle" using a flannel board. When he finished, a six-and-a-half-year-old boy who read at sixth-grade level said, "There's a problem with the story. Wondering, the teacher asked, "What problem, Tom?" Tom replied, "Well, the turtles on the flannel board are facing in the wrong direction." The teacher asked, "In what direction are they facing?" Tom quickly replied, "They're facing to the left, and they should be facing to the right." The teacher asked other children what they thought about the turtles. Most did not care which direction the turtles faced, but Tom persisted. "Let's look in the book," he said. After a thorough review of the pictures Tom decided the turtles could face in either direction. At the back of the room were two turtles in cages. Mary, determined to solve the problem scientifically, jumped up saying, "I'm going to look at our turtles." She hurried to the back of the room, looked at the turtles, and called, "It's all right, Mr. A., the turtles are facing left toward the windows." This is a perfect example of transductive thinking, which both children used although Tom was a year older than Mary.

Ned, who was in the schematic stage of art development, showed a realistic Mickey Mouse holding balloons in each hand, a blue sky, and *two* suns. The teacher said, "Ned, I really like this picture. Tell me about Mickey Mouse [the animal was unmistakably Mickey]." Ned said, "That's Mickey Mouse selling balloons at Disney World. He's so tired. He has walked around the park *all* day selling balloons." The teacher said, "Mickey has been very busy." "Yes," the boy replied, "that's why I made two suns." Ned used the two suns to show the passage of time, although he knew there is only one sun. His thinking revealed his belief in animism: inanimate objects are alive and have a purpose, which in the sun's case is to follow people as they move from place to place.

Natalie amazed her teacher one day when, at three years and two months of age, she announced, "I grew inside my Mommy's body and was borned. Jimmy [her brother] grew inside Daddy's body and was borned." The teacher told her they both grew inside her mother's body. Indignantly, she said, "No, Jimmy is a boy and Daddy's a boy. I'm a girl and Mommy's a girl." The teacher told her to ask her mother. After consulting her mother she said, unconvinced, "I still think Jimmy grew in Daddy's body. He's a boy." Although Natalie's information was faulty, her thinking was logical based upon the information she had. She had been told she grew in her mother's body. She used inductive thinking to arrive at a generalization: "I am a girl; Mommy is a girl, therefore I grew in Mommy's body. Jimmy is a boy; Daddy is a boy, therefore Jimmy grew in Daddy's body."

Even at six and a half children are sometimes confused about where they grew and how they came into the world. A sophisticated six and a half year old boy informed his teacher that he grew inside the stomach of his grandmother (who lived with the family) and that his older brother Steve grew in his mother's stomach. When his mother arrived to take John home the teacher suggested that he ask her where he had grown. When his mother told him he had grown inside her body he was surprised. She explained that she had once been a baby and grew inside his grandmother's body. "Oh," he said, "I didn't know that." Then he said, "If I grew in your stomach and Steve grew in your stomach, that makes us brothers." The teacher was surprised at this more sophisticated form of thought compared with his former, more naive remarks. Her attention was once again called to the fact that children are often naive and wise at the same time.

individual differences

If you have 20 to 25 children in your classroom you may find that learning takes off in 20 to 25 different directions. Children will choose different objects to explore, manipulate them in their own ways, and receive varied feedback from the objects. Teachers must be alert to the many directions learning may take.

During experimentation with magnets a five-year-old boy said, "I want to make an electromagnet." The teacher was surprised at his request and asked, "What will you need to make an electromagnet?" He showed a book from the library center and pointed to a picture of an electromagnet. Everything was found that Van needed except a large nail, which his parents allowed him to bring from home. He followed the directions given in picture form and soon had an electromagnet. In addition to finding out one way to make an electromagnet Van learned that books are a source of information and that pictures as well as words convey ideas. He learned that needed materials can be found at home and at school and that his teacher and his parents wanted to help him succeed in carrying out his plans.

One of the first things children discover are the properties of sand and water. Jane remarked that water was just like paint. The teacher asked, "How is it like paint?" She replied, "It's wet; I know lots of things that are wet." The teacher encouraged her to explore the playground to find things that were wet. She returned saying that the only thing she had found was wet sand. She explored the kindergarten room and asked the teacher to make a list of the things she found that felt wet—juice, milk, earth clay, paste, felt pens. This led to experimentation to remove water from substances by leaving them open to the air. Most materials dried out as the water evaporated. Although Jane used the terms "dried up" and "disappeared" she was experiencing the phenomenon of evaporation.

One child was fascinated with a small sprinkler. The teacher discussed the size of the holes and the way the water looked on Bill's hands. He wanted bigger holes and began to look for other equipment. He found sieves and sifters, which he brought to the water table. Unsatisfied, he asked for plastic bags. Using toothpicks and nails Bill made holes in each bag. He was satisfied with the results. He had solved his problem himself and commented on the big drops of water that looked like rain and the tiny drops that tickled his hand.

problem solving

Children learn when they try to find answers to problems. In problem solving in both science and mathematics, children must place objects into some kind of relationship. When a child says that there are more blue than red blocks, the relationship does not exist *in* the red or the blue blocks (physical knowledge) but is created by the child who puts them into a relationship (logico-mathematical knowledge). He or she may discover the relationship by lining up the two different colors of blocks in front of each other in a one-to-one relationship or by enumerating each set and making a comparison between the caradinal numbers. In either case the child created the relationship. In setting the stage for logico-mathematical thinking it is the teacher's responsibility to provide many interesting objects for the children to act upon and to encourage problem situations the child can solve by acting on objects and placing them into relationships.

Children's observations can lead to teacher intervention in the form of suggestions, questions, and comments. There were several round plastic containers at the water table. A five-year-old boy became very excited, "Look," he said, "the rock looks bigger." The teacher asked, "Do you think it has become larger?" "No," he said, taking the rock out of the water and showing her that it was still the same size. The teacher said, "Let's put the rock into other containers of water." She helped him find various containers and place the rock in each. Now several children had joined them. They noticed that the rock's size did not change in all the containers. The teacher asked, "Why do you think the rock looks the same size in some containers but not in others?"

The children began a discussion among themselves, and the teacher left them to solve their problem. From time to time she could hear them arguing, each giving his or her own explanation of the strange phenomenon. The next day the teacher noticed that the same type of experimentation was in progress. She joined the children, who told her, "The rock only looks bigger in round containers filled with water." One child said, "It's like our magnifying glass." The teacher asked, "Do you think other objects would look larger in the round containers?" Yes, they said, and the exploration continued. The children found that some objects stayed on top of the water. Only after the children had

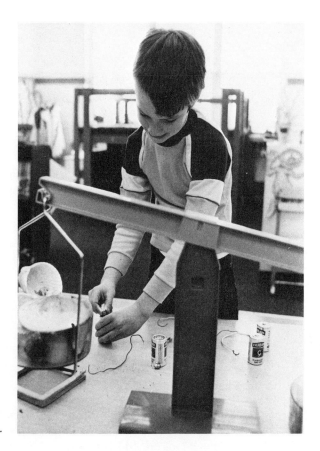

I can make the light burn.

experimented for several days did the teacher use the words "float," "sink," and "magnification," which a few children were already saying. She had wanted them to internalize their actions before she gave them verbal symbols.

Later the children discovered that when the round jars were filled with water and placed in the sunlight there was a rainbow. These discoveries led to the addition on the science table of various cut glass objects brought from home—ash trays, perfume bottles, plates. One little girl showed the teacher a book about color from the library shelf. Louise pointed to a rainbow and asked, "I don't see any cut glass in the sky. How did that happen?" The teacher read the story to her, and as she read she asked Louise questions about each page. After the teacher finished the story she asked, "What happened before the children saw the rainbow?" Louise's face lit up as she said, "It rained!" Outside, the teacher connected the hose, and the children observed the colors they saw in the spray. They enjoyed this activity and found that on cloudy days there was no color.

One day a group of four-, five-, and six-year-olds dug up some worms near their garden. They placed the worms on the grass near the sandbox and watched as many of the worms crawled into the box. Over and over the children experimented with the worms—removing them from the sandbox and watching them crawl back again. One child dug up some soil and placed it next to the sandpile. The children watched and discovered that more worms moved toward the pile of soil than toward the pile of sand. The teacher began to question the children: "Why do you think the worms like the soil better than the sand? What will happen if you take the soil away? The sand away?" Do you think the worms would like sawdust, stones, paper?" The children experimented with different materials and found that most of the worms preferred the soil. Some children verbalized their observations; others did not. The teacher was careful not to summarize their experiences for them. After several days of experimentation the children agreed that the worms liked the soil best. The teacher asked, "Why do you think they preferred the soil?" Different answers were given, but most children concluded that "worms live in soil; therefore they like it better."

process versus product

Although science for young children is presented as a process, a teacher cannot avoid product (content). If there is an animal in the classroom, children will learn from observation and experimentation much about it: how it moves, what kinds of food it likes best, what it feels like. In order to learn proper care of the animal, however, it is necessary to consult a book. The children must have facts (content) in order to care for their pet properly.

meeting goals

The evaluation scheme in chapter 1 may be applied to science and mathematics. A checklist based upon the behavioral objectives should be kept for each child. The methods previously described for collecting data are applicable to science and mathematics.

Piagetian tasks related to physical and logico-mathematical knowledge may be given to each child. Directions for giving most of the tasks are given in *Cognitive Tasks* (Osborn and Osborn, 1974). They are Conservation of Number and One-to-one Correspondence (pp. 40–45), Conservation of Quantity (p. 37), Time and Space (pp. 75–76), Time and Measurement (pp. 75–79), Location (pp. 94–97), Classification (pp. 55–59, 62–64) and Seriation (pp. 60, 61).

Copeland's *How Children Learn Mathematics* (1979) includes directions for administering the tasks and suggestions for applying the results to the teaching of young children. In addition the book discusses Horizontal and Vertical Lines (p. 317) and Perspective (pp. 365–367). Topological relationships are described in chapters 15 and 16.

Teachers should not use the results of Piagetian tasks to teach logical knowledge. The purpose of giving the tasks is to help the teacher learn more about children's thinking. A teacher who understands how children think can plan activities appropriate for the developmental level.

6
children
are creative
music and art

In recent years educators and psychologists have given increased attention to the development of creativity within the child. Research has shown that creativity is nothing special; children are born creative, some to a greater extent than others (Marsh, 1970, pp. 2–3). Creativity can be developed. The teacher's role is to help children utilize materials and ideas in ways that are original for them.

A product is judged as creative when a child has made something *new to himself* that is satisfying and useful to him (Miel, 1961, pp. 6–7). This is a broad definition of creativity that is generally accepted by those who teach young children. Marsh (1970) defines creativity as a "thought, act, or product that is original to its producer" (p. 191). Torrance (1962) chose to define creative thinking as "the process of sensing gaps or disturbing, missing elements; forming ideas or hypotheses concerning them; testing these hypotheses; and communicating the results, possibly modifying and retesting the hypotheses" (p. 16). This definition of creativity is similar to a description of the scientific process. Discovery becomes a part of the creative process since creativity is not possible without discovery. The child discovers something previously unknown to him (Marsh, 1970, p. 4).

Research since the 1950s has revealed some surprising observations about creativity which are significant for teachers: (1) All children possess creativity to a greater or lesser extent. (2) Creativity is fostered by an environment rich in ideas, experiences, materials, and equipment. (3) Creative tests and intelligence tests measure different thinking abilities. (4) Highly creative pupils are favored less often by teachers than highly intelligent students. (5) Creative thinking is divergent (takes off in different directions) rather than convergent (converging on a predetermined right answer). (6) Highly creative children often become classroom behavior problems. (7) There are many types of creativity, and a child can

be creative in one area and not in another. (8) Creativity is process as well as product. (9) Creativity flourishes in an accepting environment. (10) Creative children are open to new experiences, independent, and purposeful. (Marsh, 1970; Getzels and Jackson, 1962; and Torrance, 1963.)

Brissoni (1975) feels children are always creative because they are always ready to have a new experience (p. 19). He believes experience is the fundamental mental basic in developing creativity. Children do not create out of a vacuum; they cannot create from nothing. What children need is many varied experiences and the necessary time to elaborate these experiences. Children are kept from making good use of experiences by demanding teachers, rigid time limits, unrealistic expectations, and specific directions (pp. 20–22).

A great deal has been written about the creative process. Different steps or phases have been identified as those responsible for the creative act. Foshay (1961) discusses four phases relevant for the classroom teacher: openness, focus, discipline, and closure. The first, openness, refers to the children's tolerance of new experiences. Children are willing to take a look at all the data before making a judgment. Closely related to openness is focus. After playing with "the data" children impose structure on some of it. This process goes on as the children test and reject or accept data until they are satisfied. The third factor is discipline imposed upon children from within, not from without. They are self-disciplined and wholly absorbed in work whether the product is a piece of art, a musical composition, or a scientific formula. Closure is the end of the creative process. The children decide that they are finished or not finished, that it is all they can do, or that they are not finished and want to throw the product away. They are the creators of the product and have the right to decide what to do with it (pp. 24–40).

153

To speak of creativity is to talk about the total preschool program. The opportunity for children to "create their own thing" from their ideas is inherent in all content areas. What is necessary is a teacher who respects and understands the creative potential of each child.

Art and music are often referred to as the "creative arts." It seems that educators have always been aware of the potential for creativity in art, music, movement, and dance. Perhaps this is because artists and musicians have been described as creative whereas scientists and mathematicians, although many are highly creative, have been described as brilliant and inspired. Music and art offer children a creative challenge, for without a tinge of the child's own personality they become imitative and uninteresting.

The philosophy of "every child for music and music for every child" has permeated nursery school and kindergarten education. Teachers of young children make every effort to include musical activities in the curriculum. In spite of their belief in the importance of music, though, most teachers find it necessary to proceed by instinct. McDonald and Ramsey (1978) state that

There is little information about the kinds of musical experiences that are appropriate for the young child, the methods and techniques which might be helpful in planning musical activities, or the criteria which might be applied when choosing musical materials for young children. (p. 26)

Although a review of the literature reveals a scarcity of information dealing with music and the young child, it is encouraging that sessions dealing with music and the preschool child are currently presented at both early childhood and music conferences. Articles on young children and music are appearing more frequently in early childhood and music journals (Shelley, 1976, p. 202). This surge of interest is promising and the combined efforts of educators and music specialists should upgrade the kinds of musical activities offered for young children.

Most research in music has been concerned with the child's singing voice and, more recently, with the relationship of body movement to rhythmic expression. Research findings will be discussed under headings suggested by Smith (1970) in *Music in the Child's Education:* vocal activities, rhythmic activities, listening activities, and creative music.

singing activities

It was once believed that young children had high singing voices and that songs should be taught in the upper range. The shrill, high-pitched voices used by children in play were equated with musical sounds. Although there are a few music educators who continue to advocate teaching songs in a high range, the research evidence suggests that three-, four-, and five-year-olds have voices within a lower range of three to six notes. In general children three to five sing more comfortably somewhere in the range of middle C to A above middle C (Bayless and Ramsey, 1978; McDonald and Ramsey, 1978; Shelley, 1976; Smith, 1970; and Sheehy, 1968).

Around the age of two children join in chanting, a form of spontaneous singing. One of the common chants of childhood is the interval of the minor third ("sol-me"). The Orff and Kodàly approach to singing begins with this chant and later includes the remaining notes on the pentatonic scale. Although the Orff-Kodàly method is not widely practiced in the preschool, the song materials suggested can serve as models for teachers. Orff suggests using folk songs of children's native countries. American folk songs are particularly appealing to young children, and most are within the appropriate range for children's voices (Wheeler and Raebeck, 1972, p. xix).

Since the 1950s Robert Smith has been involved in research on young children's voices. He has worked extensively with three-, four-, and five-year-olds in an attempt to discover the natural growth of their voices. Smith (1963) found that children's voices followed developmental patterns and that with vocal training children can be taught to sing tunefully. According to Smith (1970) there are four stages in the development of singing: (1) Directional singing—children sing up and down the scale but seldom match any tones correctly. (2) Limited range—children begin as directional singers but become tuneful in a limited range of three or four notes if they have the opportunities to match tones. Three-year-olds sing tones between d' and g', four- to eight-year-olds between c' and f', and a few children sing well in a lower or higher range.* The most common range for limited-range singers is between c' and g'. (3) Lower-range stage—most three-year-olds sing in a lower range of c' to a', children between four and eight sing in a range between c' and a'. Children will move from one level to another if they sing within the proper range. (4) Upper range—this range includes tones above a' for three-year-olds and above a' or b' for older children. Children from ages four to seven will sing higher tones more easily, but approximately one-half of first graders find upper-range tones difficult to sing. Songs in this category should form a very small portion of the preschool music program (pp. 17–22). Since there will seldom be a time when all children in the same classroom sing with equal facility, it is best to select songs in more than one range.

Smith (1970) offers the following suggestions for choosing songs: (1) Songs should be selected that will appeal to children after many repetitions. (2) Songs for young children should have melodic phrase repetition. (3) The texts should have repeated word phrases to enable children to listen to the melody without being distracted by difficult word combinations. (4) The range of the song is of critical importance. The melody *must* be in the most appropriate range for children's stage of development. (5) The early childhood song repertoire should be as varied as possible (p. 24).

Carefully selected rhythm instruments will enrich singing activities. Instruments enable children to explore through a visual as well as a tonal medium. Smith (1970) recommends the use of resonator bells that the child can use to match tones. McDonald and Ramsey (1978) suggest providing visual cues by moving the hands in an up-and-down motion with the tones of a song or playing songbells held vertically. Songs should be included whose lyrics suggest melodic direction (p. 20).

---

*Smith uses the following system to designate the exact location of tones: Tones in the range from middle C up to third-line B (treble staff) are designated as c'—b' (p. 17).

rhythmic activities

According to Smith (1970) rhythm is "that element of music pertaining to the temporal quality or duration of musical sounds"(p. 349). When emotion is added to music it becomes dance.

Children explore rhythm from the day they are born. Babies coo, babble, and experiment with sounds that are pleasing. These sounds are reinforced by attentive adults who echo the sounds back to the baby. Gradually children learn to talk, and their experimentation with words often results in half-chants, half-songs. They explore objects by hitting, banging, and shaking until the resulting sounds can be reproduced to form patterns. This kind of exploration with rhythm continues throughout the preschool years.

Children enjoy rhymes, poems, and jingles. They repeat the words in rhythmic fashion just as they do big words such as "hippopotamus," "delicious," and "fantastic" (Bayless and Ramsey, 1978, p. 126). Children use various body movements as they chant, recite poetry, and carry on conversations with themselves in play. Sheehy (1968) says that "children are constantly talking to us in movement" (p. 100). Sensitive teachers are alert to children's movements and provide a rhythmic accompaniment whenever possible. They may clap, tap a stick, chant, play the piano, or use other instruments to match children's tempo.

The music-through-movement approach first makes children aware of the ways they can use their bodies in space. When they have attained a repertoire of movements and controls over their bodies, they are ready to transfer movement to music (Taylor, 1973, p. 50). A teacher invites exploration by means of provocative and open-ended questions: "Can you move from one end of the room to the other without using your feet? Can you wiggle your body without moving from your space? Make your body puff up like a cake in the oven. Can you make your body look like a ball?" Attention can be called to children who exhibit unusual body movement, "Look, Jimmy is sliding across the floor. Let's all try sliding." After trying Jimmy's way, a teacher might say, "Who would like to show us another way to move across the floor?" (McDonald and Ramsey, 1978, pp. 29–30; Bayless and Ramsey, 1978, pp. 51–55; Stecher, McElheny, and Greenwood, 1972, pp. 59–76).

Creative teachers use word pictures to create movement. Stories in movement may originate with a teacher or children. A child may describe an event that is expressed by the class through movement. "We went to the mountains in the car. The car climbed higher and higher. It went around and around sharp curves," is a story a child might tell after a weekend trip. Children can dramatize this story as they move around the room.

Opportunities for moving slowly, fast, upward, downward, and around are present. A teacher may introduce a movement story with a single theme and encourage children to continue the story as they move. The story may begin, "Let's go for a walk in the snow. The snow is very deep. We must lift our legs up high. Our legs feel. . . . " Movement stories encourage imagination and prepare children for creative responses to music (Sheehy, 1968, pp. 134–138).

Once children have had plenty of opportunities to explore movement the teacher can strike up a steady beat on a drum to accompany their movements. As the children gain more experience the teacher can ask them to respond to a beat being played (Bayless and Ramsey, 1978, pp. 53–55).

According to Smith (1970) there are three stages in the child's rhythmic response to music: (1) A teacher introduces a simple, even beat by clapping or using a drum. Children respond to the beat by clapping and/or moving about the room freely. The pattern is repeated on subsequent days. The musical elements high-low may be introduced by playing high and low notes on the piano. Next, uneven drumbeats are played which suggest skipping or galloping. The concepts fast-slow and soft-loud can be introduced as soon as even and uneven patterns are learned. (2) A child responds to music of different periods and styles ranging from the baroque period to the twentieth century. The composition chosen must have a consistent tempo and repeated rhythmic patterns. Those selected should suggest even and uneven beats. (3) Compositions should have longer and more varied musical forms. Teachers should play the compositions several times and discuss those sections with familiar sounds before introducing new elements in the music. Selections for the second and third stages may be found at the end of chapter 4 (Smith, 1970).

All too often children are told to move "the way the music makes you feel." This is almost the same as saying, "do what it says" (Sheehy, 1968, p. 104). Instead it is better to give children something to listen for—rhythm, pitch, tempo. After listening to a selection discuss it with the children and then say, "Move the way the music sounds to you" or "This music makes me feel like moving. Let's move with it" (Stecher, McElheny, and Greenwood, 1972, p. 66).

rhythm instruments

Instruments should be of good quality and should be introduced as part of the total music program. They should always be introduced for musical purposes and for legitimate experimentation (Smith, 1970, p. 165). Obviously musical instruments should be respected and not thrown about or pounded with hammers or other unsuitable objects.

There has been much controversy as to how musical instruments should be introduced. Should they be handed out to each child at the same time? Should one at a time be put out for experimentation? Should children be free to explore instruments throughout the day? The concensus of opinion is that where children show respect for instruments they should have the opportunity to handle them freely. Only a few instruments should be available to explore at one time, and simple rules for handling them must be established (Bayless and Ramsey, 1978, p. 39; Sheehy, 1968, pp. 74–75; Smith, 1970, p. 165).

Resonator bells are suggested by Smith (1970) as beginning instruments because of their large playing surface and pleasing musical sounds (pp. 165–168). Sheehy (1968) suggests a variety of drums for their versatility (pp. 69–78). Whatever instruments are used children should be free to explore their musical possibilities. Children can be guided to discover that a triangle produces a dull sound when it is held tightly in the hand and struck and a high sound when it is suspended and struck.

Teachers can guide children to help sound making become more focused and controlled by asking questions such as "Can you find a high sound? Can you find a sound that is different from that one? Does the drum always sound like that?" Children may be encouraged to create their own sound patterns with comments such as "Was your way to use the drum like Alice's? Can you use the bells to make the same sounds as the drum? Play a sound story and I'll play it back with the triangle" (Stecher, McElheny, and Greenwood, 1972, pp. 40–57).

Listening to recordings helps children to match an instrument with a musical beat. Large groups of children join in this type of activity, sometimes moving their entire bodies with the music as they play. Children sing songs with repeated phrases that can be used as cues for instruments. Some songs, such as "Jingle Bells," suggest instruments. Children can decide which instruments are most suitable to accompany a particular song.

listening activities

Listening is considered the foundation of all musical experiences. Efforts to alert the ear cannot be overestimated since auditory discrimination is basic to the development of music.

Teachers are aware of the poor listening skills children bring with them as they enter school. Bayless and Ramsey (1978) state, "There is considerable agreement between educators and psychologists that one of the major problems of children in the elementary school is lack of good listening skills. . . . Music can, and should, be a natural in helping develop good listening skills." (p. 28).

It is essential that a teacher expect children to listen. Requests should be made in a nonthreatening way. A teacher may say, "I am going to sing a birthday song for you. Listen for the things children do on their birthdays." "I am going to sing" means "I sing and you listen" and "things children do on birthdays" means "listen for what happens." We cannot expect children to listen to musical selections of our choice without giving them a reason to listen.

Children should be exposed to many types of music. A large heritage of music literature has been passed down from generation to generation. This music has an enduring quality with which children should become familiar. Teachers can assure a smorgasbord of musical selections by exposing themselves to the finest in music (Smith, 1970, pp. 119–122). Children love the recordings of Hap Palmer and Ella Jenkins. Their music has worth and is very appealing; however, a steady diet of any one type of music is not desirable.

creative music

Creativity cannot be considered a separate part of a music program. Instead it should be present in all musical activities. The first creative response of children to music is through voice sounds. As children chant they explore sound, sometimes with unexpected changes in tempo, pitch, and accent. When original chants are set to music unique songs are composed.

Sometimes children pick out melodies on the piano, xylophone, or other instruments. These original efforts to make music should be recorded by the teacher and played back. These songs can be written in musical notation, mimeographed, and sent home (Sheehy, 1968, pp. 55–60).

Children create rhythmic responses with body movements which the teacher can accompany at the piano or with percussion instruments. Rhythmic expressions may be repeated again and again by their creators and by others who enjoy them.

Rhythmic response to music should be the child's own creation. As children learn more about what they can do with their bodies in space they become freer and their movements more flexible and expressive. Alert teachers who value creativity encourage children to think for themselves and try out their own ideas.

In regard to creativity Smith (1970) says: "Every young child will thoroughly enjoy these activities which emphasize the creative process. The child will expand his musical horizons in many ways as his concepts about music are further developed by his original manipulation of musical elements and materials" (p. 197).

art

Art, perhaps more than music, offers children an opportunity to use their creative powers. While music is sometimes imitative, as in learning a song, art always reveals a child's unique way of thinking.

There are basically two approaches to teaching art to young children. The two strategies can be closely compared to the product-process approach to subject matter. The directive approach stresses the final product and the developmental approach the process of creating (Francks, 1977, p. 196).

The directive method is inappropriate for children. It does not allow for creativity because the teacher dominates children's thinking. In the developmental approach children are encouraged to think in ways that are unique for them. The teacher is a guide, motivator, supporter, and facilitator of learning (Burns, 1975, pp. 193–194). Within the developmental approach there is a place for directive teaching strategies. If a child wants to learn how to cut with scissors, direct instruction is appropriate. But "if direct guidance does not help the child to achieve his goal, then the teaching should be stopped" (Kaplan-Sanoff, 1977, p. 197). Without maturational readiness children do not profit from direct intervention.

Although there are a number of theories of child art, there is general agreement by early childhood educators that it passes through various developmental stages (Seefeldt, 1976, pp. 177–181). Lowenfeld and Kellogg are perhaps the most widely known advocates of the developmental-stage theory. Kellogg believes that children should be left alone to develop their art from within. Although Lowenfeld places more emphasis on individual learner differences, he also believes that art is an innate human capacity that unless hampered by adults, develops along biogenetically predetermined lines (Wieder, 1977, p. 8). It seems that stages of growth in children's art as outlined by Kellogg and Lowenfeld closely parallel Piaget's stages of intellectual development, particularly his investigations into the child's concept of space (Lansing, 1966; p. 33). Their developmental stages may be compared as follows:

Lowenfeld	Kellogg	Piaget
. . .	. . .	Preoperational (2 to 7)
Scribbling (2 to 4)	Scribbling (2 to 4)	Sub-preoperational (2 to 4)
Preschematic (4 to 7)	Pictorial (4 to 6)	Intuitive (4 to 7)
Schematic (7 to 9)	Pictures (5 to 7)	Concrete (7 to 11)

(Adapted from Kellogg and O'Dell, 1967; Lansing, 1966; Kaplan-Sanoff, 1977; and Seefeldt, 1976.)

Each researcher has worked independently of the others, yet their findings are interrelated. In this chapter the stages of art development and the implications for teachers will be discussed under Lowenfeld's headings of scribbling, preschematic, and schematic.

scribbling stage: approximately two to four years of age

Kellogg (1970) discovered that children all over the world pass through the same stages in their art development. She has identified 20 basic scribbles children use in their drawings. Two scribbles are united to form a "combine," and two or more combines make complex forms called "aggregates." Children do not scribble at random but place their scribbles in a definite pattern on the space they are using. Seventeen different placement patterns have been identified.

Approximately at the age of three children begin to draw a form or shape in their scribbles. The outline-of-shape stage is crucial. Kellogg believes it is at this time that children become aware of shapes in their artwork. Once conscious of their ability to create forms they enjoy experimenting and often create designs. Mandalas (figures divided into quarters), radials (lines that radiate from a point or small area), and suns (ovals or rectangles with short lines that cross the perimeter) are prominent. It is from these forms, particularly the sun, that the first attempts to make people evolve (Kellogg and O'Dell, 1967, pp. 53–61).

After four, children attempt to draw people by attaching lines to an imperfect circle. Because their concept of topological relationships, especially order and continuity, is not fully developed, the parts of the body may be scattered over a page. Children may draw a man with a nose below the eyes and a hat above the head. They may not retain a mental image of the sequence of mouth and nose along a vertical axis or of a person wearing a hat as a continuous unit (Lansing, 1966, p. 36).

Lowenfeld and Brittain (1970) recognize scribbling as a part of the total growth pattern. In their scribbles children reflect their intellectual, emotional, and physical development. They enjoy their kinesthetic sensations during scribbling, but eventually the eye directs the hand motions (p. 113). Toward the end of the scribbling stage fantasy takes over, and the marks made remind the children of something they have seen. Now they are able to give a name to their scribbles; kinesthetic thinking has become imaginative thinking (pp. 91–115).

Children do not need to be motivated to scribble. The drive to make marks on paper with a crayon or in dirt with a finger is innate. There are a few children who may have become inhibited in their attempt to scribble. These are children whose first attempts were met with a "no!" Teachers can encourage children by assuring them that it is alright to draw. If they are still hesitant teachers can invite them to draw. A child can move his or her crayon around and around on the paper as the teacher moves his or her crayon. This is not copying since the teacher is simply showing the child one way to use a crayon. A teacher might say, "It feels good to move the crayon around. Let's close our eyes and move our crayons. Now open our eyes and look at what we made" (Sparling and Sparling, 1973, p. 339).

During the initial stages of scribbling teachers should help children become aware of their movements. While observing children scribble, teachers might say, "Look at how fast your hands are moving. Can you move them faster?" "You are moving your arm up and down the page. Can you move it across the page?" When children are able to control their scribbles teachers can ask questions and make comments that call attention to their marks, such as "You put a long mark here and a small circle here." "This line moves across the paper." "This circle is almost as big as the paper." Teachers should tell children they appreciate their creative efforts: "You worked hard on this picture. You must enjoy painting. Look at that big, bright green circle. I like your bright colors," (Sparling and Sparling, 1973, pp. 336–339).

Scribbles used during the naming-of-scribbling stage do not look any different from earlier scribbles. Therefore teachers must be very careful not to ask the child what he or she has drawn. Instead Lowenfeld and Brittain (1970) say teachers should help children use their imaginative thinking. If a child says, "This is my mother," the teacher can ask "Does your mother work? What does she do?" "Is she tall? What color are her eyes? Hair?" or "I like your bright colorful picture. Would you like to tell me about it?" If children disregard the teacher's comments he or she must accept their indifference (pp. 107–108).

Children can work on large manila and easel paper (18 by 18 or 18 by 24 inches). Crayons should be dark and large, *with the wrappings removed* because children use all parts of crayons to draw. Felt pens and chalk on a blackboard are also good tools. Paint brushes should be 3/4 inch wide with long or medium handles; paint should be opaque and of a thick consistency.

Earth clay and selected collage materials are good media for this stage. Working with clay offers opportunities for both kinesthetic and imaginative thinking. Children react to clay in a similar manner as they do to crayons and paint. They manipulate the clay until shapes are found, and later name the shapes. Finger paint should not be used if children simply "play in it" and make no attempt to make marks (Sparling and Sparling, 1973, pp. 108–113).

preschematic stage: four to seven

According to Kellogg and O'Dell (1967) children begin to draw humans around the age of four or soon after they make mandalas and suns. The first people look inhuman. Children may simply lengthen some sunrays, remove others, and put marks on the top of the head. The addition to the head is not for hair but for balance. Children always strive for "balance, design, and variety within a set of self-taught, esthetic formulas" (p. 67).

Children's drawings of people are followed by pictures of animals, plants, houses, and boats. These figures, as does the human form, grow out of children's scribbles. All the world's children make their drawings—humans, trees, boats, houses—the same regardless of their environment (Kellogg, 1970, p. 23).

Lowenfeld and Brittain (1970) state that the preschematic stage grows "directly out of the last stage of scribbling" (p. 117). Humans are the first representations children make, probably because they are at the center of their world. It is clear that children are not trying to copy a visual image in front of them. Showing four-and five-year-old children pictures of humans as they draw does not change their pictures (p. 120).

Children are not consistent in their drawings of humans or other representations. They seem to be continually seeking new concepts. They enjoy using color for its own sake and do not feel the need to use it realistically. Color may be selected for its emotional appeal, or it may be purely mechanical (p. 123). Children may choose the color closest to them, the thickest paint, or the orange paint that has not been used. Adults must be very careful in interpreting the use of color as a reflection of psychological state.

Children's conception of space is very different from that of adults. Objects may appear anywhere in drawings, and have little or no relationship among them. As far as children are concerned no relationship has to be established between objects. They think of space as revolving around themselves (p. 124).

Children try to exaggerate in size the objects that are important to them. This preoccupation with ideas or images significant to them is what Piaget calls "centration." Children neglect the relationships between the primary form and secondary forms (Eisner, 1976, p. 11).

During the period of intuitive thought—the end of Piaget's preoperational stage—topological relationships are more clearly understood and Euclidean relationships are beginning to emerge (see chapter 4). Human figures are drawn more realistically, and geometric shapes may be used in the representation of objects. These forms are made by interpreting the rhythmical movements used in making topological relationships. Therefore figures may have slightly curved sides and angles of imperfect inclination (Lansing, 1966, p. 37).

Materials recommended for the scribbling stage are appropriate for the preschematic stage. Any art medium given to children should be one that provides for continuous growth. Preschool teachers sometimes introduce materials they feel are cute or novel. Activities such as finger painting with chocolate pudding, gluing sugar cereal loops, and making peanut butter clay are open to question. Are they truly art materials? Can children use them in their art expression throughout life? Are we teaching children to waste food?

Children at this stage should not be limited to large crayons or paper. Some children work large; some work small. They should be allowed to choose brushes, crayons, paper, chalk, and pencils from among a variety of sizes. Additional material to be added to the art center are collage materials of all types, earth clay, plasticine, play dough, glue, gadgets for printing, and boxes and wood for building three-dimensional shapes as in block building (Herberholz, 1974, pp. 44–164).

There is *no* place in children's artwork for stencils, tracing patterns, or coloring books. These activities stifle creativity and make children dependent on others for their ideas (Lowenfeld and Brittain, 1970, p. 141).

schematic stage: seven to nine

Kindergarten teachers and a few nursery school teachers will discover children who are in the schematic stage. Children's pictures begin to tell stories. They may put a house, children, a dog, trees, and flowers into the same picture. Before, individual objects had been placed at random, but now they are put in relation to each other. Children can use almost any art medium, and their increased dexterity enables them to control crayons and brushes more effectively. Their artwork is beginning to resemble more closely that of the adult (Kellogg and O'Dell, 1967, pp. 85–87). Forms are more realistic, and parts of a figure may be distinguished when removed from context; for example, an arm is recognized as an arm even when the rest of the drawing of a human is covered.

Piaget says that during the substage of the concrete operational stage children acquire reversibility of thought. Thus they are able to imagine the relationship between concrete objects and organize them meaningfully in their drawings (Lansing, 1966, p. 37). Lowenfeld and Brittain (1970) have called this the "schematic stage" when children begin to draw objects in a natural relationship because they draw what they conceive rather than only what they perceive (p. 37).

Topological relationships are well-developed, and objects are placed on a baseline in proximity to other objects and yet separate from them. The order of objects is correct and continuous. A skyline appears at the top of a picture. Some Euclidean shapes appear, but there are many Euclidean and projective relationships that do not appear before age eight or nine (p. 38).

Lowenfeld and Brittain (1970) recognize the emergence of schema during the schematic stage. Schema are concepts of real objects which children have developed and use over and over in their drawings. They are highly individualized and depend on personality differences and the degree to which teachers have activated passive knowledge. Lowenfeld sees schema as developing from active knowledge children have about objects; passive knowledge is knowledge they have but do not use in their drawings. Schema are not stereotyped but are flexible and undergo deviations and changes (pp. 145–147).

Teachers must help children activate their passive knowledge through interesting and challenging experiences. First-hand experiences, exposure to works of art, resource persons, films, stories, pictures, and class discussions help develop and expand concepts. Children who are interested in their world and are emotionally involved in an experience express themselves more creatively in their artwork.

During the schematic stage any art materials should facilitate self-expression. There are several musts for teachers which help assure greater creative development: (1) Allow children to finish their work uninterrupted. (2) Present only a few materials at one time. (3) Introduce materials when children are ready to use them. (4) Always have materials ready. (5) Show appreciation for children's art but never compare artwork. (Lowenfeld and Brittain, 1970, pp. 175–188).

characteristics of young children related to music and art

Listed in table 6–1 are characteristics of young children related to art and music. They represent general characteristics of children and *do not* represent the characteristics of any one child. Each child has an individual built-in rate of growth.

table 6–1
representative characteristics of young children related to art and music

From About 3 Years	to About 6 Years of Age
1. Sings up and down the scale but matches only a few tones correctly	1. Sings in the lower range—C to A above middle C
2. Experiments with rhythm—beats, taps, shakes, hits	2. Creates own rhythm—even and uneven patterns
3. Sings alone or with adult	3. Sings with an adult or group
4. Sings spontaneously—half-chant, half-song	4. Continues to enjoy singing—chants, rhymes, jingles
5. Enjoys scribbling	5. Draws objects such as humans, animals, and plants
6. Strives for balance while scribbling	6. Places objects on paper with little relationship to each other but strives for balance (preschematic stage). May be in schematic stage.
7. Thinks in terms of physical actions—kinesthetic thinking	7. Thinks in terms of images and symbols—imaginative thinking
8. Begins to understand topological relationships	8. Understands most topological relationships; begins to view figures as rigid in shape
9. Copies a circle	9. Copies a square
10. Names primary colors	10. Names primary and secondary colors
11. Practices to control scissors and direction for cutting.	11. Controls scissors and direction for cutting
12. Mixes colors indiscriminantly	12. Mixes primary colors to make secondary colors
13. Grasps crayon in fist	13. Holds crayon between thumb and forefinger
14. Primarily explores art media	14. Uses own ideas to plan final product
15. Self-centered—sees things from own point of view	15. Begins to consider viewpoints of others

goals for development through music and art

The following goals for development through music and art have been chosen as realistic ones for the teacher to select since they can be achieved by the majority of children from age three to six. Objectives are written in the cognitive, affective, social, and psychomotor domains. It is important to remember that not all the objectives will be reached by the time a child is five or six. The objectives are listed as a guide for the teacher in planning and as one source for evaluating understandings in music and art.

COGNITIVE DOMAIN. A child:

1. Sings tunefully in lower range—C to A above middle C
2. Recognizes some songs sung or played by others
3. Describes sounds as loud and soft, high and low, fast and slow, and short or long
4. Moves rhythmically in own way and responds when his or her movements are accompanied with an instrument

5. Describes musical selections as fast-slow, high-low, loud-soft
6. Adjusts body movements to accompany even and uneven beats
7. Adjusts body movements to accompaniment that involves contrasts—slow-fast, light-heavy
8. Recognizes sounds of various instruments—drum, bells, triangle
9. Listens to music and identifies a few instruments that make the appropriate sound
10. Responds accurately to tempo of a recording or another instrument
11. Suggests new words and/or uses for songs
12. Creates an original melody or tune
13. Identifies primary and secondary colors
14. Makes secondary colors from primary colors
15. Makes shades and tints with black and white paint
16. Focuses on various elements in art media and imposes form on things
17. Uses a baseline and skyline in drawings—schematic stage
18. Names own paintings or forms

SOCIAL DOMAIN.   A child:

1. Shows by actions and words that he or she is open to new ideas
2. Sings in a group and alone
3. Plays a musical selection and/or instrument alone and with other children
4. Works with art media alone and with other children

AFFECTIVE DOMAIN.   A child:

1. Discusses colors, shapes, textures, and/or sizes with peers and teacher
2. Describes an object, person, or experience as beautiful, pleasant, pretty, fun
3. Shows by facial expressions, gestures, and other physical movements that he or she enjoys a person, an object, and/or experience
4. Chooses to work with a variety of art media
5. Manipulates and experiments with rhythm instruments
6. Selects and requests favorite songs

PSYCHOMOTOR DOMAIN.   A child:

1. Holds a crayon between thumb and forefinger
2. Established preference for right or left hand
3. Cuts on a straight line
4. Places paste along the back edges of a picture

music learning centers

indoor learning center

The music center is an area where children can experiment with instruments and move rhythmically to music. This area should have enough room for these activities to take place. A music center contains a record player, rack for records, records, piano whenever possible, and stand for displaying instruments.

LOCATION.   This is an active center and should be placed near noisier centers. If there is a piano it should be part of the music center.

EQUIPMENT AND SUPPLIES.   Equipment may include:

Rhythm band set—rhythm sticks, bells, cymbals, jingle clogs, tambourine, triangle, sand blocks, snare drums, tone blocks
Xylophone
Resonator bells
Tom-tom
Record player
Rhythm instrument cart for displaying instruments
Record rack

   Supplies may include:

Record series—such as that of Silver Burdett
A wide selection of records for use with rhythms, listening, songs, stories
Songbooks

outdoor learning center

The record player can be taken outside for listening, singing, or rhythms. This is not a permanent center, but one that is set up with the help of an extension cord whenever appropriate.

teacher's role in music

SINGING ACTIVITIES.   Although teachers plan for singing as part of daily activities, spontaneous singing can occur at any time. While cutting jack-o'-lanterns a child began to sing a Halloween song, and everyone joined in. Teachers, too, can sing spontaneously. Sometimes teachers begin to sing when an activity reminds them of one of the class's songs, and children join in. When children are going outside to play a teacher can sing, "Will You Come Walk with Me?" or another appropriate song.

   Often children sing a half-chant, half-song, like the song Mark sang about washing paintbrushes. One day he was overheard half-singing, half-chanting, "I have to wash brushes. Hard! Hard! Hard! I have to wash brushes. Boo hoo hoo." The teacher joined in his song, which surprised him. He laughed, and after this experience washing brushes didn't seem to be a chore anymore. He continued to sing while he worked and made up other verses, "The paint is red, red, red. I'll wash it out soon, soon, soon."

   Teachers should encourage chanting and show their approval by singing the children's chants or creating their own. At clean-up time a teacher can sing,

We sing songs while our teacher plays the guitar.

"It's time to put toys away, now, now, now. Let's work together now, now, now." One teacher sings a welcoming song to children who come back to school after an absence. In this classroom children smile as they enter, waiting to hear the song that is "just for them." Johnny had the chicken pox, and his song was, "Johnny had the chicken pox, oh, oh, oh. Bumps have gone away, ha, ha, ha. We're happy you're in school, glad, glad, glad." When the teacher was absent and returned to school, several children took turns singing their original welcome songs for her.

Teachers can help children find their singing voices. First songs introduced should be within the range of C to A above middle C—the range children four to eight find most comfortable. Folk songs often are written in a lower range, and Smith and Leonhard's *Discovering Music Together* (1968) has songs appropriate for each of the four singing stages. When teachers find songs they like that are written in an upper range they can teach these songs in a lower key.

Since very few individuals have perfect pitch, it is best to teach songs with the help of an instrument, preferably a piano or an autoharp. When a piano is used teachers must be able to play well so that they can face children while singing; otherwise they will lose the children's attention.

There are teachers who have difficulty carrying a tune. When there is no one to play the piano, the teacher can use records to teach songs. The Silver Burdett series, Hap Palmer, Ella Jenkins, and Robert Smith have recorded songs in the lower range which are appropriate for young children. When the un-musical teach music it takes more effort and a constant search for better ways to teach. A music teacher once said to another teacher, "You can't carry a tune without an instrument but you get children to sing. That's more important." The teacher considered this a compliment but also remembered the many work-shops and talks on teaching music she had attended.

There are many ways to teach songs. Each song lends itself to a teaching technique that is more appropriate than others. Short, repetitious songs may be introduced spontaneously. The teacher sings a song and asks children to join in. This technique also applies to songs most children already know, such as "Mary Had a Little Lamb," "Jingle Bells," and "Skip to My Lou." An appropriate song for the beginning of the year in the lower range is "Hello Ev'rybody" (Hilyard and Jaye, 1971, p. 4). This song may be sung spontaneously as children enter a group.

Teachers should listen carefully to children's singing voices and try to pick out those children who are still directional singers. It is difficult to know each child's song range when children sing in a group. Teachers can play echo games to help them hear individual voices: Sing, "Good morning, Jane. How are you?" and Jane sings back, "I'm fine." Some children are reluctant to play echo games until the teacher finds something that interests them. Because children are self-centered they are more likely to respond to questions about themselves. Sing, "What do you like to play with?" and "How old are you?" Children can respond, "I like to play with ____ and I'm ____ years old."

Some children like to sing alone whereas others will volunteer to sing in small groups. When a song is learned ask, "Who would like to sing the song for us?" After everyone who wants to sing alone has had a turn, the teacher can ask, "Who would like to sing the song with someone else?" This procedure is not embarrassing to children and is not the same as singing alone.

Songs relating to special topics may be introduced by discussing the topic or theme with the children. Teachers can ask questions such as "How did you get to school today? Walk? Car? Bus? This is a song about riding to school on a bus. The bus in the song is orange, and the little girl who rides the bus is Mary Jane. Listen to the song on the record to hear what happens to the wheels on the bus." The children know what the song is about and have a reason to listen to "Riding the Bus with Mary Jane" (Smith and Leonhard, 1968, p. 8). Two verses of the song are heard and then the refrain, "Who'll ride with me?" The record can be played again and children asked to sing the refrain. The teacher can tell children to watch and that when he or she raises a hand it will be time to sing with the record. This technique is helpful in teaching new songs.

Songs whose themes are somewhat unfamiliar to children may be intro-duced with poetry or stories. The story Blueberries for Sal (McCloskey, 1948) may be used to introduce the song "The Bear Went over the Mountain" (Smith and Leonhard, 1968, p. 144). Questions about the story are related to the song: "Where do bears live? Do they like trees? Where do we find trees? Do bears live on mountains?" and "Listen to the song; the words will tell us what the bear saw when he went over the mountain." This song is short and can be sung with the record after it is heard once. Children should be thoroughly familiar with stories before they are used to introduce songs.

Short poems can be used to stimulate interest in a song that is sung immediately after the poem is read. The poem "Jump or Jiggle" (Beyer, 1961) may be read before teaching the song "Old Molly Hare" (Winn, 1966, p. 44). Questions may be asked such as "How did the snake move? The frog? The rabbit? Do rabbits hop? Do they run? Where do rabbits live? What is a hare?" "Listen to a song about a hare; where is the hare running?" Children love this song and will want to learn the other verses.

There are songbooks that have excellent pictures. They should be placed in either the music or the library center so that children can see the pictures and the musical notations. Sometimes children ask for particular songs because they like the pictures. A picture can be shown to the children and the question asked, "What do you think this song is about?"

Commercial pictures may be used to teach songs. The Silver Burdett series has large pictures that describe various songs in the series. Magazine pictures can be used effectively; for example, a picture of a large jack-o'-lantern can be used to introduce a song about Halloween.

Concrete objects are excellent to use in introducing songs. In the fall real colored leaves are more realistic than a picture of a fall tree. The song "Here Sits the Monkey" (Aubin et al., 1976, p. 2) was made more meaningful when a child brought a stuffed monkey to school. The monkey was placed in a chair and the song sung about it. Children took turns holding the monkey and then exchanging places with it as the song was sung.

When the words of a song are more complicated and there is more than one verse, flannel board figures help children remember what comes next. There is a calypso song called "Birthday Song" (Aubin et al., 1976, p. 20). Children love the tempo and melody, but there are many words to remember. Teachers can begin by asking children to think of all the things they can about birthdays. Then the teacher can play the record and place felt objects on a flannel board as each is mentioned in the song. Children can use these visual clues to help them learn the song.

There are songs that suggest rhythm instruments. "Jingle Bells" suggests bells and "Riding the Bus with Mary Jane" a variety of instruments. Children often choose instruments to accompany songs as they listen to recordings. When children sing in a group they should be encouraged to try different instruments and decide which ones are most appropriate for a particular song.

Songs should be taught first without motions. Children may become too involved with actions to concentrate on singing. This is not to say that action songs should not be taught, but that they should be sung tunefully before actions are introduced.

The words of a song are secondary to the melody and range of notes. Children can be told that some songs have silly words. "This Old Man," "I Went to the Animal Fair," and "Old Molly Hare" are called "nonsense songs." There are words in songs that children may ask about: children have asked, "What are beasts?" ("I Went to the Animal Fair"), "What does 'Hallelujah' mean?" ("Michael Row Your Boat Ashore") (Smith and Leonhard, 1968, p. 79), "What is a dandy?" ("Yankee Doodle Dandy"). After singing "White Christmas" a little girl whispered, "I always thought the song said, 'I'm dreaming of a wife for Christmas.'" Children often confuse words with others that have as much or more meaning for them.

Children should occasionally select songs they would like to sing. Most songs chosen will be those learned in class; others will be songs learned outside of school. Occasionally these songs are inappropriate or even risque. They are very funny to children and bring forth gales of laughter. It is best to ignore the words and say, "There's another way to sing that song that won't hurt anyone's feelings. We'll sing it that way." In a few cases teachers will have to tell the children they cannot sing a particular song at school. These are sometimes songs learned from older brothers and sisters.

In teaching songs to young children the following suggestions are helpful:

1. Check the range of notes first. Use C to A above middle C for songs at the beginning of the year.
2. Decide whether or not the song will appeal to children.
3. Choose the most appropriate way to introduce the song.
4. Sing the song initially with a piano or record.
5. Sing the song in same tempo song is written.
6. Allow children to sing repetitive phrases first.
7. Sing songs again, allowing children to sing any words they have learned.
8. Learn words before actions are included.
9. Sing songs several times if children are interested. Do not insist children learn words the first time a song is sung.

RHYTHMIC ACTIVITIES.   Children explore rhythm in their play as they hammer at the workbench, pound clay into a flat pancake, wash their hands, and run across the playground. Even their half-songs, half-chants have rhythm, for rhythm is the repetition of sound. It is the goal of preschool teachers to help children accompany rhythm with music and music with rhythm.

Children should be free to explore instruments in the music center. Here they learn about sounds and the instruments that produce them. A Head Start teacher chose as a project the setting up and evaluation of a music center. When the supervisor visited the classroom he suggested rhythm instruments for the center. Her reply was, "I'll have to borrow them from Ms. J. We have only one set and we share them." There were five classrooms and one set of rhythm instruments. Money had been spent on equipment for other centers, but rhythm instruments were not considered important for the music center.

Reasons teachers give for the omission of rhythm instruments is that they are too noisy and children don't know how to use them. Playing instruments with children is a good way to begin. Children model teacher behavior, listen to comments, and answer questions. "How does the drum sound when you hit with your hand? With a stick? Does it sound different when you hold it this way? Can you make a loud sound? A soft sound? Let's listen to Kay play her instrument. How does it sound?" As children experiment with individual instruments they can record various sounds on tape. When the tape is played children hear the sounds repeated and become more aware of tone and timbre. One teacher records the sound of each instrument on a large language master card and pastes a picture of the instrument on the card. Children soon learn the names of the instruments and the individual sounds they make. A game can be played by hiding an instrument behind a screen and making a sound. The child who guesses the correct instrument is the next one to make a sound for the other children to guess.

Children sometimes create their own rhythms with instruments. When teachers hear these rhythmic patterns they can choose appropriate instruments to accompany the rhythms. This action reinforces the patterns children have created and encourages them to create more rhythms.

When children are familiar with instruments and can create their own rhythms, it is time to introduce musical recordings. The music should have a definite repetitive rhythm children can hear distinctly. Marches are good selections since they have a steady beat. While some children play instruments with music, other children can move their bodies. It is rewarding to observe a small group of children playing instruments while other children are moving rhythmically to the music. It is almost as if musicians are playing for dancers, since children attach mood to their rhythmic expression.

A large repertoire of body movements enables children to respond more easily to rhythm. Chapter 1 describes activities that help children learn to use their bodies in space. When children have learned to use their bodies effectively, teachers can introduce rhythm in body movements. Begin with a steady, even drumbeat. Children listen and then pretend to beat a drum by clapping their hands. Very soon they respond with different parts of their bodies. The group may be divided in half, one-half beating the drums (hands) and the other moving with the even beats. Later children choose rhythm instruments to play with the drumbeats. As they move with the beats, the tempo changes. Uneven beats are not introduced until children can keep time with the even beats. When

Keeping time with the music.

children can move to uneven beats, contrast between even and uneven may be introduced. Children love to try to change body movements as the musical beats change.

When children have learned to respond to even and uneven beats musical selections on a piano (preferably) or records may be used. They should be distinct melodies with definite rhythmic patterns. Contrast—even-uneven, fast-slow, high-low, loud-soft, short-long—should be introduced. Children should be given something to listen for: "Is this music soft or loud? Fast or slow?" "Raise your hands when you hear the music change." "Now move your hands with the music, your head, your arms, all of your body."

When children talk about the changes in music, their imaginations take over: "I'm a butterfly! A clown! A ballerina!" Teachers can begin discussing how music makes us feel: "Is it happy music? Sad? Sleepy?" "Move the way the music sounds to you." "This music makes me feel like moving. Let's move with it." Children are now responding to music imaginatively and creatively.

LISTENING ACTIVITIES.   All music invites listening. Children cannot learn the melody or words of a song or respond to it rhythmically without listening. In our society, in which children are exposed to a great deal of auditory stimuli, screening out sounds and focusing on a few is a skill that should be taught. Teachers must have children's attention before they ask them to listen to music. Teachers use many techniques to get children's attention—finger plays, poems, games. Most of these techniques are effective. One teacher simply waited until children were ready to listen, and then she began to talk. Her presence was all that was needed. Teachers have to find the techniques that work best for them. Sometimes the problem is that the group is too large or the activity inappropriate.

When a teacher has the children's attention he or she must give them something to listen for in the musical selection. Whatever they listen for must be obvious, not subtle. As children grow in musical awareness they may be expected to listen for more sophisticated forms of music.

CREATIVE MUSIC.   Musical activity should be permeated with children's creativity. Even singing can be a truly creative experience. Children love to make up verses to songs and suggest instruments to accompany them. The song "Will you Come Walk with Me?" suggests to children other ways of moving—running, clapping, hopping, sliding. One five-year-old boy added a completely new verse to the well-known song "Six Little Ducks." The words were, "Ten little puppies that I once knew. Happy ones, sad ones, sleepy ones too. The sixth little puppy with the button nose. He led the others to the railroad track." The children loved singing this verse, which they thought was funnier than the original one. Children's original verses should be written down and mimeographed to take home. Parents and friends enjoy the songs as much as the children do.

Children suggest instruments that they want to play with songs. Sometimes the words of a song suggest the instrument; at other times it is the melody. The heavy accents and low tones of "Jumbo Elephant" suggest drums or rhythm sticks whereas the light accents and higher, softer tones of "Hey Betty Martin" (Smith and Leonhard, 1968, p. 73) suggest tambourines or bells. Sometimes children select instruments that seem inappropriate for the song or musical selection.

We can go to the moon.

This may be because they associate the selection with certain instruments or because they want to use a particular instrument. Mary chose drums to accompany "Jingle Bells." The other children protested, "Drums are low. Drums don't sound like bells." She defiantly said, "But I want to play the drum." The teacher asked, "How can you play the drum to sound like bells?" Mary replied, "lightly."

Children often make up songs, sometimes only the melody and other times both melody and words. Teachers who write musical notation can write down the songs. Often a whole class learns a child's original song. When the melody has no words children can make up words. Mimeographed books of children's original songs can be made and taken home. When teachers cannot write down the melodies, they can record the words and encourage children to sing the melody until they remember it: "That's a pretty song. I like it. I'll write the words for you." "I like your song. Can you make words for it?" Some children will not want to put words to their melodies. They prefer to hum the tune or listen to the melody on the piano. As far as they are concerned, words spoil their music.

Children make up rhythms, often creating dances. Whenever possible teachers should accompany these dances with the piano or another instrument. Teachers can encourage creative dance by providing accessories, such as scarfs, colored pieces of light material, long streamers, veils.

Children's responses to musical selections should be creative, that is, they should be tinged with the children's own personalities. Rather than tell children the name of a piece of music, ask them what they think the music is about. A teacher played a musical selection. After they had talked about what the music made them think of, he asked the children what they thought the person who wrote the music was thinking of. Some answers were "spring" (it was springtime), "Easter," "rabbits," "lakes," "woods," "geese on a lake," "ice skaters," and "trapeze artists." Most of their answers referred to quiet, light, smooth images. One child asked the name of the song, and when the teacher said, "Springtime," she said, "So that's why you played that song. It is spring."

At one school the kindergarten children took part in May Day. This was always an unpleasant experience for the teacher since she did not approve of young children acting in formal productions. She avoided some of the stress and strain associated with such performances by allowing the children to decide what they wanted to do for May Day. There was one May Day the children and teacher really enjoyed. The teacher played a musical selection that had several distinctly different parts: heavy accents and slow tempo; light, staccato accents and fast tempo; and soft, light accents and slow tempo. The children listened to the selection and talked about the changes in the music. They quickly identified three distinct parts. One child said, "The first part makes me think about children begging their mothers to go somewhere." The teacher asked, "Where do you think the children want to go?" Another child said, "For a walk in the woods." The teacher asked, "If the children ask to go for a walk in the woods, what do you think their mothers will tell them?" The unanimous answer was yes. The children continued the story as they listened to other parts of the music. Almost every child made a contribution to the story, which was:

Some children begged their mother to go for a walk in the woods. Their mother said yes. The children were happy. They ran into the woods. They saw trees and heard birds singing. Then something terrible happened. They saw a snake and ran. They got away from the snake but they were lost. Friendly animals found them and led them out of the woods into a field of daisies. The children and animals joined hands and danced and danced. They were happy. The children thanked the animals and said goodbye. They went home to their mothers and daddies.

The story was written in a large tablet which the children illustrated. One child asked, "Could we do our story for May Day?" The teacher asked the other children for their opinions. She heard, "Yes, and I want to be _____." She told them that there could be as many children, mothers, and animals as they needed. They could choose whatever they wanted to be. There were five children and three mothers; all the other children chose to be animals. There was even a chipmunk. The children's story, which they entitled "A Walk in the Woods," was printed on the May Day program.

Children should be encouraged to dramatize their ideas as they listen to music. Usually but not always children will think of those things that have meaning for them at a particular time—the circus, holidays, birthdays, and seasons. At Easter a teacher played a musical selection with two distinct parts—loud and fast and soft and slow. The children's teacher discussed the two parts, and the children moved their bodies with the music as they sat around the record player. Then they all moved around the room with the music. As they moved the teacher noticed several children pretending to hide Easter eggs. She said, "I'll go to sleep while you hide the eggs." When the music changed from soft to loud she woke up and began to hunt for the eggs, moving back and forth and pretending to look behind bushes and in the grass. Several children joined her in the pretense of hunting eggs. Soon everyone was either a rabbit or a child. When the music became quiet again the rabbits hid the eggs and the children went to sleep. As the music changed from soft to loud the children woke up and hunted for eggs while the rabbits hopped to and fro watching them.

scheduling and grouping

As in other content areas, children will group themselves naturally as they play in the music center. There should be times set aside throughout the week for singing and rhythms. It is best to plan for small groups when children participate in rhythmic activities. Children will listen more closely and discuss rhythmic selections openly in small groups. Rhythmic activities can occur during learning-center time in the music center.

Singing activities can occur at any time and anywhere throughout the day. Teachers may want to set aside time to teach songs to the whole group or, when songs are longer and more complicated, to smaller groups.

first day of school

The music center should contain a record player and a few (four to six) well-chosen records of familiar songs (folk songs), marches, simple rhythmic selections, and songs about children (Hap Palmer and Ella Jenkins have good selections). A few instruments—drums, bells, and rhythm sticks or several of one kind of instrument such as bells or drums—should be displayed. Instruments should be within easy reach on a display rack. One or two songbooks to explore should be in the music or library center. These should be books from which teachers and children can select songs written in a lower range (C to A above middle C).

music through the year

Teachers must be aware of changes in children's voices. This may be a difficult task, and they will sometimes need the help of someone more knowledgeable about music. In many schools there is a music teacher who comes once a week to each classroom including the kindergarten. When this person knows child growth and development as well as music, the teacher and the music supervisor can work as a team. When the music teacher cannot relate to children a problem arises for the kindergarten teacher and the children. A mistake teachers make is never to attend a music period with the children and the music teacher. Music teachers may not invite kindergarten teachers every week, but they should invite them several times a month. If not, kindergarten teachers can ask to come with the children. Otherwise they do not know what songs children are learning and how they can implement what they learn in the classroom. It is indeed unfortunate when teachers allow music to be set aside as a separate entity rather than a vital part of the total curriculum.

Musical selections are crucial to the development of listening and rhythm. The Silver Burdett series has many good selections with suggestions for teachers. Smith's *Music in the Child's Education* (1970, pp. 90–92) lists records for rhythmic development.

art learning centers

indoor learning centers

The art center should be placed in a tiled area. If the entire room is carpeted it may be necessary to put a waterproof covering under the easel(s). A table (rectangular) and four to six chairs, an easel, a few containers for storing art supplies, and a bulletin board or display case are necessities. Materials should always be within easy reach in clear containers. Children's artwork should be hung at their eye level.

LOCATION.   The art center should be placed as close to running water as possible. Ideally it is desirable for the science and art centers to be together since equipment and materials are interrelated and both centers require running water.

EQUIPMENT AND SUPPLIES.   Equipment:

Double adjustable easel—one or two
Easel brushes—assorted sizes—bristle and hair brushes
Easel clips
Plastic smocks
Paste brushes
Scissors—sharp and blunt points, left and right handed
Scissors rack
Stapler
Paper punch
Paint drying rack

   Supplies:

Finger paints—red, yellow, blue, black, and white
Finger paint paper
Tempera paints—red, yellow, blue, black, and white
Easel paper (newsprint)—12 by 18 inches
Felt-tip markers—washable
Poster-art chalk—assorted colors and sizes
Wax crayons—two sizes
Hard-pressed crayons—two sizes
Construction paper—assorted colors, 9- by 12-inch and 12- by 18-inch sizes
Manila drawing paper—9 by 12 inches and 12 by 18 inches
Oak tag—tag board for construction and posters
Paper paste
Glue
Plasticine clay (oil-based)
Play dough—red, yellow, blue
Earth clay—neutral color
"Beautiful" junk

outdoor learning centers

WOODWORKING CENTER. The woodworking center should be outdoors unless the room or area has accoustical treatment. A workbench, some type of cabinet or stand for displaying tools, and a container for wood scraps are a part of this center.

The woodworking center should be placed in a shaded area unless the climate is cold during school months. It should be out of the way of traffic since this is an active area where children move to and fro in their play.

EQUIPMENT, SUPPLIES, AND ACCESSORIES. Equipment may include:

Workbench
Hammer, claw—seven ounces
Saw—crosscut
Saw—coping
Brace and bits
Clamps
Hand drill and bits

Supplies:

Coping-saw blades
Sandpaper—assorted
Wheels—assorted
Dowels—assorted
Assorted scraps of wood—hard and soft (pine)
Assorted nails—large and small heads, long and short

Accessories:

Glue
Yarn
Aluminum foil
Cloth
Carpet squares
Buttons
Small boxes

ART CENTER. In warmer climates an outdoor art center is desirable. It may contain only an easel and paints. It is often difficult to move indoor equipment outside, but with children's help it is possible. A few play areas may provide for storage of art equipment and supplies, but most do not. There are materials found on the playground which are ideal as outdoor media—rocks, bark, twigs, dried grass.

teacher's role in art

Perhaps the single most important factor influencing children's art development is the teacher's knowledge of child art. When teachers do not understand developmental art stages, children's work suffers, becoming either stereotyped or stagnant. There are teachers who ask for products that "look like something." Patterns, stencils, and tracing constitute the so-called art program. Children are afraid to express themselves for fear they will "do it wrong." A kindergarten was observed where children sat quietly until all the children arrived. The supervisor suggested that learning-center time come at the beginning of the day, but the teacher preferred to begin with a group activity. The supervisor suggested that the children be given something to do while they waited. The next day when she arrived the children were dutifully tracing and attempting to cut out leaves, squirrels, and acorns. She was horrified and puzzled because the teacher had taught for several years. In talking with the teacher it was learned that she was not aware of developmental art stages but was willing to learn. As her knowledge increased the children's artwork became freer and more flexible.

The laissez-faire teacher's influence on children's art is less inhibiting but perhaps just as damaging. Children left completely to their own devices seldom progress beyond the stage they were in when they entered the classroom. In one kindergarten a few art materials were put out each day, and children were allowed to choose from a wide assortment of disorganized and poorly displayed items. The art center was observed for several weeks; it was found that the same children used the materials each week. Seldom was any encouragement given or interest shown in their work. The teacher, who was generally disorganized, was proud of her "creative" art program.

There is another type of teacher, who professes an interest in and knowledge of creative art but in reality does not practice what he or she preaches. Children's creative art efforts are encouraged on the one hand and stifled on the other. In a kindergarten children were asked to color a stencil of a child and his clothing. They were told to cut out the figures and then dress the child for the appropriate weather. Some children could not color inside the lines; others had difficulty cutting around the stenciled figures. The teacher explained that the children were engaged in a science and art activity. The activity was neither art nor science. It was not even an experience in following directions.

There fortunately are teachers who understand the stages in art development and the techniques that facilitate growth in art. These teachers explore different art media themselves in order to know their full potential for children. Teachers who have never painted with tempera paints cannot compare the sensation of spreading thick paint on paper with that of working with runny, colorless paint.

SCRIBBLING STAGE.   During the scribbling stage children learn about art media through experimentation. Materials for exploration include crayons (paper wrappers removed), felt-tip pens, pencils, paint, brushes, manila and easel paper. Art media should be offered in at least two sizes—large and small. Children can choose the size crayons and paper they want. A four-year-old boy in the scribbling stage painted his hands and made three hand prints vertically on one side of the paper. He studied the results and then chose a large brush and carefully painted a border around his picture. Next he selected the smallest brush, dipped it in paint, and allowed the paint to drip down the paper from top to bottom opposite his hand prints. The effect was unusual. This was not a planned picture but one that developed as the child experimented with brushes and paint.

Jane and Helen were children who enjoyed experimenting with paints and colors. A table was covered with newspapers, and muffin tins filled with paint were placed in the middle. An assortment of brushes and jar lids were placed next to the paints. The girls occupied themselves with mixing red, blue, and yellow paints in the jar lids. They were fascinated by the resulting colors: "I made green," "Look at my brown!" and "I know what colors make purple!" were heard as they rushed back and forth to share their findings with the teacher and children. The teacher added white and black paint to the primary colors; this encouraged further experimentation. Several prospective teachers observed the girls and remarked that "all they do is play with the paints." The teacher knew they felt she should have stopped the children when some paint landed on the walls. Even when the children washed the paint off the walls, there was disapproval on the students' faces. The teacher asked them to visit again several weeks later.

When the students returned they were surprised to find Jane carefully mixing green paint. They timed her while she worked, and 11 minutes passed before she was satisfied with the shade. Jane covered a 15- by 15-inch sheet of manila paper with green paint. Then she went to another center to play, returning frequently to test the wetness of the paint. When it was almost dry Jane chose a large brush, dipped it in white paint, and made a four-inch border along the bottom of her picture. Later she touched the white paint to make sure it was dry. Then she chose a small brush and dipped it in black paint. Gently she shook black paint over the white border, making small blotches of black on white. Jane surveyed her work and, apparently satisfied, ran to the teacher shouting, "Ms. A., come see my beautiful picture." It was indeed beautiful. The doubting observers turned into true believers. They had seen the cycle of the creative process with their own eyes: first experimentation (mixing paints), then focusing (choosing the colors to use), next discipline (carefully carrying out the plans), and last closure (deciding when the product was finished). Jane moved rapidly into the preschematic stage and, after Christmas, into the schematic stage. She was a talented, creative child who had had little opportunity to explore art media before coming to kindergarten.

Children enjoy exploring the possibilities of clay. They learn a repertoire of movements as they punch, pull, pack, pound, and polish. Children use clay in the scribbling stage much as they do crayons and paints. Their products resemble scribbles, with long clay rolls (often called snakes), coils, crosses, balls, flat and smooth pieces, and mandalas. Jimmy, a four-year-old boy, did not enjoy painting, but he liked clay since he considered it less messy. Jimmy and the teacher talked about the ways he could twist the clay to make different forms. Through his interest in clay the teacher gradually persuaded him to try to make similar forms with paints. He covered a page with large, bright crosses and other forms. Once he discovered painting was satisfying he visited the easel regularly.

ABOVE. *Children like playdough.*
LEFT. *Making a design with sponges and paint.*

Making a necklace with clay and yarn.

Teachers can become very frustrated when children refuse to work with art media. There may be one or more explanations for their disinterest. Some children have been cautioned by adults, "Don't get dirty," a few have never worked with art media, and others are dissatisfied with their own art products. When the latter is the case teachers are faced with a more serious problem. It is not difficult to introduce children to paints or to assure them that a smock will help keep them clean. It is difficult to convince them that their art products are worthwhile. Children who cannot accept their own work are often in the scribbling stage.

A five-year-old retarded child had very poor coordination and could make only longitudinal and circular scribbles. She hesitated to paint with tempera paint but enjoyed finger paint. The teacher commented on the interesting lines she made. One day Cindy went to the easel and scribbled an irregularly shaped block form with red lines attached. She showed the picture to her teacher commenting, "That's a troubled cloud with rain." At last Cindy had named her scribbles. It was a surprise to eveyone when on Halloween Cindy triumphantly showed her drawing of a ghost. She had drawn a circle with several lines extending downward. It was her first attempt to make people (ghost).

There are children who behave in ways that teachers and psychologists cannot explain. Joe was one of these children. Whenever he wanted to work with art media he moved to a secluded table. He was in the scribbling stage and seemed to take pride in his work. He enjoyed showing his pictures to the other children and the teacher, but he did not want anyone to watch him as he worked. In every way Joe appeared to be a happy child. The school psychologist observed Joe several times and talked with his parents. He finally concluded that something had happened in the beginning stage of scribbling which made Joe self-conscious. As long as Joe was satisfied with his work the teacher was advised not to force him to or even suggest that he join the other children. Joe worked by himself all year and progressed to the preschematic stage. Something probably had happened to embarrass him early in his art development.

Parents do not always appreciate children's art, particularly during the scribbling stage. A four-year-old girl drew many pictures and gave them to her teacher. She said, "Take my pictures home and put them up in your house." During a parent conference the teacher casually mentioned to her mother that she enjoyed Martha's pictures. A very surprised mother said, "She doesn't bring them home. I thought she didn't like the art center anymore." The teacher told her that Martha's artwork was prolific and she gave her pictures away. Her mother said, "I guess that's because I told her we would look at her pictures and then throw them away. I have a new house and I don't want tape on my walls." The teacher suggested a bulletin board for Martha's room. The mother bought a bulletin board, and soon Martha began to take her pictures home. Creativity is one of the best topics for a parent meeting. Many parents do not know the value of or appreciate child art.

In contrast to Martha's mother was Ruth's mother, a creative person who enjoyed crafts. To her everything Ruth made was important. When the teacher visited in the home Ruth's artwork was everywhere—on the kitchen cupboard, on the refrigerator, hanging from the living room walls, on a bulletin board, and even covering a wastepaper basket. When new pictures appeared, older ones were placed in a file. Nothing was thrown away unless Ruth discarded it herself. At four years Ruth felt her efforts were rewarded. By the end of the kindergarten year she had advanced to the schematic stage.

PRESCHEMATIC STAGE.   The preschematic stage follows soon after the name-of-scribbling stage. Children now make people, plants, houses, and transportation figures. These forms are scattered at random with no logical relationship between them. Another interesting characteristic is that parts of figures are not recognizable if separated from the whole, whereas in the schematic stage they are more realistic. It is during this stage that teachers are most tempted to say, "I like the ___ you made" and "Tell me about your picture." Children are not always anxious to tell adults about their pictures. Sometimes they prefer to talk about their pictures with other children or not to talk about them at all. Children may paint without a purpose other than to explore color, line, and design.

Instead of asking children to tell about their pictures teachers can comment with remarks such as "I like the colors you used. How did you make the green?" "I like the way you mixed white and black to make gray." "You covered the whole page with lovely colors." "The shapes you used are interesting." "I see a triangle here and a circle there." "You used many circles in your picture." When children ask teachers to guess what they have made they usually expect teachers to guess correctly. It may be better not to guess but say, "I'm not sure. You tell me."

The knowledgeable teacher will give children a wide breadth of experiences to enrich their artwork. Nature, literature, and music can be used to express art. As the seasons changed a kindergarten group looked at a tree near the school. The teachers took pictures of the tree which the children discussed in small groups. They were encouraged to make a tree like the one they saw or any other kind of tree out of art media. They could use clay, paint, crayons, felt pens, or collage materials. If they did not want to make a tree they could make another picture or none at all. Children were encouraged to keep a few pictures at school to put in their scrapbooks. The books were taken home as the seasons changed and brought back to school to include additional pictures.

One of the children's favorite stories was "The Three Billy Goats Gruff." A group of five-year-olds listened as the teacher told the story. When he finished he asked, "What does a troll look like?" Each child had his or her own version of a troll. The teacher explained that they were all correct since a troll is make-believe and can look like anything you want it to look like. He suggested that the children use art media to make trolls. Some trolls were made of clay; others were drawn or painted. The three-dimensional trolls were placed on a table near the bulletin board. A child suggested that he make a clay bridge for the trolls. Eventually the children created a scene with many trolls, a bridge, three goats, and a river of blue paper. The painted and crayon figures made by the children were cut out and a similar scene made on the bulletin board.

Many stories and poems encourage creativity in art. The imaginary fish in *McElligot's Pool* (Geisel, 1947) and the wonderful animals in *My Marvelous Menagerie* (Maguire, 1968) stimulate children's imaginations. An attractive bulletin board was a teacher-child one with a boy sitting on a bank catching imaginary fish, made by children out of paper and collage materials. The caption read *McElligot's Pool.*

There are stories, such as *A Fly Went By* (McClintock, 1958) and *Ask Mister Bear* (Flack, 1932), that have surprise endings. Teachers can read everything but the ending to a small group of children. Children can whisper their own endings in the teacher's ear. Then they can draw or paint their ideas. The next day the children's original endings can be discussed in small groups. Teachers can read the rest of the book and ask questions such as "How did the story end? Were you surprised? Was it like your ending? Did you like your ending better?"

When children have listened to many musical selections and have moved their bodies rhythmically to music, they can be encouraged to finger paint to music. First the music is played and discussed with the children: "Is it fast or slow, light or heavy, loud or soft?" Then the teacher may say, "Instead of moving your whole body with the music, move your hands and arms as you finger paint." Some children make designs or scribbles; others make pictures. A group of five-year-olds listened to a selection that was slow, light, and dreamy. Some of the paintings were of seashells at the beach (schematic stage), a house with a smile (preschematic stage), ice skaters (scribbling stage), a trapeze artist at the circus (scribbling stage), and pretty lines (scribbling stage).

Teachers must be careful that children do not feel they will have to draw a picture after each field trip or other common experience. When children say half-heartedly, "We'll have to draw a picture when we get back," teachers should take stock of themselves. Sometimes just talking about a field trip is best.

Woodworking may be done indoors or outdoors, preferably outside unless the room is acoustically treated for sound. First children should explore the possibilities of wood: "Is some wood harder than other wood? How can we make two pieces of wood stay together? Do we need a short nail or a long nail?"

Teachers should show children how to use tools properly. Not only is this safer, but children can work more effectively when they know how to use the tools properly. Most children, particularly those in the scribbling and pre-schematic stages, first make a cross, airplane, or sword by nailing two pieces of wood together. As children progress in woodworking skills a favorite form with both boys and girls is boats.

Children in the preschematic stage make more realistic and complicated forms. A few children may continue to nail two pieces of wood together without any attempt to "make something." They enjoy the kinesthetic sensation of using hammers, saws, and nails, but are not ready to use wood imaginatively. No matter how crude children's products are, the children should be allowed to take them home. When they have learned to use tools and explored the nature of wood, teachers can add a few accessories. Appropriate materials are scraps of carpet, aluminum foil, scraps of cloth, yarn, string, bark, and small twigs. One child made a dollhouse by gluing four boxes together. She used wood to make the furniture. Pieces of carpet were glued to the tops of the tables, cloth to the beds, and aluminum foil to the inside of the bathtub.

Holiday art activities are a problem for some teachers. They can talk with children in small groups about what gifts might be made from materials available in the room—wood, paint, clay, paper, collage materials, chalk, felt pens. Each child can decide what to make and tell the teacher the needed materials, which the teacher can write beside the child's name in a notebook. It may take several days for some children to decide what they want to make. A gift can be as simple as a painting or drawing or as complex as a clay trumpet. One five-year-old boy decided he wanted to make a bookcase for his father. He said he wanted to make it out of wood but gave the teacher no further information. When Christmas vacation grew near, she reminded Tom he had only three days to make his gift. He said he was not ready. She was surprised when on the day before the holiday began Tom went to the workbench and chose a long piece of wood and two short pieces. In no time he had nailed the short ends to the long piece and made a small "bookcase." He sandpapered it, wrapped it, and put it under the tree. It was the only gift he made, but the teacher was pleased that he had been formulating his plans all along.

Christmas art can be something pretty for the tree. Put out a collection of materials to make decorations with the suggestion, "Make something pretty for our tree." Children can make anything they want from a collection of straws, paper doilies, ribbons, construction paper, cotton, colored rice or grits, pipe cleaners, pine cones. There are no patterns to trace or cut out. Each child, regardless of developmental stage, can make something attractive. Some decorations are elaborate; others are as simple as a cotton ball glued onto a small piece of red paper. The decorations may be taken home and shared with the family.

Children associate traditional colors with holidays; however, they should be encouraged to use any color that appeals to them. May's red and green valentine outlined in white and surrounded with gray was truly beautiful. The heart was not realistic; in fact, it looked more like a "whale's mouth" as one child expressed it. But it won first prize at the children's art exhibit because the combination of colors was so unusual. We stifle children's self-expression when we insist on realistic or traditional colors in their artwork.

SCHEMATIC STAGE.*   In this stage children's art is more realistic. Figures resemble actual objects and are often the same color as in nature. A baseline and skyline are present or implied. Children are developing their individual styles. Ruth, a five-year-old, made lovely, intricate drawings and clay figures. She worked with small paintbrushes, covering a small area of paper. James covered the entire page with brightly painted designs. Bonnie usually added white to her paint, which made light, pastel colors. Robert drew people—small, detailed figures of spacemen and rockets. Julie, a very talented child, worked with all art media creating pictures that were advanced for her age. One of her most outstanding paintings was a row of tall trees growing along a river, their bright fall colors reflected in the water.

Julie's creativity amazed her teacher. One day he observed Julie sawing wood at the workbench. She carefully collected the sawdust on a newspaper and placed it with the wood in her locker. The next day Julie made a border of glue around the piece of wood. She carefully sprinkled sawdust on the glue. The teacher was curious, but he had learned not to interfer with Julie when she was involved with a project. She always had a plan and usually carried it out without

*Many five-and six-year-olds are still in the preschematic stage.

adult help. Julie waited until the next day to continue her work. She drew a picture on the wood with felt pens. As usual, when she finished an art project she brought it to the teacher. This time he saw drawn on a piece of wood a beautiful Thanksgiving turkey surrounded with a border of sawdust colored with a green felt pen.

Shortly before Carol's fifth birthday she painted a Halloween picture. Although young, she had been in the schematic stage for several months. The teacher kept a running record of her movements as she used red, black, and yellow paint to make a baseline in the form of a hill. Then she painted three children going for "Trick or Treat." The children wore colored costumes and carried bags. The figures were large and completely covered the width of the page. Next Carol painted the empty spaces with black paint. The result was three children running up and down a hill carrying their "Trick or Treat" bags on Halloween night. It had taken Carol 28 minutes to complete her picture.

There are highly creative children who, even in the schematic stage, are made to feel uncomfortable about their art. When Jim came to kindergarten he was self-conscious and often apologetic about his artwork. The teacher commented on a picture he had painted of a large egg with a rabbit inside. She said, "I like your picture, especially the bunny's ears." Jim walked away and then came back to his picture. He whispered to the teacher, "I really know bunnies don't hatch from eggs." She answered, "Chickens hatch from eggs, but we think of eggs and rabbits at Easter. I like the bunny and egg together." He smiled and asked, "Is my picture alright, then?" Someone, adult or child, had found fault with his efforts toward self-expression.

When children are doubtful about their artwork they sometimes copy other children's work. This tendency seems to be prevalent in children who are moving into or are in the schematic stage. Perhaps this is because they are less self-centered and more conscious of what others think of them.

Ginny copied whatever other children did including their artwork. When children asked her to stop copying them she continued, unperturbed by their complaints. The teacher had seen her earlier drawings and knew that Ginny was in the schematic stage and could draw as well as the other children. She was puzzled by Ginny's tendency to copy. She knew Ginny's parents had come to the United States from an Asian country and, although they had lived in America for several years, continued many of their country's customs. The teacher went to dinner at Ginny's home. She enjoyed the foreign dishes and the folk music that was played during dinner. Ginny told her she had chosen the dessert, the only nonforeign dish they ate. Ginny's parents told her they had asked Ginny to take her nursery rhyme records to school but she had said, "No, the children won't understand them. The words are in another language." They were concerned because Ginny often said, "I'm not like the other children at school." It was decided that Ginny's parents would prepare more American foods and buy her popular records. They would not give up their customs, but they would try to do more things the way Ginny wanted. Gradually Ginny became more sure of herself as she established her identity. Her need to copy other children decreased and her art began to change. She created her own pictures and seldom compared her drawings with others'.

Children are very susceptible to what they see, particularly if the art product is made by an adult or older child. This is why it is destructive to make a product of any kind and show it to children as an example. On Halloween a teacher showed the children a paper bag mask made to look like a cat. She told them how she had constructed the mask and then said, "Make any kind of mask you want to make." As expected, most children made cats and all of them resembled the teacher's.

One year, at Christmas a kindergarten group and their teacher stopped to admire a third-grade bulletin board. Later several children painted Christmas pictures for the room. That afternoon, when the teacher took them off the drying rack she noticed that every picture contained a large amount of blue paint. She was surprised since normally the children were not influenced by each other's work. Then she remembered the third-grade bulletin board. She looked at it again and saw that each painting was predominantly blue. She was struck by the realization that young children are very easily influenced by the artwork of others.

During the schematic stage children may show a preference for one art medium over others. A teacher taught three talented children whose father was an artist. The oldest child enjoyed all art media; the second loved clay and showed little interest in any other medium; the youngest made intricate drawings with crayons and pencils. All three children could choose from a variety of art media at home, but they chose the same media at home that they did at school. Teachers should encourage children to sample a variety of media, but when they are especially gifted in an art form teachers should help the children develop their talents with that medium.

Art is an extension of the total personality, and children express themselves in their own individual ways. Research has shown that the art of children with severe emotional and mental problems has certain characteristics. Teachers must be very careful, however, not to read things into children's art. A teacher became concerned because a child chose to paint exclusively with black. She observed Dick closely but could find no evidence of emotional disturbance. She talked with his parents, who said he seemed satisfied at school and had not used black in his artwork at home. This puzzled the teacher, and finally she did what she should have done earlier. She asked Dick why he chose black instead of other colors. He replied, "I like black. I don't have any black crayons at home and they didn't have black in nursery school." Dick had never seen or used black paint before. His obsession with black was over within a short time.

Charles played mostly by himself. He seemed content to pursue his own interests. One day he showed the teacher a picture he had drawn of two houses. On the roof of each house he had drawn a boy. He pointed to one boy and said, "This little boy is sad because he has no one to play with. He wants to play with the other little boy." The teacher thought about Charles's picture and wondered if he were as satisfied playing alone as she had thought. During a parent conference she showed Charles's picture to his parents. They thought the picture was significant since Charles had said he didn't have any friends. The teacher made every effort at school to involve him with other children, and his parents invited children to play with Charles at home. In this case a child's artwork gave the teacher a clue to behavior.

scheduling and grouping

Art activities occur naturally during learning-activity time both indoors and outdoors. There is no special time or period set aside for art. Group art activities should not be used in the nursery school and should be kept to a minimum in the kindergarten. A topic should be broad so that all children have an opportunity to express themselves. Children should never be forced to stick to the topic but should be free to make something different.

first day of school

Art materials appropriate for the first day of school are crayons, felt-tip pens, and manila drawing paper. Unless there is adequate supervision painting at the easel can be postponed until the second week of school. If paints are used, two primary colors should be out with the third added later. Children learn to mix secondary colors themselves.

It is best to wait for several weeks to introduce the workbench. Saws, hammers, nails, and wood scraps should be available. Woodworking needs close supervision, especially at the beginning of the year. This center may be limited to four to six children.

art through the year

Teachers should keep a folder of children's artwork. It is sometimes difficult to gather artwork because children like to take their products home. They sometimes forget to take them home, however, and pictures can be rescued for their folders. A technique that often works is to ask children to make something for school and to take home. They are less reluctant to give up a picture when they know they have one to take home. Examine art folders regularly and observe children as they work to determine their developmental stages. When teachers know children's levels of development they can plan for their needs. Children in the scribbling stage need to use crayons, paper, and paint rather than finger paint and a variety of collage materials. Children in the schematic stage should be encouraged to use a wide variety of materials.

Certain art media may be available at all times. These include unwrapped crayons; earth clay; plasticine; "beautiful" junk; felt-tip pens; red, yellow, blue, white, and black paint; colored construction paper; and manila and easel paper. Children usually choose the materials most appropriate for their developmental stage. In addition, finger paint, gadgets for printing, colored chalk, and other media can be put out at the teacher's discretion.

Teachers must analyze art activities they plan carefully so that they can supervise them adequately. At Christmas a kindergarten was in utter chaos. Children were making tree decorations, preparing Christmas presents, painting pictures, finger painting, and decorating paper wreaths to take home. Any one of these activities would have been sufficient. One teacher consistently involved children in many art activities; very few were carried out well. Her comment was, "I know I do too much. I get started and I just can't stop." It seemed the art activity was planned for the teacher and not for the children.

Materials should be ready for children to use when they first come into the room. There is nothing more frustrating than to stand and wait until the materials are ready to use. There should be enough materials for every child to have a turn. When it is not possible for some children to have a turn, because of shortage of time, teachers can write their names down and make sure they are offered a turn the next day.

Artwork should be displayed at the child's eye level. Examples of all children's art should be included. There are teachers who choose "the best or most adult-like art" to put on the bulletin board. This practice is damaging to children and exposes teachers as ones who know little about child art.

The most effective bulletin boards are child-centered. These are the loveliest and most interesting. A lovely display was a bulletin board covered with soap paintings of various colors. Children had placed their own paintings on the bulletin board. A few paintings overlapped, and others stuck out over the borders; however, the effect was attractive.

Teacher-made bulletin boards have little place in the preschool curriculum. They exhibit adult art, which children cannot and should not model. Children seldom comment about teacher-made bulletin boards, and it is doubtful that they even notice them. In an unpublished study it was found that most children in a laboratory setting ignored two teacher-made bulletin boards. One displayed posters and pictures of a circus that was in a nearby town and the other, photographs from Disney World and a large poster of Mickey Mouse. Only 3 out of 10 children remembered these bulletin boards.

There is a place for child-teacher bulletin boards. At Christmas a teacher put a picture of Santa and his reindeer on a bulletin board. She suggested the children add anything they wanted. The children made stars and a large house with a chimney. They pushed a table against the bulletin board and covered it with cotton for snow. They drew and cut out people and houses and stood them up in the snow. Then they broke off small evergreen twigs and stuck them in tiny balls of plasticine clay. These "trees" were placed near the house. Now the children had a display that showed Santa and his reindeer riding over a village. The effect was very realistic.

meeting goals

The evaluation scheme in chapter 2 may be applied to art and music. A checklist based upon the behavioral objectives can be kept for each child. The methods described for collecting data are applicable to art and music.

Children's developmental stages in art and music should be determined soon after the beginning of school. A folder with samples of children's artwork should be kept throughout the year.

7
children are talkative

language arts

It has been said that children, like some adults, enjoy hearing themselves talk. They, talk mostly about themselves or about events directly related to them. A four-year-old was asked to tell about his picture. He took his photograph from the teacher and showed it to each child in turn. Again and again he said, "Look, this is me!" Children of six or seven may be content to "tell about their picture" but younger children need the reassurance that everyone knows, "That's me." As young children mature and become less egocentric they learn to use language not only to express their thoughts but also to exchange ideas. Communication in all its forms is referred to as the "language arts."

It is useful to discuss the language arts in categories—speaking, listening, writing, and reading—but they are not separated in the learner's mind. To a child "language and the world must be indivisible" (Smith, 1979, p. 125).

speaking

Observations of many children show that the acquisition of speech is a natural process. Even when children have limited resources to aid them they learn to speak the language they hear (Cohen and Rudolph, 1977, p. 65). As soon as they learn to verbalize the speech sounds of their language they learn how the various parts of speech are put together to express meaning, even though the rules are not taught and remain unstated. When children say, "I wented yesterday" or "I have two foots," they are implementing the rule that in English "ed" denotes past tense and "s," plural number (Editorial, *International Journal of Early Childhood Education*, 1974, p. 3).

Despite the opinion that children can be taught to correct their language usage by hearing and then imitating correct forms, research does not show this to

be true (Hess and Croft, 1975, p. 225). It is true, however, that children who hear little speech or only the speech of those who are limited in language are likely to have a language that differs from children surrounded by a sea of enriched language.

There is no evidence that lower socioeconomic and culturally different children lack the capacity to learn language (Robbins, 1970, p. 11). What they apparently lack is the kind of standard English needed for success in a school designed for middle-class children; the problem is one of different language usage. Some differences between standard English and black dialect may be found in *Teachers of Young Children* (Hess and Croft, 1975, p. 229).

It appears that children learn to communicate best when they see a reason or purpose for language. Since children must see a reason for language it is doubtful that pattern drill or rote drill helps them make sense out of their world. "Pattern practice or rote drills may be available and efficient but are they functional?" (Schery, 1978, p. 74).

Strickland (1973) found that preschool children become bored with uninteresting repetition and practice. She developed a program to encourage children who spoke a dialect to imitate standard English in a natural, childlike way. Teachers were taught to read stories that encouraged emotional identification, followed by creative dramatics, choral speaking, puppetry, and role playing. In their dramatic play children used the standard English heard in the stories. It appears that a natural, childlike approach to teaching standard English is appropriate for young children (pp. 79–88).

There are children who speak another language and know little or no English. Teachers who teach non-English-speaking children must be bilingual in order to help them learn the new language in its oral form. Mechanical

191

approaches that require memorizing have not been successful. Cohen and Rudolph (1977) state, "While children do need a carefully thought out series of steps into a new language, with much opportunity for repetition and drill, failure to relate this technical need to the children's level of development leads to failure in engaging the children's interest and imagination. The result can only be disappointment" (p. 86). They suggest teaching English as a second language in a meaningful context combining interests with concrete experiences (pp. 86–87).

Experiences with language at the preschool level are best when they occur in a natural context. Hess and Croft (1975) recommend the use of expanded discourse (p. 23). Instead of saying, "It's time to go outside," the teacher can say, "It's time to go outside now. There are two new things for you to do on the playground. You may play at the water table or paint at the easel."

Opportunities to develop language through play situations are numerous. Schickedanz (1978) cites research that indicates that in sociodramatic play situations children are more verbal than usual and use language to structure and sustain their play. She discusses ways teachers can help children gain first-hand experiences to aid them in their dramatic play (pp. 713–717). Cazden (1974) feels that children unconsciously reflect on language as they play with sounds during nonsense games and rhymes. Playing with language calls children's attention to its phonic and semantic elements (pp. 12–24).

listening

Children spend more time listening than reading, writing, or speaking. Therefore the ability to listen discriminately should be one of the most important skills fostered in schools. Although listening is receptive it is not passive. It demands the active involvement of the child.

In order to meet the listening needs of children teachers must decide in advance what it is they want children to listen for. In this way they create "a mind set for listening" (Tutolo, 1979, p. 36). Teachers also must create a "mind set" for listening *to* children. Because of their egocentrism children consider most important the conversations they instigate. When teachers listen attentively to children they contribute significantly to the children's attempts to express themselves. Teachers who do not listen may find that children stop communicating with them entirely. This means a breakdown of communication between teacher and child (Whisnant and Hassett, 1974, pp. 15–16).

What teachers say to children and how they say it is as important as how they listen. Sometimes teachers say something quite different from what they intend. Teachers who say, "Now we all need to rest and be quiet, don't we?" create confusion in children's minds. Some children may not want to rest; however, they are being told they *need* to rest, but only if they want to. If teachers want children to listen they must say what they mean to say (Hess and Croft, 1975, pp. 216–219; Cohen and Rudolph, 1977, pp. 89–95).

writing

Writing begins with children's first scribbles. Later they draw pictures and then copy letters and words. Children eventually learn to read the words they write; thus the surest way to reading may be through writing (Durkin, 1978, p. 185). Platt (1977) found that moving children from pictures to word symbols was an effective way to encourage them to copy words and in time to read them. In this study a recognizable image on children's drawings was singled out and labeled. The term "word pictures" was used by Platt, as the words were written directly on the pictures. These words were read to the children. Then the children copied the words and later wrote them spontaneously on their pictures (pp. 264–265).

Manuscript writing is recommended for young children because it is composed of circles and straight lines. Sometimes children write in manuscript using only capital letters. This is easier since all the letters are the same height. When children observe teachers writing in upper- and lower-case letters they gradually begin to use both. Reversals are common at this age. If there is no visual difficulty they will disappear with proper teacher guidance. Most children are right-handed. When children are ambidextrous teachers can encourage them to use their right hands (Leeper et al., 1979, p. 265).

reading

What is reading? This question is not as simple as it sounds. Experts cannot agree on an answer. Some describe reading as a decoding process, the sounding out of letters and the forming of words from letter sounds. Thus little or no importance is attached to an understanding of what is read (Cohen and Rudolph, 1977, pp. 294–295). Others believe that a broader definition of reading is needed, one that includes bringing meaning to the printed word. Sullivan (1976) states that "the meaning phase is the process whereby meaning is attributed to the graphic symbol, based on the past experiences of the reader. Reading, therefore, consists of decoding the printed symbol and then making that symbol meaningful to the reader" (p. 47). Wadsworth (1978) describes reading as "a process of deriving meaning from written symbols" (p. 122). Therefore reading means perceiving written symbols and at the same time comprehending their meaning.

The term most often associated with reading at the preschool level is "prereading" or "reading readiness." This is a much discussed and often misunderstood term. Durkin (1978) says children's ability to read involves "(a) their capacity in relation to (b) the instruction that will be available" (p. 162). Therefore the best way to assess readiness is to "provide children with varied opportunities to read" (p. 166). Leeper et al. (1979) feel that readiness for reading has to do with the best time for beginning reading instruction. They state that "the problem becomes one of assessing readiness and providing instructional opportunities that 'provide the best match for the capacities and interests of the children to be taught' " (p. 255).

Factors influencing learning to read are age, vision, visual perception, eye-hand coordination, visual recall, hearing, emotional-social factors, language development, mental and intellectual factors, and attention span (Leeper et al., 1979, pp. 226–254). Wadsworth (1978) deals with the skills a child needs to make sense out of the printed word. He lists cognitive development (logical operations), visual discrimination, spacial relations, auditory discrimination, and eye control (pp. 134–143). Rupley (1977) identifies reading prerequisites as "(1) language development and verbal meaning, (2) perceptual skills, (3) attending skills, (4) listening skills, and (5) thinking skills" (p. 450). In this chapter the ability to learn to read will be discussed under the headings language development, visual discrimination, auditory discrimination, knowledge of letters and words, eye-hand coordination, and cognitive skills.

language development

Children's readiness to read has long been identified with their facility with language. Robinson, Strickland, and Cullinan (1977) state,

A child's language is the raw material for reading. It contains the meaning the child knows and forms the base for the necessary pairings a child makes between oral and graphic symbols in learning to read. . . . Oral language is not only the vehicle but, in another form, [is] printed language [, and that] is *what* we teach children to read. (pp. 22–23)

Oral language's importance in kindergarten programs and relation to reading was found in a study by Loban (1963). Children who were high in general language development were also high in reading ability. Those who were low in language ability were low in reading ability (p. 87). Loban's conclusion that proficiency in oral language is basic to achievement in reading is in agreement with other studies (Sampson, 1962; Morrison, 1962; Strickland, 1972; Fox, 1976).

Some researchers have explained how specific areas contribute to language development and reading. Fasick (1973) found that a strong literature program provides a richer learning environment than television. Sentences heard on TV were simple whereas those in children's books were more complex. Chomsky (1969) found that children who were read to and read on their own had a significantly higher knowledge of complex sentences than those who heard and read fewer books. Flood (1977) investigated the relationship between parental style of reading to children and children's performances on selected prereading-related tasks. It was found that the reading episodes between parent and child were most effective when the following occurred: (1) Warm-up questions were used to settle children in preparation for the story and to stimulate interest in content. (2) Children were allowed to speak, ask and answer questions, and relate content to past experiences. (3) Positive reinforcement was used to encourage participation. (4) Evaluative questions were used after reading (pp. 866–867). The author cautions that books alone do not teach the child to read, but the more effective way to read stories is to involve children verbally.

Chaparro (1978) suggests capitalizing on patterns that are already part of children's language backgrounds. Mother Goose rhymes are an integral part of our culture and may be utilized in the following ways: (1) choral reading or reciting in unison; (2) assigning parts for which there is dialogue, such as in "*The Three Little Kittens*"; and (3) creative dramatics, for which such rhymes as "*Humpty Dumpty*" are suitable (p. 93). Pretend play can also be effective in language development. Yawkey (1979) found that play situations during and after a story were more effective than discussions in aiding the development of aural language (listening) and recall. Five-year-olds listened better and recalled more when puppets were used to rehearse during a story and body action movements to rehearse after a story than when body actions were used during a story and puppets after a story. It may be that puppets hold children's attention better and help them to recall more and that body actions are more effective for acting out the whole rather than the parts of a story (pp. 132–133). This study suggests that the use of puppets with stories may enhance children's aural language ability.

visual discrimination

In addition to normal visual acuity children must be able to distinguish between and among letters and words. Durkin (1978) states that

Reading is a visual task; consequently, visual discrimination ability is a prerequisite for success. . . . For those preparing children for reading, the specificity indicates that the only way to help them learn to discriminate among letters and words is by using letters and words—*not* pictures, shapes, numerals, or anything else. (p. 181)

Research in visual discrimination and its relationship to reading supports Durkin's insistence upon experiences with letters and words (Barrett, 1965; Paradis, 1974).

Samuels (1973) found that prereaders are more successful at learning letter names and at visual discrimination when features of letters are pointed out to them. Hall (1976) suggests exposure to experience reading (children's oral words written down) to help children understand that language can be written down and read by others. Experience reading also helps with visual discrimination, left-to-right orientation, visual memory, and language concepts (p. 8). It would seem that contact with the child's own words written down is an effective way to help children discriminate among letters and words.

auditory discrimination

In addition to normal acuity of hearing children must be able to distinguish among and between sounds. Cohen and Rudolph (1977) state, "Children's capacity to deal with segments of speech is a basic requirement for the successful applications of phonics learning" (p. 302). Robinson (1955) suggests that the influence of auditory and visual discrimination together is greater than that of intelligence in learning to read (p. 265). Gates and Bond (1958) found high correlations between the ability to learn and "tests of oral abilities, such as repeating letter sounds, nonsense words . . . , telling whether two words spoken in rapid succession were the same or different, guessing the letter which represented a particular letter sound, and the like" (p. 64). Other studies have found that auditory discrimination correlates positively with reading achievement (Durell, 1958; Dykstra, 1966; de Hirsch, Jansky, and Langford, 1966; Chall, 1967).

Downing (1970) found that the term "sound" was poorly understood by five-year-olds. Fifty percent of the children in the study did not think "of 'a sound' as being exclusively the phoneme," as one might in the context of teaching reading (p. 111). In everyday life the term "sound" is used for a variety of noises, and children's experience of spoken language does not encourage an awareness of sound segments as words or phonemes (units of sound).

Robinson, Strickland, and Cullinan (1977) suggest "playing with language" as appropriate for children in preschool programs to foster linguistic growth, including auditory discrimination. Play with alliteration as well as rhymes and jingles are suggested (p. 16). Rhyming games, songs, stories, poetry, and dramatic play can be used to improve sound awareness (Cohen and Rudolph, 1977, p. 309).

knowledge of letters and words

According to Rude (1973) the one skill most consistently measured by reading readiness tests is letter recognition, which remains the most valid predictor of success from readiness tests. In a classic study by Durrell (1958) tests of letter names at school entrance were the best predictors of February and June reading achievement (p. 18). Children who knew letter names, however, had shown an early interest in letters and learned on their own rather than through direct teaching and drill. Durkin (1970) found that children who learned to read before first grade had shown an early interest in the alphabet and words (p. 539).

Do we need to teach letter names in kindergarten? Cohen and Rudolph (1977) say

Children surrounded by story books, signs, alphabet blocks, etc. *do not need to be taught their letters.* They will learn them as they are ready. . . . Focus on print, for all children must be meaningful, as in hearing stories read from a book, or seeing one's spoken words transformed to print. (pp. 299–300)

In order to stimulate interest in the printed word Lowes (1975) suggests

Labeling with children's own names anything that needs to be identified as theirs . . .
Writing accounts of group experiences . . .
Keeping an up-to-date calendar of room duties assigned to individual pupils
Recording periodic observations made in science products . . .
Creating songs, stories, and poems, and preserving them for future use
Composing announcements and directions that may need to be duplicated and taken home to parents
Writing group letters, invitations, or simple greetings as the need arises (p. 330)

It would seem that preschool programs that attempt to teach children letter names through oral drill, workbooks, and mimeographed materials are a waste of time.

eye-hand coordination

Authorities believe that there is a positive relationship between motor control and reading readiness. Betts (1957) states, "reading activities usually require precise oculomotor control for making rapid and accurate fixation, fairly accurate eye-hand control for pencil and paper activities, and general motor control for turning pages and the careful handling of books" (pp. 135–136).

De Hirsch, Jansky, and Langford (1966) found that children's ability to write their first names was significantly related to end-of-second-grade reading achievement (p. 31). Durkin (1978) found that children who read before first grade wrote before they read.

Names are the easiest words for children to read and write. When they can write their names they can copy other words: names of colors, names of family members, numerals, and highly emotional words, such as "love," "I," "me," and "Halloween." Words can be copied in manuscript on lined or unlined pieces of paper. In the beginning spelling will come from the teacher; later labeled pictures can provide assistance (p. 185).

cognitive abilities

It is generally assumed that a high IQ ensures success in beginning reading, yet there are good readers among children with average IQs and poor readers among children with high IQs. Neither IQ tests nor reading readiness tests assess a variety of cognitive abilities related to reading achievement (Elkind, 1974; Wadsworth, 1978). The following cognitive abilities associated with Piaget's theory of intellectual development appear to be related to beginning reading.

classification and class inclusion

In reading the ability to relate the whole to its parts (words to letters and sentences to words) and the parts to the whole (letters to words and words to sentences) involves an understanding of class inclusion. The ability to understand that a letter can be both a letter and/or a vowel or consonant involves an understanding of multiple classification. Researchers have found a low but positive correlation between reading achievement and an understanding of multiple classification and class inclusion (Kaufman and Kaufman, 1972; Simpson, 1972; DeVries, 1974).

conservation

In reading conservation abilities are required for children to understand that the same letter, for example, "C," can have more than one sound depending on the word ("cat" or "Cindy"). Children also must understand that $A = a = a$ and $G = g = g$.

Researchers have found a low positive correlation between reading performance tests, reading readiness tests, and measures of conservation. The most frequently measured conservation task has been that of number (Almy, Chittenden, and Miller, 1967; DeVries, 1974; and Dimitrovsky and Almy, 1975).

seriation

In reading children must see the letters in a word in the correct sequence in order to recognize the same word again. Children who are still in the preoperational stage may see a letter in relation to a preceding word or space rather than in relation to other letters in the word. Scott (1969) found high positive correlations between the ability to seriate and total reading readiness scores. In a study by Kaufman and Kaufman (1972) the correlation between seriation and reading was almost as high as the correlation between reading and the total score of a Piagetian battery. The correlations between reading and seriation were higher than the correlation of reading with mental age (MA) or IQ (p. 58). Although studies are limited the results with seriation and reading are impressive (Waller, 1977, p. 23).

perceptual decentration

The ability to decenter (to consider more than one aspect of a problem at a time) is necessary for an understanding of class inclusion and conservation. No longer concentrating on only one form of a letter or word, children take into consideration different forms and recognize them as the same letter or word. The ability to decenter also enables children to consider at the same time the whole word and its parts and the parts in relation to the whole word. In other words, the ability to decenter helps children in more than one aspect of learning to read. Waller (1977) states that "the only systematic investigation of the relationship between perceptual development and reading is represented in empirical and theoretical work of Elkind." (p. 20). Elkind and his coworkers (Elkind, Horn, and Schneider, 1965; Elkind, Larson, and Van Doornick, 1965) have provided evidence that the decentration factor is different from intelligence and that decentration training improves at least the recognition aspect of reading performance.

topological perspective

In addition to classification, seriation, conservation, and decentration, correct perspective is important in learning to read. Wadsworth (1978) suggests that children who view forms from a topological rather than a Euclidean perspective may have reading difficulties. These children may not see the difference between shapes that are topologically similar. They may see "b," "d," and "g" as all being the same since the children are unable to view shapes as rigid. Problems with letter reversals, inversion, and rotation occur (p. 139).

In summary, the results of research studies indicate a positive relationship between reading performance and performance on tasks requiring concrete operational thought. "There is more evidence relating reading to number conservation than to any other conservation task. Second, seriation, rather than conservation or classification, appears to be most highly related to reading performance." (Waller, 1977, p. 23).

reading in the kindergarten

Most educators agree that formal reading instruction—a situation in which all children are taught the same prescribed material at the same time and at the same rate—is not appropriate in the kindergarten (Leeper et al., 1979, p. 255).

Cohen and Rudolph state, "There is ample evidence that a *range* of readiness for reading exists in children between five and seven, with the greatest readiness for most children closer to seven than five" (p. 307). Although formal teaching of reading is not recommended, opportunities for children who show readiness to read should be provided. The most appropriate approach for beginning reading is the language-experience approach, which is the "child's own words written down" (Durkin, 1978, p. 107). When children show an interest in reading it should be taught as a natural outgrowth of the kindergarten day. For teachers who have children who come to school reading or are ready to read, the book *The Kindergarten Child and Reading* (Ollila, 1977) is recommended.

characteristics of young children related to language arts

Before formulating goals for the language arts it is necessary to review the characteristics of young children. Listed in table 7–1 are characteristics of young children related to language arts. They represent general characteristics of young children and do not represent the characteristics of any one child; each child has an individual built-in rate of growth. It is important to keep in mind that the table is a summary of a group of children and does not represent any one child.

table 7–1
representative characteristics of young children related to language arts

From About 3 Years	to About 6 Years of Age
1. Uses simple words and short sentences (three to four words), "to be" verb forms, negative sentences, interrogatory sentences, inflections.	1. Uses complex and compound sentences, "if" and "so" clauses.
2. May carry on a monologue.	2. Uses language for communication and learning.
3. May recognize a few letters.	3. Names most upper-case letters and some lower-case letters.
4. Is aware of gross likenesses and differences in words.	4. Identifies words that look alike and different.
5. Enjoys word play.	5. Continues to enjoy play with words. Identifies rhyming words.
6. May recognize name.	6. Recognizes a few words—name, signs, TV words.
7. Is unaware of initial consonant sounds.	7. May identify words that begin with the same sound.
8. May write name or a few letters in name.	8. Writes first and last name in manuscript.
9. Grips pencil or crayon in fist or between fingers and thumb.	9. Holds pencil or crayon between thumb and forefinger.
10. Attention span is short and varies with activity. May attend in a small group for 5 to 10 minutes.	10. Attention span varies with activity. May be expected to attend in a small group for 15 to 20 minutes.
11. May have difficulty with some sounds—Z, S, V, R, J, F, G, K, sh, ch, th.	11. May still mispronounce some sounds—th, ch, gr, cl, lf, r.

table 7–1 (continued)

From About 3 Years	to About 6 Years of Age
12. Thinking is centered—attends to an aspect of one object or event rather than considering two or more aspects simultaneously.	12. Continues to center on one aspect at a time; decentering varies among children and may occur earlier in some.
13. Thinking is irreversible—is unable to follow a process from beginning to end and retrace steps back to starting point.	13. Thinking is still irreversible; reversibility varies among children and may occur earlier in some.
14. Thinking is static—ignores transformations or changes and instead centers on separate states.	14. Continues to ignore transformations; dynamic thinking varies among children and may occur earlier in some.
15. Beginning to understand topological relationships of proximity, enclosure, order, and separation.	15. Understands most topological relationships; begins to view figures as rigid in shape (Euclidean geometry).
16. Sorts objects according to likenesses—simple form of classification.	16. Uses multiple classification; a few understand class inclusion.
17. Verbally compares two or more objects.	17. May seriate as many as 8 to 10 objects according to given criteria, such as color, length, size.

goals for development through language arts

The following goals for development through the language arts have been chosen as realistic ones for the teacher to select since they can be achieved by the majority of children from age three to six. Objectives are written in the cognitive, affective, social, and psychomotor domains. It is important to remember that not all the objectives will be reached by the time a child is five or six. The objectives are listed as a guide for the teacher in planning and as one method for evaluating language arts understanding.

COGNITIVE DOMAIN.   A child:

1. Uses multiple classification—considers more than one possible classification for an object
2. Introduces words previously not used in his or her conversation
3. In a group situation, verbally describes an experience
4. Listens to and carries out verbal instructions
5. Carries out a meaningful conversation with peers and teacher
6. Uses compound and complex sentences and "if," "so," and "because" clauses
7. Makes speech sounds correctly
8. When shown a set of objects, duplicates it with another set in the same order
9. Writes first name in manuscript
10. Copies a few words and/or short sentences in manuscript
11. Dictates sentences and words describing a picture he or she has drawn or an experience he or she has had

12. Looks at a book from left to right
13. Recognizes own name written in manuscript letters
14. Identifies rhyming words
15. Identifies a few beginning consonant sounds
16. Names some upper- and lower-case letters
17. Recognizes a few sight words—5 to 10
18. Recognizes likenesses and differences in letters and words
19. Separates objects according to some criterion, such as length, color, size
20. Shows in drawings and descriptions of objects an understanding of topological relationships
21. Identifies shapes such as triangle, square, circle (five years old)

AFFECTIVE DOMAIN. A child:

1. Shows interest in books by asking someone to read to him or her
2. Chooses books to look at
3. Asks someone to write experience stories
4. Shows an interest in letters and words by writing and/or copying them
5. Shows an interest in learning letters and words by asking, "What does that say?"
6. Verbalizes his or her experiences

SOCIAL DOMAIN. A child:

1. Contributes ideas and feelings while interacting with others
2. Listens to other children's ideas
3. Willingly takes turns with other children
4. Is open to the ideas of others

PSYCHOMOTOR DOMAIN. A child:

1. Holds a brush, pencil and/or crayon between the thumb and index fingers
2. Establishes a preference for either the left or right hand
3. Has the necessary hand-eye coordination to write name

indoor learning centers

library center

The library center should invite children to look at books. It can be made interesting with colorful, oversize pillows and/or a table with an attractive plant. Bookshelves must be at children's eye level, with the covers of the books showing, so that they can tell at a glance which books they want to explore. It is desirable to include a bulletin board where children can display their experience stories and/or a teacher can put pictures related to children's books.

LOCATION.   The library center should be located in a quiet area of the room. An ideal location is next to the language arts center and near the writing center. The three centers can be combined when headphones are used in the language arts center.

EQUIPMENT AND SUPPLIES.   Equipment may include:

Round or trapezoidal table(s)
One or two straight chairs
A rocking chair
Bookshelf
Selection of books that may be ordered for the room or borrowed from the school
    and/or public libraries
Room divider

Supplies may include:

Oversized pillows (two)
Bean bag chair(s)
Plants

Books available should include stories about children at school, animals, the ABCs, counting, poetry, and nursery rhymes. Book lists may be found in *Kindergarten and Early Schooling* (Cohen and Rudolph, 1977) and *Good Schools and Young Children* (Leeper et al., 1979). A children's picture dictionary and an adult dictionary should be in the library or writing center. After books are read or stories are told from books, these books should be placed in the library center. Teachers can observe children looking at books and/or retelling stories from pictures.

language arts center

The language arts center includes activities related to reading and writing, such as listening and speaking. In this center are found mechanical equipment such as a listening center, language master, and/or typewriter. Headphones should be provided to avoid noise pollution.

LOCATION.   This center should either be next to the library center or part of it. Both centers should be close to other quiet centers.

EQUIPMENT AND SUPPLIES.   Equipment may include:

Language master
Manuscript typewriter
Cassette tape recorder and player
Listening center
Headphones (three to five sets)
Filmstrip viewer

Filmstrips
Cassette stories with books
Small flannel boards (8 by 12 inches)
Wooden letters
Magnetic board and letters
Plastic letters
Removable letters in form boards—wooden or rubber
Flannel board, figures, and letters

Supplies may include:

Large and small language master cards
Cassette tapes

Familiar flannel board story characters should be placed in the language arts center. Children can place the figures on the flannel board and tell stories as they move the figures. Sometimes children ask teachers and other children to listen to or participate in their stories.

writing center

Teachers must decide whether or not to include a writing center in the classroom. The decision will depend on the experiential background of the children and their present interests and capabilities. Sometimes a writing center is included toward the end of the school year, when more children are writing their names and other words.

LOCATION.   The writing center should be next to the library and language arts centers.

EQUIPMENT AND SUPPLIES.   Equipment may include:

Wooden letters—upper and lower case
Sandpaper or beaded letters
Rectangular table with four chairs
Storage unit for paper and pencils
Picture dictionary, child
Picture dictionary, adult

Supplies may include:

Assortment of thick and regular-size pencils
Assortment of crayons
Felt-tip pens
Unlined easel paper or other unlined paper
Paper with wide lines
Teacher-made name cards

teacher's role in language arts

speaking

In order to speak children must have the opportunity to talk. Teachers destroy the incentive to talk when they do most of the talking and/or put words into children's mouths. During one "show and tell" kindergarten session a record was kept of the words spoken by the children and teacher. Ninety-five percent of the 45-minute period was dominated by the teacher. Not only did she do the talking, but without knowing it she also told the children what to say. The dialogue went something like this: Teacher, "What is your doll's name?" Child, "Susan." Teacher, "Where did you get Susan?" Child, "At the store." Teacher, "What color is Susan's dress?" Child, "Blue." The teacher spoke in sentences but the child's speech was limited to phrases encouraged by the teacher's endless questioning. This description of a "show and tell" period is typical of many so-called class discussions. Obviously "show and tell" is not the answer to language development.

Opportunities for language expression occur naturally when children have something purposeful to talk about. A group of five-year-olds prepared to visit a grocery store in order to buy fruit for snack. The children were divided into three groups with either the teacher, the aide, or a parent in each group. They talked with the children about selecting "good" fruits to eat. Several fruits in varying conditions were given to the children to handle and observe. Meaningful discussions evolved concerning what to look for when buying "good" fruits. These discussions gradually led to the necessity for safety rules to follow during the trip. Each group made its own rules, which were written on experience charts. Through these experiences and others like them children find a *reason* to express themselves *in their own way*.

Sometimes teachers unthinkingly answer their own questions before children have an opportunity to respond. One teacher asked a five-year-old, "What did you do for Halloween? I bet I know. You went for 'Trick or Treat.' What did you wear? I bet you were a ghost." As the teacher talked on, Sam shook his head. As she knelt down beside him Sam said, "No, that's not what happened" and walked away.

Another child enthusiastically began to tell a teacher about her new pet. The teacher interrupted asking, "What color is your pet? Is it brown, black, or white? Do you keep it inside or outside?" This line of questioning brought a quizzical look from the child and the remark, "I don't know anything else about my dog." A good rule for teachers to follow is to listen first and let the child do the talking.

When children are given a choice it must be a *real* choice. "Do you want the red or the blue crayon?" is a sincere question since the teacher does not care which crayon is chosen; however, "Would you like to go outside now?" is not giving children a choice since the teacher plans to take them outside anyway. Since young children are literal-minded some statements teachers make must be perplexing. Common expressions used by some teachers are "Put on your thinking caps," "Button your lips," and "Listen with your ears not with your mouths." No wonder one child remarked, "I didn't wear a cap to school today" and another, "I don't have any buttons on my mouth."

A teacher's gestures and facial expressions convey messages to children just as do verbal expressions. One child asked a teacher if he could paint at the easel. Since Bill often painted the teacher preferred that he choose another activity. She shrugged her shoulders and said, "Yes, you may." Bill received two very different messages from his teacher. Which one did she *really* mean? There are a few teachers who speak with soft, pleasant voices but never smile. One wonders what message they are sending children. Then there are those teachers who smile and say they "like children." These same teachers, at the slightest provocation, become annoyed and scream at children.

A mother tried to explain to her five-year-old Jimmy that Ms. H. really loves children but has a habit of yelling at them. In response Jimmy shook his head and said, "No, she doesn't love us. She screams at us and says, 'I know you don't like me, but you'll be glad when you go to first grade and know your letters.' She doesn't love us; all she wants to do is teach letters." How sad for Jimmy and his classmates. Teachers must ask themselves periodically, "What did I say today? Why did I say it? How did I say it? What did it mean to the children?"

There are children who come to school with immature speech and/or speech defects. Immature speech usually disappears by the time a child is six or seven. When it interferes with communication, however, a speech therapist should be consulted. The speech of an immature, shy, and overprotected four-year-old was unintelligible. He was unable to make many initial consonant sounds, and as a result he could not communicate with the teacher or the children. He became withdrawn and refused to try anything unfamiliar. Speech therapy during the summer months improved Dan's speech so markedly that in the fall he had learned to make most speech sounds. By Christmas he no longer needed therapy. Although he was not ready for first grade at the end of the kindergarten year, the confidence he had gained through the added dimension of articulate speech enabled him to assume the role of leader as well as follower. He changed from a shy to a confident, outgoing boy.

Every child should have a speech test during the nursery school and kindergarten years. What a teacher calls "baby talk" or immature speech may be a speech defect. Jack had a slight lisp his teacher referred to as "baby talk." An examination by a speech therapist revealed that Jack had been born with a piece of skin attached to the back of his tongue. A simple operation corrected the lisp.

Children who do not speak standard English are not always understood by their peers or teachers. A teacher's own speech is crucial since children learn standard English by modeling. When speaking standard English is not effective a teacher must give additional help. One method is to repeat in standard English what children say in their dialect. Record both on a language master or tape recorder so that children can hear them. By listening to another way to say the same thing children hear standard English but learn at the same time that the teacher accepts the way they speak.

The vocabulary of disadvantaged children is often restricted, and words understood by most children are unknown to them. A teacher tried to teach color names to a five-year-old boy from a low socioeconomic background. As Dean manipulated objects the teacher named the color of each. For several days they matched objects of the same hue; however, when the teacher pointed to an object, Dean still was unable to tell her the color name. One day, in great excitement, Dean pointed to a red crayon and yelled, "color red, color red!" He ran around the room pointing out everything red that he saw, each time saying, "color red!" The teacher now realized that Dean did not know the meaning of the word "color." When she asked, "What color is the crayon?" Dean could not answer because he had not asociated the word "color" with the hue of an object.

Often teachers assume that children understand certain concepts when they have little or no understanding of them. Peter in his second year of Head Start could write and recognize his name. The teacher assumed that he knew what the term "word" meant and that he could identify printed material as composed of words. She was shocked one day when Peter pointed to a word in a book and asked, "What's that?" She said, "What do you mean?" Peter continued to point to words in the story asking, "What's that?" She answered, "Those are words." "What are words?" Stunned, she wrote his name and told him it was a word. With a puzzled look he inquired, "My name is a word?" She answered, "Yes" and told him to find the word on his locker that said "Peter." He found his name and repeated after her, "That word is Peter." They spent the rest of the summer writing experience stories and talking about letters, words, and sentences. Peter gradually learned that words express ideas and that his ideas could be written down for others to read. Apparently no one had ever told Peter that printed and written words tell us what to say when we read.

listening

Teachers sometimes complain that children become restless and bored when they are in a group. This behavior is usually the result of unrealistic teacher expectations. Young children cannot be expected to sit still and listen to the teacher or other children for long periods of time. They are much too egocentric to focus their attention on the verbalizations of others. Small-group activities and discussions are more meaningful to children and give them opportunities to participate and in turn to *listen*. A teacher divided 20 kindergarten children into 2 groups with 10 in each. The groups were led alternately by the teacher and aide. Each group talked about the kind of pumpkin they wanted to buy for Halloween. As the children discussed the pumpkins, different opinions were given. Some children wanted big orange pumpkins, others small orange ones. A compromise had to be reached. In one group the teacher said, "All of us want an orange pumpkin but we have different opinions about the size. I'm going to draw a pumpkin on a sheet of paper. Watch me, and when I draw one you like tell me." As the teacher sketched a pumpkin a few children suggested a larger one. The drawing was made larger and the children agreed that this size was satisfactory. Every child was listening and contributing to the group discussion, which lasted for approximately 10 minutes.

There are many opportunities for preschool children to talk in small groups. Before taking a trip it is necessary to talk about "things to remember during a trip." The rules can be discussed and written on experience charts. Here is a reason for listening and for talking, and children's ideas can be put into immediate action.

Identifying children with hearing problems may be difficult since these children learn to compensate by reading lips and facial expressions. Signs of hearing loss are being inattentive, failing to follow directions, shaking the head, rubbing the ears, and sometimes crying and/or having temper tantrums.

Sue was a cooperative, apparently happy five-year-old who one day unexpectedly had a temper tantrum. After rest the teacher asked Sue several times to put her rug away. She was looking in another direction and ignored him. He knelt beside Sue and asked her again to put her rug away. At first she smiled, but when she realized that the other children had folded their rugs she suddenly began to kick and hit the teacher. She would not stop and had to be restrained with the teacher's arms held loosely around her. The teacher could not understand these actions, which were just the opposite from Sue's typical behavior. After carefully analyzing the situation he suspected that Sue had not heard him when he asked her to put away her rug. She had been embarrassed when she discovered she was the last one. Sue later had an audiometer test that showed a 20 percent hearing loss in each ear. She was fitted with a hearing aid that she wore into adulthood.

Some children come to school with hearing problems that have already been diagnosed. Marjorie could hear low and moderate frequencies, but high frequencies were painful and difficult for her to hear as speech sounds. Her loss of hearing became more pronounced during the year, but her parents refused to accept that situation. They were asked to help with classroom activities in order to observe Marjorie as she interacted with other children. Slowly they accepted the fact that further diagnosis was necessary. Marjorie stayed in the class but in addition spent part of each day is a resource room where she gradually learned to read lips.

Jane was a five-year-old who had been mainstreamed into a Head Start group. She was deaf from birth and could not speak or hear. For the first weeks of school she was loud, restless, and constantly moving about. The teacher placed her fingers on her lips and then on Jane's. Gradually Jane learned a signal that meant to keep her lips closed. She became less frustrated as she learned the class routines and knew what to expect next. The teacher followed the example of the resource room teacher, who had encouraged Jane to touch a speaker's lips. Jane often touched the teacher's lips and then her own in order to imitate lip movements. The teacher encouraged this behavior. One miraculous day Jane made her first intelligible sounds. She never learned to say words clearly, but the teacher and children understood what she meant. There was hope that with further therapy Jane would one day communicate more effectively.

writing

There are children who write their names and other words before beginning kindergarten, and then there are those who do not write until first grade. The latter are usually children whose eye-hand coordination has not developed sufficiently to enable them to hold a crayon and/or copy lines and circles. Every

Making letters out of clay.

effort must be made to give these children opportunities to use their small muscles.

Dick was a five-year-old who could not write his name, draw, paint, tie his shoes, or hold a crayon between his thumb and forefinger. Fortunately he enjoyed woodworking, and the teacher found nails with large heads that Dick could hammer into a tree stump. Dick was generally immature and remained in kindergarten a second year. By the end of the year he could write the letters in his name.

Walt, another five-year-old boy, could not hold a crayon without dropping it. He was clumsy, sometimes bumping into furniture and other children. His parents sought medical help, which provided them with the hope that one day Walt would be able to write. Walt's parents worked on prescribed exercises at home while the teacher worked on large- and small-muscle development at school. In third grade Walt was able to take paper-and-pencil tests. Until this time tests had to be given orally.

Children's development may be uneven, as in the case of Dick and Walt, whose physical development lagged behind other forms of development. Bill, a five-year-old, had excellent large and small motor development but was somewhat intellectually immature. Although he recognized letters he refused to write his name in upper- and lower-case letters. Whenever it was suggested he write with both his answer was, "I'll do it when I get to first grade." By Christmas of the first-grade year Bill wrote in upper- and lower-case letters. Teachers who insist that children must recognize letter names and learn to write letters before first grade often are wasting time and effort. It is the interest in letters and words that is important.

reading

It is in the preschool that children are exposed to the prerequisites that eventually lead them to read with ease and normal progress. There are a few children who come to kindergarten or nursery school already reading and others who will learn to read during the year. Preschool teachers *are* teachers of reading since everything they plan for children involves skills and/or cognitive processes that relate directly to reading.

LANGUAGE DEVELOPMENT. For true communication to occur children must see a reason to share with and receive ideas from others. Therefore teachers must provide children with something to talk about. An environment rich in meaningful experiences stimulates an exchange of ideas. One morning a group of children found two gerbils in a cage on the science table. They were immediately attracted to the animals and asked, "What are they? Where did they come from? Can we keep them? Can we hold them?" The teacher answered some questions and asked others: "Why do you think I put the gerbils in a cage? How did I know what kind of food to buy for them? How can we find out whether or not gerbils bite? Do you think they would get away if we held them?" This line of questioning began an exchange of ideas about the care of gerbils from "Gerbils drink milk" to "No, they don't! They only eat seeds." The teacher asked, "How can we find out more about gerbils?" "The books might tell us a lot," one child said, pointing to books about gerbils in the science center. The children learned that most answers to their questions were found in the books. They learned from their books that gerbils eat parts of plants. They wondered, "Would the gerbils like green grapes? Spinach? Nuts?" During informal group discussions it was decided to take any remaining food out of the cage and place only one food in the gerbil's dish. If the food was partially eaten, it was decided that the gerbils liked that food. The teacher asked, "How will we remember what the gerbils like and dislike?" "Let's keep a record with a 'yes' and 'no' column," was one child's suggestion. A chart was made and a check mark placed in either the "yes" or "no" column under the name of each food tested. There was not only something meaningful to talk about but also a reason for writing things down.

A group of children experimented with batteries and bulbs. They wanted to remember what they had discovered about batteries, wires, and bulbs. When they wanted to record a discovery they dictated sentences for the teacher to write in a book entitled *What We Know About Batteries*. A question arose, "What's inside a battery?" The teacher said, "How can we find out?" Suggestions were made: "Ask your mother and daddy," "Look in a battery book," and "Open a battery and find out." The answers were not found in available books or from parents so the children asked to open the batteries. The teacher checked with a science teacher to make sure that the contents of a flashlight battery were not harmful if care was taken not to get the material in the eye or mouth. Reassured, she allowed the children to saw open several batteries. "What is the black stuff in the batteries?" was the next question asked. This time the children suggested writing the people who made the batteries to find out what was inside. They dictated a letter to the Burgess Battery Company which the teacher rewrote on stationery and reread to the children. The letter was addressed, stamped, and mailed at the corner mailbox. An answer arrived within two weeks with the answers to their question and materials to make their own batteries. They had learned to communicate through listening, speaking, reading, and writing. Most important, they had learned that there were many uses for language.

Expanding vocabulary is a part of language development. In the experiences with the gerbils and the batteries and bulbs described above the children were exposed to the meanings of many new words: "battery," "gerbil," "chemicals," "conductor," "metal," "maze," and "experiment." Words already known by the children—"lettuce," "cage," "light," "animal"—took on a new meaning. One child said, "I know lots of animals and, guess what, a gerbil is an animal too." Other comments heard were, "I like lettuce and so does the gerbil," "Gerbils need food just like us," "The light burns brighter with two batteries," and "String isn't a conductor of electricity."

In order to increase vocabulary children must encounter words in many concrete ways. To understand the words "top" and "bottom," both essential to beginning reading, children can put blocks on the *top* and *bottom* shelves, find the *top* and *bottom* of a page, help clean the *bottom* of the gerbil cage, and wash the *top* of the counter.

Children who are very verbal and have a wide background of experience may use words in surprising ways. One child said, "Doesn't Miss Jackson [class aide] look sophisticated with her dark glasses on?" and another child said, "I was perplexed when I couldn't find the crayons." Children may use mature words in the wrong context. A principal visited a classroom for the second time and said hello to a child. He looked at her with surprise and said, "Oh, Miss L., I didn't realize you with your glasses on." She answered, "You didn't recognize me, did you? I look different from the last time you saw me." These attempts to use grown-up words are indications that children's vocabularies are expanding.

There are children who may be described as creative with language. Susan expressed herself in ways that were unusual. One day three children were jumping rope as Susan approached singing "Jingle Bells." She accidently walked into the rope, which made the other children very angry. Susan put her hands on her hips, looked at the children, and said, "Well, that's one way to keep Christmas from coming." Another child in describing his trip to his grandmother said, "I didn't get homesick. I got people sick." Both children dictated long, highly creative stories. Their stories were mimeographed and made into books for them to take home.

Language experience stories are children's words written down. They should originate with children and not with teachers. Teachers can ask, "Do you want me to write something for you?" instead of "Tell me what you want to say and I'll write it down." The latter implies that the child should have something to say. Children have been heard to comment, "Oh, do I have to tell about my picture?" and "We'll have to write about our trip."

Children who are exposed to experience charts dictated by them for a definite purpose are more likely to see a reason for written expression. They begin to understand that language expressed as writing is important. Therefore what they have to say about themselves or their work can be important. A sign on a block construction, "Please don't tear down this building," conveys a message to all the children. In an atmosphere where written language expresses ideas that are meaningful to them, children naturally ask, "Will you write it for me?"

Visitors enjoy experience stories too.

Children use language in their dramatic play. The more involved and realistic play episodes precipitate the use of enriched language. Careful teacher guidance and a common background of experiences are crucial. Dramatic play and the teacher's role in play are discussed in chapter 3.

Creative dramatics may be used to encourage language development. This type of play situation differs from dramatic play since the teacher suggests the theme and the roles children will act out. In preparation for Halloween one teacher asked a policeman to talk about safe ways to "Trick or Treat." After the policeman's visit the teacher set up a center with Halloween masks, flashlights, and a stand-up mirror. When children visited the center they tried on the various masks, looked at themselves in the mirror, and talked with the teacher about the importance of carrying flashlights on Halloween.

The next day the teacher added three cardboard houses to the center. She talked with small groups of children asking questions such as "How do you think you'll feel on Halloween night?" "How will you dress?" "Will you 'Trick or Treat' by yourself?" "Will you take a flashlight?" "What will you do when you go to a house?" "What will you say?" The children talked about their feelings as "a little afraid," "excited," "good," "scared," "shy" and suggested things to say to their friends, such as "Hello," "Trick or Treat," "May I come in?" "I can sing a song," "I know a finger play," and "Thank you." The teacher pretended to live in one of the houses and invited the children to come to the house for treats (nuts wrapped in foil). Gradually children took the teacher's place in the houses and the play continued.

After Halloween the play became more realistic and more verbal. Occasionally the teacher introduced ideas that changed the direction of the play. "Pretend it's raining. What will we do?" The children built a car with blocks.

"Pretend no one is home." The children came home empty handed and sad. They decided to have a party at home. "Pretend someone dressed like a monster opens the door." Some children screamed and ran. Others laughed and said, "Who are you?" or "You're not really a monster. You can't scare us." The children began to create their own situations. In this way their play became more imaginative and creative.

Another form of creative dramatics is acting out or dramatizing a story. One of the best ways to begin dramatization is to first read the story and then tell it later using flannel board figures. When children are familiar with the story, a teacher can tell it encouraging children to "talk for" the story characters. Later, as the teacher tells the story, children can act it out using their own props. Finally, children act out the story on their own without a narrator.

As Valentine's Day approached a kindergarten group listened to a legend about Saint Valentine. They loved the story and asked to hear it several times. The teacher suggested that as he told the story, the children act it out. Ten characters were chosen, two boys, Saint Valentine, six neighbors, and a dove. The dove was included since it brought messages to Saint Valentine. A few days later the children were observed acting out the story on their own. They made up their version to include five boys, two doves, Mr. Valentine, a doctor (for Mr. Valentine when he was sick), and several neighbors. In their adaptation the boys cooked soup and brought it to Mr. Valentine, who was in bed recuperating from an illness. The teacher was delighted that the children had used their imaginations to create additional characters and situations that seemed logical to them. They knew their story was somewhat different from the original and renamed it "Saint Valentine and the Children."

When children act out stories or poems it does not matter how many characters are involved. There can be more than three bears and one Goldilocks. By allowing children to choose what they would like to be they have an opportunity to try out many roles. Twelve children dramatized "The Three Billy Goats Gruff." The outdoor jungle gym became the troll's bridge and the playground the green hill. There were three big goats, two middle-size goats, four baby goats, and three trolls. The children were not disturbed by the number of goats or trolls since the essentials of the story were the same.

VISUAL DISCRIMINATION.   When children have adequate visual perception they have no difficulty discriminating between objects such as crayons and pencils or triangles and squares. Teachers should spend more time providing experiences that help children see likenesses and differences between and among letters and words.

Teachers can begin by writing children's names on sturdy oak tag. Three sets of name cards may be made, two sets to be used at school and one to take home. When a language master is available teachers can write children's names on language master cards. Names can be recorded using both the teacher's and the children's voices. When the cards are placed in the language master, children hear their names spoken by themselves and by their teachers. Polaroid pictures can be taken of children during the first week of school and these pictures placed on the language master cards with masking tape. By associating the pictures, names, and voices children learn to recognize each others' names as well as their own.

Meaningful labels help children learn letter names and sometimes words. When children see their names on lockers, artwork, clothing, and experience stories, they learn that their names say the same thing whenever they see them. They begin to compare their names with those of other children. Familiar comments are heard such as "My name looks like John's," "I have letters in my name just like Gene's," and "I see the same letters in my name as in Ronnie's name." Teachers should encourage children to compare name cards: "Which letters are alike? Which ones are different? How are they different? Do the words look exactly alike? Do they say the same thing?"

Children's work and objects of interest can be labeled with words describing them. Johnny brought a stalk of sugar cane to school. On placing it on the science table he asked the teacher to write, "This is Johnny's sugar cane." The sentence strip was placed in front of the sugar cane. When children see objects labeled at their own suggestion they begin to notice other words and letters that look alike. One child told his teacher that he had found the word "school" four places in the room. They counted together and found the word on a language master card, on a sign in the block center, in a sentence on the science table, and in a book in the library center.

Experience stories lend themselves to the recognition and comparison of letters and words. Whenever a small group writes an experience story a word may be chosen from the story and written on a card. Children can use the card to find the same word in the story. They enjoy finding the word and telling how many times it occurs in the story. Sometimes children call attention to sentences and/or phrases that are repetitive, such as "We saw a ___." "We are thankful for ___." "We want to ___." These experiences give teachers opportunities to

The children wrote a story about their dinosaurs.

point out differences as well as likenesses. Teachers can say such things as "Find a word that is different." "Find words or letters that are alike." "How are they alike?" "Do the words say the same thing?" "How is this word different from this one?" One child pointed to the period at the end of a sentence and asked, "What is this? I never saw a letter like that. What's its name?" This incident told the teacher that Bill had advanced rapidly in his understanding of the terms "alike" and "different" and that he was interested in the printed word.

Some of the terms closely associated with reading are "left," "right," "beginning," "middle," and "end." When children write their names, a small x may be placed on the left-hand side of the paper to encourage left-to-right orientation. When children know left and right, teachers can use this knowledge to help them see differences in letters. The lower-case "b" can be described as the letter with the circle on the right side of the straight line and the lower-case "d" as the letter with the circle on the left side of the straight line. The lower-case "p" is the letter with the straight line below the line and the circle on the right. Words have a beginning, a middle, and an end. "Do these words begin with the same letter? Do they end with the same letter? Are the middle letters the same or different?" are questions that can be asked while comparing words.

When children begin to compare letters and words their interest is unlimited. They can use wooden, magnetic, or felt letters to make words and sentences. They may write words, and in order to copy them correctly they must notice likenesses and differences. Children who write from memory and/or copy from books or experience stories show a readiness for more systematic approaches to reading.

AUDITORY DISCRIMINATION.   When children acquire adequate hearing they have little or no difficulty discriminating between sounds such as doorbells and buzzers, drums and rhythm sticks. Gross differences among words are more difficult since words sometimes sound very much alike, for example, "where," "here"; "pirate," "parrot"; "tag," "bag"; "think," "blink." Children show by their actions and/or questions whether or not they understand what is said to them. One child was asked to get his coat to go outside. Puzzled, he brought the wooden boat from the block center. Another child was told he could help make pumpkin pie. As he helped mix the ingredients he laughed and said, "Oh, we are making pumpkin pie. I thought we were going to make *punkin* pie. I never heard of that."

Children sometimes misunderstand what is said because the teacher does not enunciate clearly or because they have acquired poor listening habits. Teachers must pronounce words distinctly and not fall into the habit of using lazy speech. Careful listening may be encouraged by playing games such as "Simon Says" and Magic. In Magic children close their eyes, are quiet, and listen to the sounds around them. When a minute has passed they open their eyes and tell what they think happened around them while their eyes were closed. Sounds that may be heard are the heat coming on, clock hands moving, or a gerbil playing on its wheel. Outside sounds may be a car horn tooting, a bird chirping, children playing on the playground, or a lawn mower working. Teachers and children can make up their own sound stories by presenting a sequence of sounds that tells a story. Children can close their eyes and listen while the teacher walks to the library center, takes a book off the shelf, sits down in the chair, and opens the book. When the children open their eyes they describe in correct sequence what the sounds told them the teacher was doing. Children love sound stories and enjoy making their own for other children to guess.

When children are aware of gross differences among sounds, teachers can introduce rhyming words. In most instances five-year-olds will notice words that rhyme as they play with language. Through nursery rhymes teachers can discover those children who are sensitive to rhymes, by asking questions such as " 'Jack and Jill went up the hill to fetch a pail of water.' 'Hill' sounds like ____?" " 'Jack fell down and broke his crown.' 'Crown' sounds like ____?" Two or three pictures may be shown, and children can choose the one that rhymes with the end of each phrase.

Objects that rhyme can be named for children to match. Later pictures can be placed in boxes and the objects that rhyme with the pictures put in the correct boxes. One box has a picture of a cat and the other a bed. Objects to be placed in the respective boxes may include a bat, mat, rat, head, sled. At first it is better to use words of one syllable. Later two- or three-syllable words may be used. Teachers should call the children's attention to the fact that "rhyming words sound alike at the *end* of the word."

Children can make up their own rhymes. After reading a rhyming book a kindergarten teacher asked children to think of a rhyme. The children illustrated their rhymes, and they were made into a large book. Some rhymes were "a bear without hair," "a plane in a lane," "a fellow eating Jello," "a duck in a truck," "a fox in a box," "a fly looking at the sky," and "a shoe painted blue."

Initial consonant sounds should be taught as parts of the whole word and not in isolation. Children vary in their ability to hear beginning sounds. Some children enter kindergarten aware of words that begin alike; others do not hear these likenesses until later in the year or during first grade. Teachers can help children hear initial consonant sounds by calling attention to words that "sound alike at the beginning of the word." When children notice words that look alike teachers can compare not only their physical appearance but also their sounds. Peter noticed his name "looked like Pam's name." The teacher wrote both names and Peter compared them. He decided that the first letter in his name and in Pam's looked "just alike." The teacher told him to listen as she said each name. She told him that the words sounded alike at the beginning. Later Peter said, "I know another word that sounds like my name, 'Pete.' " Although "Pete" was almost identical to his own name, Peter was beginning to show an awareness of initial consonant sounds.

Several five-year-olds in a multiage classroom became interested in making their own picture dictionaries. They thought of words that began with each letter of the alphabet. Then they wrote the letters in upper- and lower-case letters at the top of the pages. Pictures were drawn or cut from magazines to describe the words. A few four-year-olds in the group attempted to make picture dictionaries but quickly lost interest. Instead they cut out or wrote a few letters on the pages of their books. This experience made the older children aware of initial consonant sounds and helped the younger children learn letter names.

Teachers can use concrete objects to teach initial consonants by asking children to find the objects that begin with the same sounds. Games may be played with the objects in the same manner as described for rhyming words.

Matching upper- and lower-case letters.

KNOWLEDGE OF LETTERS AND WORDS.   Children should have easy access to a variety of concrete letters. Upper- and lower-case wooden letters can be held in the hand, traced with the finger or pencil, used to make words and the ABCs. Magnetic letters are three-dimensional. Although they can be placed upside down, they cannot be put backward without falling off the magnetic board. Children can also have tactile and visual experiences with felt, beaded, sandpaper, and plastic letters. These letters can be used to make words from memory or match printed words. A four-year-old grouped several letters and asked the teacher, "What does this say?" The letters did not make a word, but the teacher said, "Those letters look like a word. If you change one letter and add one more you can make the word 'sail.' Let's make more words. Get your name card and find letters that make your name." Paul could not spell words, but he had the concept that letters put together make a word, an important concept in learning to read.

Children learn letter names as they explore the printed word. Since children's names are important to them teachers can begin by naming the letters as they write children's names. Writing and letter naming are closely related. When children learn to recognize their names they attempt to write them. The letters may not be in the correct sequence; however, the interest in making letters is an important step toward letter and word recognition. When children ask, "What letter is that?" or "What does that say?" they are taking their first steps toward reading.

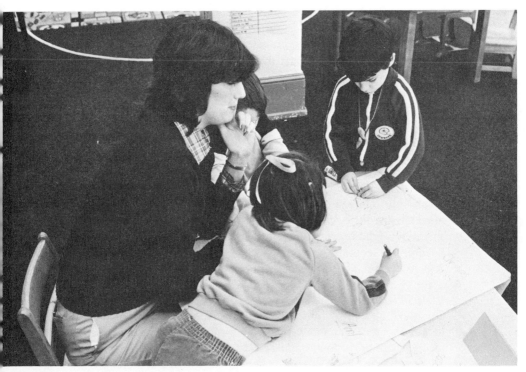

I can sign my own story.

EYE-HAND COORDINATION.   When teachers write children's names they should sit next to them so that the children observe that letters are written from left to right. It is not important for children to form each letter according to a step-by-step procedure. It does not matter whether the circle or straight line is made first. What is important is that teachers encourage children to write from left to right. Teachers must remember, however, that reversals and mirror writing are common at four and five. Putting a small mark on the left-hand side of the paper and saying, "Start here to write your name," aids children in writing their letters in correct sequence. It also is helpful to tell children to start at the top and pull down to make their letters. When children have adequate motor coordination there is no harm in showing them their name card and asking them to compare it with the way they wrote their name. They are quick to say, "Oh, I made that letter upside down" or "My name is backwards."

A gifted six-year-old was able to write experience stories on chart paper as children dictated their sentences. John wrote carefully but found that he could not fit all the letters in the word "hotel" on the same line. He said the word, then exclaimed, "I'll put the hyphen between the o and the t." He continued to hyphenate words as needed. The teacher gave this child every opportunity to write his own stories and those of other children.

Children associate certain words with special occasions. Teachers can write these high-interest words on cards for them to copy. At Halloween several children wrote sentences using word cards. Each card had a picture and an identifying printed word. Some of the sentences were "I am going for Trick or Treat," "I am a witch," "My brother and I saw a witch on Halloween," and "We made a jack-'o-lantern at school." Although teacher guidance was sometimes necessary, the children were able to do most of their own work.

The writing center should be the hub of writing activities. Children's name cards may be kept here so they can refer to them when needed. A picture dictionary can be used, with the teacher's help, to look up words they don't know how to spell. Once an interest in writing has begun children will copy words and sentences from books, labels, sentence strips, and experience stories. A few children will be able to copy or type their own experience stories.

COGNITIVE ABILITIES.   Certain cognitive abilities as well as specific skills are apparently related to success in beginning reading. The cognitive abilities associated with success in reading are classification and class inclusion, conservation, seriation, and perceptual decentration. Each category and activities to develop these understandings are discussed in chapters 4 and 5. Activities related specifically to reading will be reviewed briefly here.

CLASSIFICATION AND CLASS INCLUSION.   By calling attention to the letters that make up their names and other words, teachers can help children get the feeling that letters make words. When experience stories are read to children teachers can move their hand from left to right across the page, briefly pausing after each word. Sentences are made up of words, and there is a physical space between each printed word and a pause between each spoken word. Teachers can ask questions such as "Listen as I say the name of your story. How many words will I write?" and "Does it take more letters to write 'you' than 'birthday?' " Another activity is to relate the letters to the words: "Let's look at your name. How many letters are there? If you write the letters in each corner of the page, can we read your name? No, because the letters must be together in the correct order to make a word." These activities present a challenge to most children; however, they should not continue when children become uninterested or frustrated.

CONSERVATION.   Very few young children understand that a letter can represent more than one sound. This concept is not appropriate for kindergarten and may not be understood by first graders. Teachers can, however, give children experiences in recognizing letters and words in various forms and contexts.

Letters and words should be written on white or cream-colored paper with a black or brown marker so that children can see them distinctly. Children who recognize upper- and lower-case letters learn that both forms of "C" "(c)" say the same thing and that the words "cat" and "Cat" have the same name.

Printed labels used by the teacher should begin with small letters unless they are proper names. When captions on bulletin boards are sentences they should begin with a capital letter, followed by lower-case letters, with a period at the end of the sentence. Teachers should explain that upper-case letters may be used at the beginning of a sentence but stress that the words say the same things when written with either upper- or lower-case letters. Teachers must be consistent in referring to letters as either upper- and lower-case, capital and small, or large and small letters. A good policy to follow is to ask first-grade teachers the terms they use.

SERIATION. Children learn the sequence of letters as they write their names and other words. At first they do not realize that the order of letters in a word is important to the meaning. A child may write "Jcak" for "Jack" and insist that he has written his name. It is not until children "see" the differences between the way they write their names and the way the teacher writes them that they understand the importance of the sequence of letters.

Teachers should encourage children to "spell" their names as well as write them. When children ask how to write a word teachers can either spell it verbally or write it on paper naming each letter as they write. The concept that the order of letters changes the pronunciation and/or meaning of a word is essential in reading.

PERCEPTUAL DECENTRATION. The inability to consider more than one aspect of a word or letter at the same time limits children's ability to understand class inclusion and conservation. A child who centers on the letter "e" in the word "the" does not see the word as a whole and has difficulty recognizing it. He or she therefore considers the whole word *or* its parts but not the relationship between them. Children are also handicapped when they center on only one form of a letter or word. A child who recognizes "A" but not "a" will have difficulty learning letters and words. As children have many experiences with both written and concrete forms of words and letters they gain a clearer understanding of the forms letters and words can take. The experience story probably best helps children understand the part-whole relationship between letters and words and between words and sentences.

TOPOLOGY. When children continue to make reversals and inversions in letters and words and cannot remember the difference between words such as "dog" and "boy" and "boat" and "goat," it may be because they still view the world from a topological perspective. Teachers should examine children's drawings to help them understand the children's spatial orientation. Piagetian tasks using closed and open figures are also helpful in determining a child's understanding of topological and Euclidean relationships (Copeland, 1979, pp. 285–290).

A name card for each child may be kept in the writing center. Children can consult the card whenever they want to write their names or the names of other children. They have a model to copy and their attention focuses on the correct way to form the letters and vowels. Children may trace letters on paper. This is permissible because a letter always has the same form. Stencils of objects and people should be avoided since they give a stereotyped way to represent forms in artwork.

scheduling

There will be occasions when teachers will want to work with specific children during learning-center time. Jenny and Susie recognized their names when written but did not know the names of the letters. The teacher made a lotto game using only the letters in the children's names. She asked them to play the game in the language arts center before moving to other centers. In this way the teacher used a game to teach letter names, avoiding unnecessary drill and possible frustration.

The best time to schedule small-group activities is during learning-center time. The same type of activity may continue for several days, until all the children have had an opportunity to participate. A filmstrip, for example, may be shown over a period of 5 to 10 days. Children can enter and reenter the center as often as they like. The teacher or aide discusses the film periodically with the children in the center.

grouping

Children group themselves naturally in language arts just as they do in other content areas. Small groups are formed depending on children's interests and abilities. A teacher surveying the preschool room might find the following activities happening simultaneously: children placing a label on a block construction, copying from name cards in the writing center, dramatizing a story in the dramatic-play center, looking at books in the library center, dictating an experience story in the art center, looking for pictures of an insect in the science center, and listening to a taped story in the language arts center.

During the year a few children may show signs that they are ready for a systematized approach to reading. The language experience approach to teaching reading through the children's own language written down is recommended for young children. Although this approach requires individual instruction, teachers will sometimes want to work with small groups. Three kindergarten children had sight vocabularies of 50 to 60 words. The teacher noticed that these children were particularly interested in the class guinea pig. She talked with the children about the guinea pig and then asked them if they would like to write an experience story about their pet. The children dictated what they wanted to say. After the story was recorded the children looked for words they all knew, such as "black," "white," "guinea pig," "the," and "name." Word cards were made for words the children did not know, such as "lettuce," "Abyssinian," and "nocturnal." Similar small-group activities continued throughout the year.

first day of school

The library center should contain a few well-selected books. Good selections are stories about children, school, animals, counting, the ABCs, poems, and nursery rhymes. This center can be made inviting by including large, brightly colored pillows, a plant, a flannel board with familiar figures (Three Bears, Three Little Pigs, nursery rhyme characters), hand puppets, and/or a few large and colorful pictures (children looking at books, nursery rhymes, familiar stories). The books must be within easy reach, with the front covers in full view. A few books should be opened on a table and/or pillow to suggest, "Sit down with a book."

The language arts center may be a part of the library center or an adjacent center divided by a partition from the library center. Since most preschool classrooms have only an aide and a teacher on the first day of school, it is best to introduce mechanical equipment at a later date. If a language master is available, cards can be made ahead of time (possibly pictures of children in school, with appropriate recordings, such as "We paint at school," "We eat a snack at school," "We play outside.") and played by the children with the help of the teacher or aide. Children should be introduced gradually to any type of equipment with mechanical parts, such as a typewriter, language master, tape recorder, or listening center.

The writing center should be set up when children show an interest in writing their names and copying words. Unlined paper, an assortment of large and small pencils, and wooden letters invite children to name, trace, or write letters and words.

language arts through the year

Children's ability to communicate effectively, listen attentively, write, and recognize letters and words varies considerably from child to child. For some children progress means the ability to talk in complete sentences and name a few letters; for others it means gaining a sight vocabulary, learning initial consonant sounds, and copying experience stories.

When children begin to recognize and copy words in experience stories, they are beginning to read. There are different ways to approach experience reading. One way is to ask a child to choose a word from an experience story that he or she would like to learn. The teacher writes the word as the child watches. The next day the child is shown the word. If he or she does not know the word it is written again and put away until the next day. If the child recognizes the word it is placed in his or her word box. In either case another story is dictated and the child again chooses a word to learn. When there are 50 sight words in the word box the child is encouraged to use them in combination with other words.

Experience stories can be dictated in a separated area of the room called a reading center, or when space is limited, the writing or language arts center may be used. A few children may be able to read books on the library shelf. The teacher can check children's comprehension by asking questions about the stories.

When children who are already reading come to school they should be given an informal test to determine their instructional level. Teachers can work with first-grade teachers and/or a reading specialist to provide reading experiences for these children. It shoud be stressed that children who enter kindergarten or nursery school already reading are in the minority. A teacher may have no children reading at the beginning of the school year or at the end of the year. It is not, and should not be, the purpose of the preschool teacher to teach all children to read. The best preparation children can have for success in first grade is a program that meets their present developmental needs.

meeting goals

The evaluation scheme in chapter 1 may be applied to the language arts. A checklist based upon the behavioral objectives should be kept for each child. The methods suggested for collecting data are applicable to the language arts.

Samples of children's work should be kept on a regular basis. The area of language arts includes materials such as experience stories dictated by the children, stories, labels, sentences and/or names written by the children, and taped conversations with children.

The teacher should be cognizant of children's performances on the Piagetian tasks that have a direct relationship to reading. These are class inclusion; seriation; conservation of number, amount, and length; and topological relationships. Directions for giving the first five tasks may be found in *Cognitive Tasks: An Approach for Early Childhood Education* (Osborn and Osborn, 1974) and for topological relationships in *How Children Learn Mathematics* (Copeland, 1979, pp. 285–290).

8
children are both dependent and independent

discipline

Preschool children are an interesting blend of dependence and independence. They may dress themselves but ask for assistance in zipping their coats; ask for a toy but, when refused, demand, "Make him give it to me"; insist that "I can do it" and then say, "Help me. It's too hard." These contradictions in children are a normal part of growing up. They show both their desire to do things for themselves and their need for understanding and support.

Much has been written and said about classroom discipline, or "child guidance" as it is often called. Discipline in the nursery school and kindergarten is easier to understand when viewed as a child's struggle for autonomy. Discipline should be carefully planned and carried out in ways that allow children to grow in autonomy.

Effective discipline is dependent upon setting realistic limitations. It is when restrictions are placed in all areas of school life that children become dependent. Excessive strictness limits the possibilities for independent thought and action, thus leading to feelings of helplessness, guilt, and dependence. What children need is neither demands for conformity nor freedom to do as they please, but careful guidance and understanding. Cohen and Rudolph (1977) state:

Good discipline, as we see it, incorporates affectionate acceptance and understanding of children at their stage of development; respect for individual and group needs; order and sufficient supervision so all can feel safe; and a satisfying range of interesting things to do without unduly repressing individuals. (pp. 372–373)

In the 1920s and 1930s a strict authoritarian approach to child discipline was in vogue. It gave way to the Freudian and Dr. Spock "free expression" point of view in the 1940s, 1950s, and 1960s. Children reared under the strict

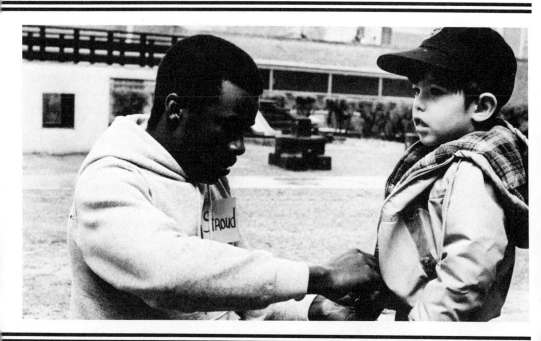

authoritarian point of view conformed to parental and teacher demands often out of a fear of punishment rather than an understanding of the situation. The free expression point of view, although never clearly defined, gave way to the practice of sheer indulgence. In a dilemma, parents and teachers were afraid of damaging children's psyches and often allowed the children to do as they pleased, with few or no restrictions. This pattern of adult behavior was probably more harmful than the strict authoritarian approach since children were not made aware of the realistic limitations to which they must later conform.

In *Discipline and Classroom Management,* Osborn and Osborn (1977) discuss three modes of child discipline. The first describes children surrounded by a wall of "no"s. No matter in which direction they proceed they cannot break down the wall: the adults in their world make the decisions for them and the children learn, "We cannot succeed. We cannot do anything right, so we must be bad." In the second mode children are allowed to move freely in any direction, for there are no walls and there are no "no"s. Children are free to do what they please, but they do not know in which direction to move since any avenue is acceptable. In this kind of environment children become frustrated, insecure, and sometimes hostile. In the last mode children are described as surrounded by low walls with doors that can be opened to go in and out. This environment is called "freedom with control." Children are aware of the limitations that are set for them but are free to make choices within the avenues open to them (pp. 24–31).

The authors caution teachers that the freedom-with-control mode is not sufficient without a warm, caring, and understanding teacher (pp. 32–34). In their research they have found that teachers may appear to be permissive when in reality they assume a do-nothing or uninterested attitude. As a result children are uncertain about what is expected of them and may feel the teacher is uncaring and indifferent. On the other hand, the Osborns have observed teachers in moderately strict classrooms where children are independent and do achieve autonomy. These children had caring and understanding teachers. It seems that children are flexible and can grow in autonomy within a moderately wide range of controls as long as there is love and understanding. Osborn and Osborn (1977) state, "the key question is not one of control, rather it is one of love and understanding" (p. 35). Teachers should ask themselves, "Is my discipline viewed by the child in an atmosphere of love, warmth, and caring, or does the child view my control as the action of a hostile, indifferent adult?" (p. 34).

All teachers have problems with child guidance or discipline at one time or another. Yet some teachers have less trouble than others, perhaps because their approaches to child guidance are based "upon knowledge of child development, learning theories and sound pedagogy" (Hipple, 1978, p. 183). Those approaches that are grounded upon sound basic assumptions are as follows:

1. The development of internal control (self-discipline) is more productive than reliance upon extrinsic control.
2. It is preferable to find out the causes of or purposes for undesirable behavior.
3. Knowledge of several guidance approaches or strategies is more effective than a reliance on one strategy.
4. Positive reinforcement is more effective than negative reinforcement (p. 184).

In this chapter these assumptions will be discussed under the headings Self-discipline, Purposes of Behavior, Guidance Techniques, and Positive Reinforcement.

self-discipline

the teacher

A warm, supportive, and responsive teacher is a source of comfort to children. They need someone to count on and to trust in when the going gets tough. When children trust teachers they develop a dependence that is beneficial, helpful, and, if handled skillfully, temporary. "As the children experience the fact that they can depend on you, and as their self-confidence becomes stable, it sometimes seems that it is their very dependence on you that forms the basis for a new, almost surprising air of independence" (McCarthy and Houston, 1980, p. 164). This change from dependence to independence occurs as teachers encourage children's steps away from them by rewarding independent behavior.

It is sometimes difficult for teachers to reward independent behavior because of their own hang-ups. They are afraid to relinquish authority because of their own experiences with a boss-type authority, their fear of losing control of children, or their concern about appearing to be too permissive and tolerant.

Teachers must face these feelings and ask, "What is best for the children?" They must act with confidence when they impose limits—if these limits meet children's needs and not their own (Read, 1976, pp. 325–326).

Osborn and Osborn (1977) suggest that teachers ask themselves, "Why am I teaching anyway?" They may discover unacceptable reasons, such as need to have power over others, inability to work with adults, or desire to satisfy their egos through children's triumphs (p. 3). Other questions teachers should ask are: "What do children do that upsets me?" "Is my classroom behavior influenced by my own childhood experiences?" "Am I tired or upset?" (pp. 3–4.) Answers to these questions may provide insight into discipline problems.

the environment

In order to develop inner control children should feel safe to explore their physical and social environments. Teachers must create an emotional climate that says: "You are safe here. I may not always like what you do but I will always like you." "It's alright to make mistakes. Everyone does." "I will not expect too much of you, and you can trust me." (Swanson and Jenkins, 1969, pp. 4–6.) It is only in this kind of safe, supportive environment that children feel the freedom to risk themselves and do things on their own.

Carefully planned learning situations are safeguards against discipline problems. When children encounter activities that are too difficult or too easy for them they become either frustrated or bored. Dissatisfaction with learning experiences often results in undesirable, disruptive behavior (Howell and Howell, 1979, p. 83). Teachers must be concerned with what is sometimes referred to as the "problem of the match." How well does an activity fit a child's particular developmental needs? A closer match between a child and an activity assures a higher degree of absorption in learning. A child who is involved with learning is less likely to become a behavior problem. It is the teacher who determines the kinds of activities and the variety and amount of available materials. Hess and Croft (1975) say, "By such means, perhaps unintentionally, teachers regulate the arrangement of stimuli and opportunities, and so control behavior in their classrooms" (p. 279).

purposes of behavior

When discipline problems do occur teachers who understand the purposes of behavior have a better chance of changing it. Teachers can sometimes, through a concentrated study of a child's behavior, determine not only the purposes of the behavior but also the underlying causes. The reasons for behavior are complex, however, and may not be discovered by teachers. In such cases teachers must recognize their limitations and seek professional help (Osborn and Osborn, 1977, pp. 20–23). This chapter deals with the four goals of misbehavior (that may interfere with the rights and welfare of others) suggested by Baruth and Eckstein (1978). These goals are attention, power, revenge, and inadequacy.

attention

Children who are misbehaving to get attention believe they are important only when people are involved with them. It is natural to want some attention; however, it becomes a mistaken goal when the child demands attention at inappropriate times (Baruth and Eckstein, 1978, p. 44).

power

Children who misbehave to demonstrate power usually feel important "when being the boss or when maneuvering and manipulating to get one's own way" (Baruth and Eckstein, 1978, p. 44).

revenge

Children who are vengeful usually feel hurt and want to hurt others. These children often feel life is punishing them and in turn seek to punish others (Baruth and Eckstein, 1978, p. 46).

inadequacy

Children who feel inadequate often feel they cannot do anything right. They are victims of repeated failures, pampering, or having things done for them (Baruth and Eckstein, 1978, p. 46).

Before teachers attempt to determine the purposes of behavior they should ask themselves, "Is the child physically sound?" Children who are not physically healthy may exhibit all types of behavior, from biting (due to painful teeth and gums) to falling asleep (due to malnutrition). Only when physical causes are ruled out can the teacher proceed with appropriate guidance techniques (Osborn and Osborn, 1977, pp. 8–10).

guidance techniques

Since the goals of misbehavior differ, no single guidance technique will be effective with all children. Teachers must first determine the purpose of the behavior and then use those techniques that seem appropriate in a given situation.

attention

Children who are attention getters usually feel secure and important only when they have the teacher's and/or peers' undivided attention. They may be children who receive too much or too little attention outside the school environment.

One way to cope with attention getters is to convince them that they are important to their teacher. Children must believe that teachers like them, are interested in their welfare, accept their shortcomings, and will treat them fairly (Swanson and Jenkins, 1969, pp. 3–6).

Children are not fooled by teachers who pretend to like them but in reality are judgmental and unaccepting. Children intuitively sense teachers' authenticity. The old adage, "It is not what one says and does, but how one says and does it," manifests itself in teacher-child relationships. If a teacher frowns and says, "I'm glad to see you today," it is the frown that will be noticed rather than the positive comment (Wallen and Wallen, 1978, pp. 270–282). When children receive contradictory messages they tend to disregard positive information and assume the worst.

When children have confidence in teachers a willingness to cooperate prevails. Read (1976) states:

Because relationships are so important, we will want to consider the effect of what we do as we work with children on the friendliness and confidence it builds between us and them. Good relationships make the acceptance of authority easy—and a lack of good relationships makes it difficult. (p. 333)

When children have adequate teacher attention their inappropriate demands for it often cease. There are children, however, whose appetite increases with more teacher attention. When this is the case it is often best to ignore attention-getting behavior and acknowledge only behaviors teachers want to maintain. When this technique is used children should realize that when they want attention, they will get it—for socially acceptable behavior.

Another way of dealing with the attention getter is to give him or her two options. One option should be related to the inappropriate behavior. A teacher may give a child a choice of sitting on a chair outside the group until the child decides he or she can return without interrupting or listening to a story quietly from the outset. When this technique is used the decision is up to the child, who does not thereby lose face with the teacher or other children (Baruth and Eckstein, 1978, p. 44).

power

Children who misbehave to obtain power usually feel important only when they are boss. The important thing for teachers to do is to avoid getting into a power struggle with these children (Baruth and Eckstein, 1978, pp. 44–45).

An effective technique for dealing with power getters is, as in the case of attention getters, to offer children a realistic choice, for example, "Would you like to eat with us at the table without throwing food or would you prefer to eat alone at another table?" Children make the choice, and if they choose to continue with inappropriate behavior, suffer the consequences. A confrontation between children and teachers thus can be avoided.

Teachers should avoid requests that open the door for a power struggle. Instead of saying, "I want you to . . ." or "You must . . .," say "Let's go . . ." or "It's time to. . . ." It is never wise to give commands or imply that children must do something because the teacher wishes it (Baruth and Eckstein, 1978, p. 45).

It is sometimes necessary to stop children from continuing their present behavior. When their actions are dangerous to themselves and others restraint may be the only workable approach. Verbal restraint may be all that is necessary. Statements such as "I can't let you hurt anyone" and "I can't let anyone hurt you" are realistic and reassuring to children. Physical restraint is used only when absolutely necessary. It should never be done in a punitive or aggressive manner. Hitting, shaking, grabbing, or pushing children is never acceptable teacher behavior. Instead children should be held calmly but firmly, sometimes with the teacher's arms around the top part of the child's body (Hipple, 1978, p. 187).

Taking "time out" or removing children to a quiet place should be seen not as punishment but rather as a means of giving the children a chance to reestablish control over their behavior. The "quiet place" should be a room apart from the classroom (or if a separate room is unavailable, an isolated part of the classroom), but a place from which children can be seen and can see the class. The quiet place needs only a table, chair, and a few playthings. The children should decide when they are ready to leave it and rejoin the group. A given length of time may be set using an egg timer or a 60-minute timer. At the end of this short period of time the children can be asked if they are ready to return to the class. If they say no, the procedure may be repeated until the children are ready (Gallagher, 1973, pp. 6–7).

In any discipline situation teachers must mean what they say. Inconsistency of response makes children insecure, and they may double their efforts to test their limits. One way to avoid conflicts is to make only those rules that are absolutely necessary and consistently maintain them. Occasionally a rule may be changed for the welfare of the group, but this should not be a common practice. Howell and Howell (1979) state, "If a rule is important enough to classroom functioning to make in the first place, then it is important enough to enforce consistently" (p. 29).

As children become more mature they begin to think of rules "being made *for* the group and *by* the group, with punishment having as its goal the restoration of group unity" (Artmann, 1979, p. 33). Therefore it is important that older preschool children have a part in making rules for the class. When rules come from children and not entirely from teachers they are more likely to be internalized. Particularly for power seekers, personalized rules are easier to follow since they belong to the children (Curwin and Mendler, 1980, pp. 25–26).

revenge

Vengeful children usually feel hurt and as a consequence want to hurt others. Teachers should avoid punishing vengeful children for misbehavior since this will make them want to hurt others more. These children often come from homes where they have been physically and/or emotionally abused. Some children withdraw in that situation whereas others become aggressive and hostile. When constraint is necessary teachers should remain firm but friendly (Baruth and Eckstein, 1978, p. 46).

Vengeful children need emotional support and a feeling that their teachers understand them. One method of dealing with inappropriate behavior is to give a child an I-message. An I-message has three parts: teachers' nonjudgmental description of a problem, its effects upon them, and their feelings about the behavior. This intimate form of communication lets the child know how teachers feel, in order to help the child interpret the effects of his or her behavior

(Hipple, 1978, p. 185). This technique is based upon the belief that children often are not aware of the effect their behavior has on others.

Another related technique is to encourage children to reflect upon their feelings. This strategy is used to convey empathy to children. The teacher may use statements such as: "I know how you feel. You can talk to me about it" "It's OK to feel the way you do." "I like you, but I don't always like what you do." "Let's talk about what else you can do when you feel like hitting." Osborn and Osborn (1977) caution teachers, however, that reflective techniques may contribute to a disturbance rather than have a calming effect, therefore teachers must choose situations in which these techniques are most appropriate (p. 64).

inadequacy

All student misbehavior is not due to hostile intent or the desire to disrupt the teacher in class. Often it may be covering up feelings of inadequacy (Howell and Howell, 1979, pp. 84–85). Inadequate children usually feel they cannot do anything right (Baruth and Eckstein, 1978, p. 46). They need *encouragement* to do something. A distinction should be made between encouragement and praise. Praise is given after a task is completed, and encouragement before and during a task. Praise focuses on the self and may lead children to always expect to be rewarded for their efforts or to feel let down when they complete a task and are not rewarded for it. On the other hand, encouragement helps children focus on their inner strength and ability to cope. Children who feel inadequate need encouragement to begin and complete tasks. When they finish tasks satisfactorily a feeling of confidence emerges (Baruth and Eckstein, 1978, pp. 80–83).

positive reinforcement

Despite materials printed on the ways humanism and behaviorism differ, teachers should not cling to either extreme as the sole means of changing behavior. Howell and Howell (1979) state:

Although the distinction between behaviorism as training and humanism as education has been made, we do not feel that they are mutually exclusive. Behavioral techniques can possibly improve the humanistic program; and the behavioristic teacher cannot be truly successful if unresponsive or insensitive to the needs of students. (p. 82)

Reinforcement is a powerful tool that cannot be ignored. Often undesirable behavior is unknowingly reinforced by teachers who do not understand reinforcement. Reinforcement can be positive (a reward) or negative (a punishment). Whenever a response is positively reinforced there is greater likelihood that it will not occur again.

The three types of positive reinforcement are token (food, star, toy), activity (experience that is enjoyed), and social (smiles, praise). Negative reinforcement may take the form of ignoring, "time out," scolding, nagging, taking away a privilege or possession, and physical punishment.

Research has shown that in most cases positive reinforcement is more effective than negative reinforcement. Osborn and Osborn (1977) recommend the use of social and activity types of reinforcement rather than token reinforcement (p. 58). They suggest the following ways in which teachers can successfully use positive reinforcement:

1. Observe children carefully. Establish baseline data (frequency and circumstances under which behaviors occur).
2. Decide on the behavior to be changed and set up attainable goals (those children can realistically reach).
3. Reward the behaviors you wish to maintain. Use social or activity reinforcers.
4. Ignore the behaviors you wish to discourage.
5. Reinforce incompatible behaviors. Reward the behavior that is opposite from the undesired behavior, such as rewarding walking in order to stop running.
6. Recognize that some negative reinforcement may be positive; for example, repeatedly telling a child to stop throwing blocks may gain the attention desired and in turn increase block throwing.
7. Reinforce desired behavior immediately.
8. Require an undesired activity first in anticipation of a more desired activity.
9. Initially reinforce behavior continuously.
10. Reinforce behavior consistently.
11. Reobserve the child and evaluate goals. Determine whether or not the teaching strategies used are effective (pp. 40–54).

Teachers must remember that the ultimate goal of control by external forces is control from within. Reinforcement techniques are useful only to the extent that they lead to self-direction.

working with parents

Until approximately 15 years ago administrators and teachers held the commonly accepted view that the role of parents in public education was to drop their children at the school door in the morning and pick them up at the end of the day. In the mid-1960s federally sponsored compensatory education programs such as Head Start and Follow Through caused educators to look at the nature of learning and development in a new light. In most cases they became convinced that the home was an important influence on the child's total development. Parent education and parent involvement became a vital part of early childhood education. Three factors brought about a rapid change in attitude from "parents stay out" to "parents get involved." First, the large body of research revealed a positive link between parent-child relations and children's learning styles, attitudes toward school, and general cognitive development. Second, researchers found that compensatory programs with parent-involvement components have a more than temporary desirable effect on children. Third, there was an upsurge in direct political pressure for community involvement in education. These factors, combined with a series of innovative experiments in parent education, helped educators realize the benefits of parent involvement (Evans, 1975, pp. 338–340).

Forms of parental involvement vary considerably from school to school and are dependent upon the age of the children and the type of program. They vary from maximal involvement of parents as decision makers in determining curriculum to minimal involvement of parents in periodic observations and parent conferences.

Regardless of the type of program and the goals of a parent-education program, certain strategies are useful. These are discussed in this chapter under the headings Home Visits, Parent Meetings, Parent Participation, and Parent Conferences.

home visits

Home visits should have as their primary objective meeting with and relating to parents. Parents often are most at ease in the home, and teachers can see how the family lives (Leeper et al., 1979, p. 471). During home visits teachers must remember that families may be sensitive to their expressions or nonexpressions of emotion. Teachers must not show negative reactions to a family's value system, the ways in which their needs are met, the independence of the family members, or the cultural influence upon them (Broman, 1978, p. 422). Unfortunately, in a few cases teachers will not be welcome in a child's home and home visits may not occur.

parent meetings

To establish rapport with parents teachers must get to know them from the beginning of the school year. Sometimes an informal meeting at an open house breaks the ice. At this time teachers can convey their goals for the year, the purposes of equipment and materials, and the nature of school adjustment (Cohen and Rudolph, 1977, p. 403).

Throughout the year parent meetings should be informal and informative. Topics should focus on parent concerns about children. Parents can help plan and actually participate in the meetings. The most successful meetings are those in which children have a part. Wenig and Brown (1975) describe two night meetings planned by children especially for parents. One was a "Mothers' Tea" and the other a "Dads' Night." At these events children not only prepared and served refreshments, but also showed their parents around the room and played games with them. The outstanding value of this kind of meeting is that it shows the parents what children are doing at school (pp. 375–376).

parent participation

Parents may visit the school to observe their children or to become involved actively in the school program. Special talents and resources are found among parents of all social and economic levels. Teachers may need to seek out parents who play a musical instrument, are skilled at carpentry, raise their own vegetables, or are involved in other interesting activities (Hess and Croft, 1975, p. 100).

It is difficult for parents to observe since the activities of the classroom invite participation. They should make an effort occasionally to remain in an observational role, however. They will see their children in a new light as they watch their interaction with other children. Perhaps for the first time they will have the opportunity to compare their child's development with that of others. If problems arise they can talk with teachers about them. They can realize that the problems of their children are not unlike those of many other children (McCarthy and Houston, 1980, pp. 306–309).

parent conferences

Parent conferences represent one of the most effective ways to unite parents and teachers in a desirable partnership. If they are to be successful teachers must prepare carefully. McCarthy and Houston (1980) give the following suggestions for effective preparation:

1. Go through the child's school file.
2. Go through your own file on each child (notes or significant events in the child's school career).
3. Take notes on the child to refer to during the conference.
4. Begin the conference by thanking the parent(s) for coming and reaffirm your desire to work with them as partners.
5. Listen to what parents have to say about their children and family problems.
6. Suggest school services if needed.
7. Be sympathetic and supportive to family problems.
8. Discuss the child on a positive note.
9. Refer to difficulties as areas of development to focus upon.
10. Ask parents' advice about how to handle a particular problem.
11. End the conference on a positive note (pp. 309–312).

There should be several planned conferences held during the year, each one building upon the points raised by the previous conference. Parents and teachers must agree upon courses of action to be taken. A record should be made after each conference and placed in the child's folder. Suggestions for recording individual parent conferences may be found in *The Early Years in Childhood Education* (Broman, 1978, pp. 426–427).

teacher's role in discipline

self-discipline, the teacher, and the environment

A perceptive person walking into a classroom can almost immediately sense the emotional climate of the room. In one classroom a teacher, on the false assump-

We can share this book with our teacher.

tion of creating independence, allowed children to make most of the decisions. One day there was a goat on the playground which had been borrowed, at the children's request, from the local nature museum. No plans had been made to feed or house the goat. It began to rain, and the goat had no shelter. He stood in the rain all day while the children watched. Two days later he was taken back to the museum. What had the children learned from this experience? Certainly they had not learned responsibility or compassion for animals. As the year progressed the decisions placed upon the children became too much for them. They became loud, aggressive, disrespectful, bored, and indecisive. As one child put it, "We can do anything we want to do. But what do we do next?" As long as the children continued to make the decisions the teacher was confident she had a good program. After all, wasn't it child-centered?

There are teachers who always know what is best for children. They make most of the decisions and tell children what to do. One teacher repeatedly said: "Now be quiet for Ms. Y. She likes it when you are quiet." and "Who's talking now? That's right; it's Ms. Y.'s time to talk. You can talk later." These children eventually became obedient robots. They were unable to become involved in activities without saying: "Is it alright, Ms. Y.?" "Do you like my picture?" "Was I good today?" Many of the children lost confidence in themselves; a few tuned out school completely. The following year, in a new situation one of the children who had been turned off by Ms. Y. said to his mother, "Well, I finally got a good teacher."

In a child-centered classroom teachers value the uniqueness of each child. They firmly believe that children go through developmental stages at their own rate. With the teacher's guidance children select activities best suited to their needs. They meet with success because the activities are challenging but not too difficult to master. Sometimes children are capable of tasks they have avoided because they lacked the confidence to try them. One four-year-old boy refused to pick up blocks because he felt "tired." The teacher knew the child was afraid of failure. She said, "It takes strong arms to lift blocks. You have strong arms. Please put the blocks on the shelf." He lifted the blocks and said with surprise, "I *am* strong."

Sometimes children are not challenged. Four boys, ages six to six and one-half, spent the greater part of their time in dramatic block play, sometimes throwing blocks and knocking down other children's buildings. Two of the boys read at second-grade level, and the other two read approximately 50 sight words. In order to interest them in reading experiences the teacher made a Mickey Mouse tape and invited the boys to listen to it. At first they listened reluctantly, but when the voice of Mickey Mouse asked them to write a story about him, they became interested. Each boy was able to write his own story or dictate one to his teacher. They were delighted when she suggested sending their stories to Mickey Mouse and were overjoyed when they received an auto-graphed picture from Mickey.

Nothing succeeds like success, and in a child-centered environment each child has the opportunity to succeed. Therefore children have the opportunity to develop positive feelings about themselves.

purposes of behavior and teaching strategies

ATTENTION GETTERS.   It is desirable and natural for children to want a certain amount of attention. It is inappropriate, however to demand attention by inter-rupting the class and/or disturbing other children. It is the teachers' responsibility to stop disruptive behavior and at the same time teach children acceptable ways to get attention.

Frequently the attention getter is the class clown, who spends most of his or her time putting on a show for the class. Henry was an attention getter who by the third week of school had become the center of attention. He constantly interrupted group activities with his antics. He would turn around, make a face, and then fall on the floor in a fit of laughter. This feat was accompanied by gales of laughter from the other children. During learning-center time he continued to disrupt by engaging children in play activities that disintegrated into comic antics accompanied by colorful language.

Ignoring Henry's behavior was ineffective since the entire class reinforced it through their laughter. "Time out" was useless since Henry considered it a treat to be removed from the group. He would say, "Boy, oh boy! I get to leave!"

The teacher had tried every strategy she knew to change Henry's behavior. Finally she asked the school psychologist to observe. After several observations he decided it was the children who were reinforcing Henry's behavior. He also suspected that his behavior was being reinforced at home. During a three-way parent conference they learned that Henry, the youngest child, was the family pet. His comic behavior was encouraged at home. His parents and siblings thought he was cute, clever, and funny. His father said, "We love to laugh at him. He's so clever." These were intelligent, well-meaning parents who did not realize that they were fostering undesirable behavior in their child.

After several sessions with the psychologist and a talk with the older siblings, the family's reactions to Henry changed. They no longer laughed at him when he was cute, but told him he was too old for this kind of behavior. They reinforced more mature behavior when it occurred. Gradually Henry's behavior changed at school. When begged by the children to "be funny" Henry resisted and sought praise in more desirable ways.

Jane was a child who wanted all the teacher's attention. She followed her teacher wherever she went, held her hand, and sat on her lap. Her behavior puzzled the teacher because Jane liked other children and sometimes played with them. She was talented in art and enjoyed using art media. She often said to the teacher, "I like you. I want to go home with you." Although Jane was apparently insecure the teacher felt her problem was deeper than an exaggerated attachment for her. She suggested that instead of sitting on her lap Jane sit beside her. Later she told Jane to sit with the other children and she would sit nearby. Jane stopped clinging to the teacher but still demanded a great deal of attention. She interrupted other children and asked for help when unnecessary. The teacher gradually withdrew her support. Instead of demanding less attention Jane demanded more through inappropriate behavior.

Parent conferences revealed little insight into the problem. One day Jane cried, climbed in the teacher's lap, and said, "I feel awful inside. I took $10 from my mother's pocketbook. Will I go to jail?" The teacher asked her when it had happened and she said, "Yesterday, but I take money whenever I find it." She knew then that Jane had a deep-seated emotional problem. She assured Jane that she would not go to jail and that she would talk with her parents about what had happened.

It was several months before the parents were convinced that Jane had a serious problem. Although the psychologist and teacher were never sure what caused Jane's behavior, they suspected it was that her older sister received most of the attention at home. They felt Jane received little or no parental love and guidance.

Joan was a different kind of child. She was independent of the teacher but tried to get the children's attention in any way she could. One day she cut her dress, which brought forth "Look what Joan did." Joan's play resembled that of a two-year-old. She repeated the same motions over and over. She put magnets in a box, emptied it, then refilled it. In the homemaking center she dressed and undressed the dolls. The teacher began to suspect brain damage, and further testing revealed that Joan had a progressive brain disease. She was placed in a special education class and later in a special school.

Ricky and Billy were children who read at an early age. They became fast friends and at the same time behavior problems. They got attention by monopolizing group discussions and generally knew the solution to any classroom problem. The others resented them and sometimes said, "Ricky and Billy think they know everything." During a field trip to a store Billy talked a great deal and answered questions before the other children had a chance. The manager said, "I know you're smart. You answer so many questions." When Ricky heard this he turned to his teacher and said, "I think I'm as smart as Billy, don't you?" She said, "You both know how to do many things and so do the other children." This conversation convinced her that the boys were not being challenged at school. She asked them what they would like to read about, and they agreed on space. They helped set up a learning center that all the children could use. Each day the teacher made task cards that the boys could work and put into their folders. They were learning a great deal and were respected by the other children for the information they could share.

Children seek attention for different reasons. Billy and Ricky were gifted children who were bored with school and relieved their boredom by annoying other children. Joan suffered from mental retardation and compensated by showing off. Jane had a deep-seated emotional problem and as a result, clung to the teacher and demanded her attention. Henry was a perfectly normal child who had learned how to get the attention of the class by acting silly. The symptoms were the same, but the causes of behaviors were varied and required different teaching strategies.

POWER.   There are children who feel important and secure only when they are boss. Teachers must try to avoid a power struggle with these children, who may feel helpless while teachers feel beaten and frustrated.

John was a child who had to be boss and first in everything. He was the tallest and heaviest child in the class. His size and his behavior made him formidable to most children. In an argument he did not hesitate to hit or push. He

Taking turns and sharing toys.

constantly insisted on having his way by saying things like: "I want to be leader." "Why can't I have the tricycle first?" "Give me that puzzle." "Get out of my way so I can climb on the jungle gym." Unfortunately children gave in to John. Whenever the teacher saw this about to happen she intervened and gave him a chance to choose another activity she felt he would like. This type of intervention avoided conflicts and gave other children freedom to continue their activities, but it did not change John's behavior. The fact that the teacher gave him a choice of doing something he enjoyed only reinforced his ability to get his way. The teacher tried other techniques to change John's behavior. She began by giving him the opportunity to choose from two activities each day; later she allowed him to choose from three. Although John knew he would be able to do some things he wanted to do, his behavior did not change. He continued to make demands and whine when he didn't get his way.

"Time out" was used when his behavior became aggressive and harmful to the other children. Removal from the group situation had little effect since he saw it as a means of controlling the teacher.

A parent conference indicated that John's parents were concerned about his behavior but blamed it on a prior nursery school experience. They described John as the youngest and smallest child in a multiage group and insisted that he was "getting back" for the times he had been pushed around by older children. Further conferences revealed that the parents and a teenage sister gave in to his every whim with the explanation, "It really doesn't matter to us. He's been made to feel so inferior."

The same parental attitude prevailed throughout the year. Although John hit less he still demanded his way. The teacher felt that with the cooperation of the parents, John could have been helped. Unfortunately his attitude continued throughout the elementary school years. Without parental cooperation teachers can help change behavior somewhat but are not as successful as they can be when home and school work together.

Harvey was a consistently aggressive child. He hit and/or verbally attacked children and adults without provocation. He would use a toy as a weapon and strike out at any child near him. At these times the teacher would restrain him until he had control of himself.

Since he showed little interest in school activities, offering him acceptable alternatives to his inappropriate behavior was not effective. The safety of other children became a crucial factor in determining whether or not Harvey could remain in a regular classroom. The teacher asked the resource-room teacher to observe Harvey and decided to ask a graduate student from a nearby university to work with him in the classroom and resource room. Harvey was allowed to remain in the classroom with the understanding that he could not hurt anyone. Frequently he still had to be removed to prevent injury to another child.

Conferences with the parents, the classroom teacher, and the resource teacher revealed that the parents considered the problem to be school-related. They said that Harvey's behavior had been fine in the nursery school he had attended the previous year. Further questioning revealed that Harvey was seldom in the classroom. He had been allowed to roam the building and grounds at will. The nursery school teacher could not cope with him in the classroom but unfortunately had never told the parents.

Further conferences revealed that the parents left most of the family decisions up to Harvey. They felt they had given him a child-centered home, which indeed they had. Unfortunately they had also given him responsibilities with which no child his age could cope. He felt he had to control the school situation too. When he could not he struck out at everyone.

Harvey improved somewhat during the year as outside controls were placed on him at school and more responsibility was taken from him at home. It would be a long time, however, before he would become an emotionally stable child.

Ann was an attractive, petite, bright five-year-old. She enjoyed other children and played well with them as long as she had her own way. Whenever she was thwarted she hit or kicked. On the third day of school she kicked five children in the stomach within a three-hour period. Alarmed, the teacher asked the parents to come in for a conference.

During the parent conference she learned that Ann had been striking out at other children since she was three. Her behavior had not changed during two years of nursery school experience. Her parents were desperate and agreed to try anything the teacher might suggest. She asked them what they did at home when Ann hurt other children. She learned that sending Ann to her room was effective for short periods of time. Since Ann disliked being separated from other children they decided that "time out" at home and school might be the best way to change her behavior.

The next day the teacher told Ann that when she hit without provocation she would have to take "time out." She listened carefully and said, "I know it. My mother told me. I won't hit unless someone hits me." The teacher felt Ann understood why she could not hit. She explained that a teacher had a responsibility to all children. She wouldn't let them hurt Ann and she couldn't let her hurt them.

During the next five weeks Ann was asked to take "time out" twice, sitting on a chair in the doorway, where she could see and be seen. She disliked being removed from the group, and the teacher saw Ann hit her hand several times saying, "Don't hit." Ann needed external controls before she was able to control her own behavior. Within two months her behavior changed, and "time out" was seldom used for the remainder of the year.

Ginny controlled other children by whining and crying. This behavior was reinforced by her mother, who comforted her saying, "What's wrong with my poor little girl? Tell me what happened to make you cry!" This family had lost a six-year-old child from a rare illness when Ginny was three years old. The shock to the parents, grandparents, and two younger children had been great.

At the first parent conference Ginny's mother said, "When Cathy died I made Ginny my baby to take her place. They reminded me of each other." Ginny's mother was a well-educated intelligent person who had worked with young children. She quickly saw that she was reinforcing Ginny's immature behavior and discussed the problem with her husband and her parents, who she felt were also reinforcing Ginny's behavior. They decided to ignore crying and whining and to reinforce acceptable behavior. With the cooperation of the grandparents the family's reactions toward Ginny's behavior were consistent. At school the teacher rewarded only behavior that did not involve crying and whining. Although it wasn't until first grade that her immature methods of control changed significantly, Ginny did eventually learn appropriate ways to relate to other children.

Children use power to control others for different reasons. Sometimes a child has severe emotional problems (Harvey), but more often unacceptable behavior has been unknowingly reinforced by the significant others in the child's life (Ann, Ginny, and John). When parents and teachers work together a child's behavior can change, but without parental support, as in John's case, little change may occur.

REVENGE.   Vengeful children feel hurt and want to hurt others. They may be aggressive or withdrawn. Sara was an aggressive child who verbally attacked her classmates. When she arrived at school each day she accused the first child she saw of hitting her the day before. She would say, "J., you hit me yesterday. Miss A., J. hit me yesterday." The bewildered child would reply, "Miss A., I didn't see Sara yesterday. She's crazy." Unfortunately it appeared to most of the children that Sara was crazy "because she talks crazy." Sara saw disaster in most situations. If she saw two dogs playing on the playground, she announced, "They're going to kill each other." If she saw a plane, she said, "It's going to crash." When someone did something she didn't like, she announced, "The witch will get you." Sara was obsessed with witches, ghosts, goblins, and bad omens. No amount of reassurance would convince her that disaster did not lie in wait for her and for others.

After several parent conferences it was decided to get outside help from the school psychologist. Sara's parents felt her problems stemmed from a witch she had seen in a funhouse two years before. This explanation seemed too simplistic to explain Sara's fears. Although both parents were concerned, the mother seemed to view Sara realistically while the father tended to dismiss the situation as normal for a child of five.

The teacher continued to give Sara emotional support by listening to her when she was upset and reassuring her as much as possible. At the psychologist's suggestion she tried to make Sara aware that the terrible things she said would happen seldom, if ever. This technique had little effect, and she continued to accuse others of things they were not responsible for and to predict disasters. One child said to her, "Sara, you don't like anything. I bet you don't even like Miss A."

The teacher learned that Sara's mother had attempted suicide. This incident revealed more about Sara's upper-class family than the psychologist had been able to learn. He now found that Sara's parents were heavy drinkers. The mother had wanted a divorce for several years, but the father would not give her one. Sara had been constantly subjected to quarreling parents. No one meant to hurt Sara, but the damage was done. It was not until a year later, when the parents divorced and Sara went to live with her mother, by that time a reformed alcoholic, that Sara's fears subsided.

Tom was an attractive five-year-old from a middle-class family, but he was a sullen child who seemed unhappy at school. His behavior alternated between periods of withdrawal and outbursts of temper directed at other children. He had few friends since the children said, "You're too mean. We don't want to play with you." Tom seldom hit, but he called children by every name he could think of. As he watched them play the expression on his face would change from contentment to anguish. Then suddenly he would begin his verbal attacks, apparently without provocation.

It was during learning-center time that Tom disturbed other children. As long as an activity was teacher-directed he was cooperative. The teacher decided to give Tom two choices during learning-center time. After he finished the first activity she talked about other choices he could make. This procedure kept him occupied, and there were no outbursts of temper. She purposely gave him choices that did not involve other children. Gradually she introduced Tom to commercial games that he liked but could not play alone. He learned to enjoy these games, but the teacher's presence was still needed to keep him calm.

Tom talked negatively about his three-year-old sister. He told the teacher he didn't like her and said, "You wouldn't either. She's a girl." At the first parent conference Tom's mother said he was jealous of his sister. She said she dreaded the times Tom was at home because he fought with his sister constantly. She referred to "my poor little girl with that bully for a brother." The teacher suggested that she use a hidden tape recorder to record conversations between the children and herself. She did not tell Tom's mother that she suspected she treated her children differently.

At the next conference Tom's mother brought the tape and played parts of it. She said, "I seem so nice when I talk to Susie, but I sound impatient when I talk to Tom." There was an obvious difference, not only in the way she talked but also in the way she handled the children. Tom was blamed for any friction between the children; however, the tape revealed that Susie often provoked Tom's behavior. Not all mothers would have listened to a taped conversation as perceptively as this mother. Fortunately, with continued effort, she changed her behavior; as a result Tom became a happier child.

On the first day of school Joe walked into the block center, picked up a block, and threw it. The block hit Pat on the head, and when Pat began to cry, Joe cried too. The teacher comforted Pat and then turned to Joe, who through his tears said, "I hate this school. I'm never coming back." The teacher said, "We would like you to come back. We'll miss you." He replied, "Well, I'm not coming back." She ignored his remark and said, "We have a rule about the blocks. Use them to build." He stalked out of the block center, sat down at a table, and worked a puzzle. Later, on the playground, he deliberately pushed a child down the slide. The teacher asked him to come inside until he could play without hurting other children. He ran back into the building calling, "I don't like you and I won't be back tomorrow." Several times during the morning the teacher noticed that Joe had become interested in playing with equipment. She felt reasonably sure he would want to return the next day. When he left he reminded the teacher, "I'm not coming tomorrow."

Joe and his family had just moved from Texas to South Carolina. Joe had many adjustments to make—a new house, town, school, children, and teachers. Instead of coming to school the first time with his parents, he had been allowed to walk by himself. There were too many new things to cope with at school, and Joe couldn't handle them. No wonder he rebelled. He was hurt and bewildered. Joe came back to school the next day. This time he was quiet and withdrawn. After several weeks and additional emotional support from his teachers, Joe adjusted and eventually loved his school.

Sara, Tom, and Joe were children who hurt and wanted to hurt others. They each struck back at other children and at their teachers, but for different reasons. Sara felt responsible for the constant quarreling between her parents. Tom felt rejection because his sister was preferred over him. Joe reacted as any normal child might when too many changes occurred in his life. Teacher insight and in some cases professional assistance were needed to help these children.

INADEQUACY. Inadequate children feel they can do nothing right no matter how hard they try. They have met with failure too often or have had so much done for them that they have never been allowed to "try their wings." These children are usually quiet and withdrawn. These are the children who, if the teacher is not careful, fade into the woodwork. On the other hand, with too much supervision they can suddenly explode into aggressive behavior problems.

Mary Elizabeth was five years old, tall for her age, and hesitant about trying anything new. Her reason was "I can't do it." One day she said to her teacher, "I'm not little, am I?" The teacher said, "No, you're a tall five-year-old girl." She replied, "I'm taller than Margaret and she's in first grade. She's only five like me, but they thought she was smarter." The teacher asked about Margaret and was told that she lived next door. Mary Elizabeth often talked about her, reminding the teacher that Margaret was in first grade.

One of the first questions asked at the first parent conference was, "Who is Margaret?" The teacher learned that Mary Elizabeth and Margaret were best

I can scrape my own plate.

friends and had been together in nursery school. Since Margaret could read, she skipped kindergarten and went into first grade. The girls continued to play with each other after school. The teacher told the parents that just because Margaret could read it did not mean she was brighter than Mary Elizabeth. The parents were surprised since they had naturally assumed that Margaret had to be brighter than their child. She suggested they invite children from kindergarten to play with Mary Elizabeth after school.

Mary Elizabeth enjoyed having visitors at home, and for a while she became more active and interested in school activities. Then she reported to the teacher that Margaret came to her house when she had company and played with her friends. Mary Elizabeth again became withdrawn and talked about Margaret. She definitely felt inferior to her in every way.

At another parent conference the teacher suggested that when Mary Elizabeth had company, no other children be present. She let them read the anecdotal records she had been keeping. The parents were convinced, as was the teacher, that most of Mary Elizabeth's poor self-concept was due to her feelings of inferiority toward Margaret.

Mary Elizabeth remained Margaret's friend but did not see her often. She made new friends at school and by Christmas had stopped comparing herself with Margaret. She was no longer the shy, withdrawn, uncertain child the teacher had first known.

Charlie was a young five-year-old with very poor motor coordination. He had been overprotected by both parents, particularly by his father. Jimmy, a large boy for his age, was Charlie's idol. Charlie copied everything Jimmy did that was not too difficult for him. This frustrated Jimmy, who told Charlie, "Leave me alone and stop copying me." Rather than taking offense Charlie began following Jimmy everywhere. Finally Jimmy hit Charlie, saying, "Stay away from me." This time Charlie's feelings were hurt, and he spent several days telling the teacher, "Jimmy won't play with me. Make him play with me." She told Charlie that Jimmy was busy and that she would help him find something to do.

Since Charlie acted babyish and whined when he talked, the other children were reluctant to play with him. He was unhappy at school because he wanted to belong most of all. His size, poor physical coordination, and dependence on adults were all handicaps in his social development.

Every accomplishment, no matter how small, was positively reinforced by teachers. When a new boy came to school Charlie immediately became attached to him. Richard liked Charlie and did not mind his attentions. Richard was physically agile and well coordinated. Since Charlie admired Richard he was encouraged to try some of the activities Richard engaged in. By watching Richard, Charlie learned to hit a nail, jump off a box, climb the jungle gym, and walk down steps alternating feet. Charlie remained in kindergarten a second year, and by the end of the year he no longer depended on one child but had several friends.

Jake, a four-year-old, played roughly with other children, sometimes hurting them. He told the teacher, "Nobody likes me." The teacher talked with Jake about why he thought he wasn't liked. He said, "Because I hit them. I hit them so they'll think I'm tough." Jake wanted to be feared by the children but not disliked. He came from a low-socioeconomic neighborhood where being tough meant being accepted. Since the same values were not upheld by his classmates he felt inferior and confused.

The teacher noticed that Jake enjoyed feeding the guinea pig. With her he was gentle and kind. The teacher said, "Jake, the guinea pig likes you. She always makes a sound when she hears your voice." Jake beamed and told the other children, "Rosette likes me. She talks to me." The teacher continued to talk with Jake about Rosette, stressing how gently he picked her up and brushed her hair. She allowed Jake to clean Rosette's cage, and in group time she stressed how gently he picked her up and brushed her hair. The children were surprised when they learned that even Jake could be gentle. They were also amazed when Jake carried Rosette on his shoulder. Gradually Jake's reputation changed. He was no longer thought of as the class bully. He was the boy the guinea pig liked best. Through his love for an animal Jake had learned that kindness and gentleness were qualities he possessed which other children liked.

Mary Elizabeth, Charlie, and Jake were children who felt inadequate. Mary Elizabeth because she felt inferior to her best friend; Charlie because his poor coordination, immature development, and overprotective environment kept him from attempting new skills; and Jake because being tough did not give him the status he sought. Children who feel inadequate can be helped only when they are made to feel they are accepted by teachers and children.

positive reinforcement

There are teachers who say they don't use reinforcement techniques. If they stop and think about it they find they do use some type of reinforcement throughout the school day. When teachers smile at children (positive reinforcement) they are saying, "That's fine," and when they frown (negative reinforcement) they are saying, "That's not so good" or "Don't do that again." A friendly hello in the morning (positive reinforcement) tells a child, "I'm glad you're here today." In the examples of teaching strategies given in this chapter social and activity reinforcement were sometimes used to change behavior. For teachers who need help in understanding and using reinforcement techniques *Discipline and Classroom Management* (Osborn and Osborn, 1977, pp. 36–54) is recommended.

teacher's role in working with parents

It is when parents and teachers work together that children profit most from their school experiences. Without parental support teachers deal with many unknowns that interfere with their effectiveness. "If only I had known about C." is a frequent refrain. If a teacher had known, it might have made the difference between helping a child and being unable to help.

Even when teachers are aware of children's backgrounds there are limitations. Some parents are direct, open, objective, and sincere about wanting to help their children. Others easily take offense and feel under attack when their children have problems. Unfortunately a few parents do not care about their children. Teachers must take a positive view of parents. Their attitude should be, "I can help these children" and "Parents will help me as much as possible. I can learn from parents. I cannot give up."

HOME VISITS.   Home visits may occur before or during the school year. Some teachers feel a home visit prior to school gives a mental set before they have an opportunity to know children in the school environment. Others feel they gain insight into children's behavior that helps them plan more effectively at the beginning and throughout the year. Whenever visits occur they give teachers a more complete picture of children.

One five-year-old was on the whole very thoughtful of other children; however, Jane gave commands to children, such as "Bring me my coat," "Find my sweater," and "Help me put on my boots." Her inconsistent behavior puzzled the teacher. When she visited in Jane's home she learned that the family employed three maids around the clock. She watched as a maid brought Jane her coat. Later she watched as Jane put her toys away and put her clothes in the clothes hamper. She realized that Jane had responsibilities and fulfilled them willingly. The difference between Jane and most of the children was in the kinds of responsibilities required of them. The teacher asked Jane if she could put her boots on by herself. She said, "I don't know, but I'll try." As soon as she learned how to handle her own clothing she no longer asked other children for help.

A four-year-old wanted to keep his cot with him as he played. He moved the cot from place to place, sitting on it as he worked in the manipulative center. Since it interfered with constructive play Larry was told that the cot must stay in its place until rest time. The teacher suspected Larry did not have a bed of his own at home. When she visited in the home she learned Larry had no bed. He and his brother slept on a thin mattress on the floor. The next day the teacher told Larry that he could not take his cot into the playroom, but that he could lie on the cot whenever he wanted to rest. Larry used the cot regularly for several weeks. His interest waned as he became certain no one was going to take it away from him.

Pete was a child who showed no interest in art media. He firmly said, "I'm not going to the art center, not ever." His teachers were puzzled since Pete used other centers and did not care how dirty his clothes got on the playground. During a home visit the teacher was surprised when she saw Pete's art displayed throughout the house. Now she understood what was happening to him: he did artwork at home and wanted to do other things at school. When Pete's mother visited school the teacher suggested he paint a picture for her. He proudly gave his mother the picture he painted for her. Gradually Pete began to show an interest in the art center.

Home visits should be made at the convenience of the parent(s). When both parents work it may be necessary to visit in the late afternoon. There will be a few homes where teachers are not welcome. The refusal to allow a teacher in the home may be due to timidity, disinterest, poverty, or resentment. As the year progresses and teachers get to know parents better they may find they are welcome in homes previously closed to them. Parents sometimes respond to requests to bring school-related material to the home. This can be a newsletter, a policy handbook, a toy for a child, or a child product to share. When a home visit is impossible teachers must strive to involve parent(s) in other ways. One teacher writes a letter to parents asking for help in making teacher-made materials. The directions and necessary materials are enclosed in a large envelope.

Parents who never come to school have participated in these projects. In this way every parent is asked to take part in classroom activities.

PARENT MEETINGS.   Parent meetings have a twofold purpose: to help parents and teachers get acquainted and to help parents understand the school program. It is sometimes best to begin with a get-acquainted meeting. A Head Start group had a watermelon cutting at a local park. The purpose of the meeting was to bring teachers, parents, and children together in a location familiar to everyone. Eighty percent of the parents attended with their children. The second meeting was an open house at the school. The purpose of this meeting was to allow children to show their room to their parents. In this way parents were introduced informally to some aspects of the school program.

A nursery school teacher took slides of children in various activities and showed these slides at the first school parent meeting. Parents were motivated to come to school to see their child's pictures. The teacher seized this opportunity to explain the program through pictures. Later in the year the parents formed a program committee. They sent questionnaires to parents to learn what kinds of programs they wanted during the year. For this group of parents reading was the first concern, followed by discipline, sibling rivalry, and moral values. The meetings became a series of discussions led by either a parent, teacher, or a resource person. High school students provided care for the children during the night meetings.

Teachers are a part of the parent-teacher group, and they can voice their concerns to parents. A teacher was disturbed by a lack of materials in the classroom. When they learned there was a shortage of equipment, fathers built a workbench and a sand table and made missing puzzle pieces. The mothers made doll clothes, dress-up clothes, and oversized pillows for the library center. Occasional workshops were held where parents made picture books, toys, and other materials to use with their children at home. Younger siblings could also profit from the materials.

PARENT PARTICIPATION.   Teachers should not only know the occupations of parents but also their hobbies, which may range from growing plants to writing poetry. They should be encouraged to share interesting hobbies in the class-room. Some hobbies shared by parents have been reading poetry, setting up an aquarium, making Chinese noodles, teaching folk songs, telling stories, making paste and play dough, and flying kites.

One of the best ways to get parents involved is to invite them to school at the beginning of the year during a special week set aside for parent visits. Visits do not have to be scheduled during this week. Parents can drop in and leave at any time. They may be encouraged to become involved in whatever their children are doing, from playing games to working with play dough. Teachers must remember that school policies differ on visits and some schools require parents to notify the school beforehand.

Sometimes parents are reluctant to participate but want to observe their children. Observation is one of the best ways parents can learn about children. Laboratory schools and some public schools have booths where parents can

Sometimes parents help at school.

observe without being seen. When there are no booths they may observe as unobtrusively as possible. Often parents expect every child to be like their own. When they compare their child with other children they are often surprised. A child was generally immature, and his motor development lagged behind that of other children his age. The teacher felt Dan's parents did not understand his immaturity. She urged them to observe Dan frequently. At a parent conference they were convinced that he should stay in kindergarten another year. They had seen for themselves and said, "Dan can't sit still long enough to listen to a story. He shows no interest in writing. Most of the children are writing their names. We are surprised at what we didn't know about Dan." Another parent said to a teacher, "I am amazed at all the different personalities you have to relate to. I thought most children were like my child." This comment had an impact on the teacher. She had not realized how little many parents knew about the problems teachers face in a classroom.

PARENT CONFERENCES.   Most schools have two regularly scheduled conferences a year; however, conferences should be held whenever teachers or parents feel they are needed. They should take place at school, not in a home or a public place. Sometimes parents meet teachers casually after school hours and want to talk about their children. When this happens a teacher can discourage further discussion by saying, "I want to talk with you about K. Let's make an appointment to talk at school. I'll call you." In this way a teacher shows an interest in a child but lets the parent(s) know that discussing children is a professional matter.

Teachers should prepare for parent conferences by listing positive things to say about children and also concerns. There are times when teachers cannot voice all or any of their concerns. A teacher had many concerns about a child who was overprotected. She knew, however, that if she voiced an opinion or made a suggestion the child would be taken out of school. It was more important to keep him in school than to change parent attitudes. There are teachers who, in order to protect children from parental abuse, cannot be completely honest with parents.

Fortunately most parents at all socioeconomic levels do care about their children and want to cooperate with teachers. One effective way to begin a parent conference is to ask, "How does A. like school?" and another, "Tell me about A.'s day. What is it like?" Since neither question is threatening, most parents easily respond. Another way to begin is to show parents something their children have done in school, such as a drawing, painting, clay model, or block construction. A tour of the room is helpful since it gives parents a better idea of what their child's school is like. One parent exclaimed, "Oh! I didn't know you had a guinea pig. I thought B. made that up."

The more teachers listen to parents and the less they talk the more they may learn about children. The teacher's concerns are often raised by parents. A teacher was worried about a five-year-old boy who preferred girls' roles in dramatic play. During a parent conference his father said, "Larry says he dresses up like a girl at school. Why does he? He doesn't do that at home." The teacher pointed out that at school there were boy and girl dress-up clothes. At home Larry had no dress-up clothes. They talked about the way Larry walked—mincingly, rather like a girl. The teacher felt this was a physical disability. Larry was checked by a physician, who confirmed her suspicions. Larry had a slight case of cerebral palsy, which explained his walk. This knowledge about their child reassured the parents.

Teachers must be tactful with parents. There is a difference between saying, "The children don't like John" and "John sometimes has difficulty playing with other children." It is not always what is said but how it is said that offends parents. Words spoken sarcastically or harshly have no place in parent conferences.

It is crucial that parents feel teachers like their children. Teachers who talk positively and enthusiastically about children convince parents that they value their children and sincerely care what happens to them. A father once said, "I didn't know teachers could care so much about the children they teach."

references

chapter 1. good teachers are planners

Althouse, R., and Main, C. 1974. The science learning center: Hub of science activities. *Childhood Education 50*(4), 222–226.

Frost, J., and Kissinger, J. 1976. *The young child and the educative process.* New York: Holt, Rinehart and Winston.

chapter 2. children are active

Block, S. 1977. *Me and I'm great: Physical education for children three through eight.* Minneapolis, Minn.: Burgess Publishing Co.

Charles, C. M. 1974. *Teacher's petite Piaget.* Belmont, Calif.: Fearon.

Flinchum, B. 1975. *Motor development in early childhood: A guide for movement education with ages 2 to 6.* St. Louis: Mosby.

Gallahue, D. 1976. *Motor development and movement experiences for young children.* New York: Wiley.

———. 1977. Editor's corner. *The Physical Educator 34,* 58–59.

Gee, E. G., and Sperry, D. J. 1978. *Education and the public school: A compendium.* Boston: Allyn and Bacon.

Ginsburg, H., and Opper, S. 1969. *Piaget's theory of intellectual development.* Englewood Cliffs, N.J.: Prentice-Hall.

Godfrey, B., and Kephart, N. 1969. *Movement patterns and motor education.* New York: Appleton.

Herkowitz, J. 1977. Movement experiences for preschool children. *Journal of Physical Education and Recreation 48*(3), 15–16.

Kirchner, G., Cunningham, J., and Worrell, E. 1970. *Introduction to movement education: An individualized approach to teaching physical education.* Dubuque, Iowa: Wm. C. Brown.

Lillard, P. 1972. *Montessori: A modern approach.* New York: Schocken.

Milne, C., Seefeldt, V., and Reuschlein, P. 1976. Relationship between grade, sex, race and motor performance in young children. *Research Quarterly 47*(4), 726–730.

Montessori, M. 1965. *Dr. Montessori's own handbook.* New York: Schocken.

Osborn, J., and Osborn, K. 1974. *Cognitive tasks: An approach for early childhood education.* Athens, Ga.: University of Georgia.

Sinclair, C. 1973. *Movement of the young child ages two to six.* Columbus, Ohio: Charles E. Merrill.

Weber, E. 1969. *The kindergarten: Its encounter with educational thought in America.* New York: Teachers College Press.

Yardley, A. 1974. *Structures in early learning.* New York: Citation Press.

chapter 3.   children are full of pleasure

Anker, D., Foster, J., McLane, J., Sobel, J., and Weissboard, B. 1974. Teaching children as they play. *Young Children 29*(4), 203–213.

Caplan, F., and Caplan, T. 1973. *The power of play.* Garden City, N.Y.: Anchor Press (Doubleday).

Dewey, J. 1913. On play. In *A cyclopedia of education,* ed. Paul Monroe. New York: Macmillan.

Gallahue D. 1976. Editor's corner: why children play. *The Physical Educator 33*(3), 114.

Good, C. V. (Ed.) 1973. *Dictionary of education* (3rd Ed.). New York: McGraw-Hill.

Hartley, R. 1952. *Understanding children's play.* New York: Columbia University Press.

Herron, R. E., and Sutton-Smith, B. 1971. *Child's play.* New York: Wiley.

Holme, A., and Massie, P. 1970. *Children's play: A study of needs and opportunities.* London: Michael Joseph.

Isaacs, S. 1968. *The nursery years.* New York: Schocken.

Miller, P. 1972. *Creative outdoor play areas.* Englewood Cliffs, N.J.: Prentice-Hall.

Mitchell, E., and Mason, B. 1948. *The theory of play.* New York: A. S. Barnes.

Piaget, J. 1962. *Play, dreams and imitation in childhood.* New York: Norton.

Pulaski, M. A. 1971. *Understanding Piaget.* New York: Harper & Row.

Smilansky, S. 1968. *The effects of sociodramatic play on disadvantaged preschool children.* New York: Wiley.

Spodek, B. 1972. *Teaching in the early years.* Englewood Cliffs, N.J.: Prentice-Hall.

Sund, R. B., and Bybee, R. W. Piaget and the teacher. In *Becoming an elementary science teacher: A reader,* eds. R. Sund and R. Bybee 1973. Columbus, Ohio: Merrill.

Whiren, A. 1975. Table toys: The underdeveloped resource. *Young Children 30*(6), 414–419.

Wolfgang, C. H. 1976. Teaching preschool children to play. *Quest,* monograph 26, 117–127.

chapter 4.   children are social

Ansello, E. F. 1975. Ageism—the subtle stereotype. *Childhood Education 54*(3), 118–122.

Association for Supervision and Curriculum Development Yearbook. 1949. *Toward better teaching.* (1949 Yearbook.) Washington, D.C.: ASCD.

Birns, B. 1976. The emergence and socialization of sex differences in the early years. *Merrill Palmer Quarterly 22*(3), 229–253.

Bryan, T. 1974. An observational analysis of classroom behaviors of children with learning disabilities. *Journal of Learning Disabilities 7,* 26–34.

Canady, H., and Darnley, F. 1977. Mr. Albonese builds a special bridge. *Dimensions 6*(1), 11–12, 26.

Cohen, D., and Rudolph, M. 1977. *Kindergarten and early schooling.* Englewood Cliffs, N.J.: Prentice-Hall.

Copeland, R. 1979. *How children learn mathematics: Teaching implications of Piaget's research.* New York: Macmillan.

Crase, D. R., and Crase, D. 1976. Helping children understand death. *Young Children* 32(1), 21–25.

Dunlop, K. H. 1977. Mainstreaming: Valuing diversity in children. *Young Children* 32(4), 26–32.

Elkind, D. 1976. *Child development and education.* New York: Oxford University Press.

Evans, E. D., and McCandless, B. R. 1978. *Children and youth psychosocial development.* New York: Holt, Rinehart and Winston.

Fagan, P. L., and Osborn, D. K. 1975. Femininity and masculinity in young children. *Dimensions* 3(3), 73–75.

Furman, E. 1978. Helping children cope with death. *Young Children* 33(4), 25–32.

Gottlieb, J., and Budoff, M. 1972. Attitudes toward school by segregated and integrated retarded children: A study and experimental validation. *Studies in Learning Potential 2,* no. 35. (ERIC Document Reproduction Service no. ED o85 967.)

Greenwald, H. J., and Oppenheim, D. B. 1968. Reported magnitude of self-misidentification among negro children—artificial? *Journal of Personality and Social Psychology 8,* 49–52.

Hammer, T. 1976. A psychological resource for the future. *Dimensions* 4(2), 30–32, 50.

Hymes, J. L., Jr. 1968. *Teaching the child under six,* p. 89. Columbus, Ohio: Charles E. Merrill.

Jantz, R. K., and Fulda, T. A. 1975. The role of moral education in the public elementary school. *Social Education* 39(1), 24–28.

John, M. T. 1977. Teaching children about older family members. *Social Education* 41(6), 524–529.

Johnson, G. O. 1962. Special education for the mentally handicapped—a paradox. *Exceptional Children* 29(2), 62–69.

Jones, R. L. 1974. Student views of special placement and their special classes: A clarification. *Exceptional Children* 41(1), 22–29.

Madsen, J. M., and Wickersham, E. B. 1980. A look at children's realistic fiction. *The Reading Teacher* 34(3), 273–279.

Mitchell, E. 1973. The learning of sex roles through toys and books: A woman's view. *Young Children* 28(4), 226–231.

Moore, C. L. 1976. The racial preference and attitude of preschool black children. *The Journal of Genetic Psychology 129,* 37–44.

Nilsen, A. P. 1977. Alternatives to sexist practices in the classroom. *Young Children* 32(5), 53–58.

Osborn, J., and Osborn, K. 1974. *Cognitive tasks: An approach for early childhood education.* Athens, Ga.: University of Georgia.

Porter, J. D. R. 1971. *Black child, white child: The development of racial attitudes.* Cambridge, Mass.: Harvard University Press.

Pulaski, M. A. S. 1971. *Understanding Piaget.* New York: Harper and Row.

Rohrer, G. K. 1977. Racial and ethnic identification and preference in young children. *Young Children* 32(2), 24–33.

Rosen, H. 1977. Genetic epistemology: Basic concepts and overview. In *Pathway to Piaget,* ed. Jerome Platt. Cherry Hill, N.J.: Postgraduate International, Inc. pp. 3–32.

Sayre, S. A., and Ankney, P. 1976. Piaget, justice and behavior in the classroom. *Childhood Education* 52(5), 238–241.

Seefeldt, C. 1977. *Social studies for the preschool-primary child.* Columbus, Ohio: Charles E. Merrill.

———, et al. 1978. The coming of age in children's literature. *Childhood Education 54*(3), 123–127.

Storey, D. C. 1977. Gray Power: An endangered species? Ageism as portrayed in children's books. *Social Education 41*(6), 528–533.

Timberlake, P. 1978. Classroom holidaze. *Childhood Education 54*(3), 128–130.

Wadsworth, B. W. 1978. *Piaget for the classroom teacher.* New York: Longman.

Webster's New Collegiate Dictionary. 1975. Springfield, Mass.: G. and C. Merriam.

Wren-Lewis, J. 1975. Breaking the final taboo. *Psychology Today 8*(12), 14–15.

Wynne, S., Ulfelder, L., and Dakof, G. 1975. *Mainstreaming and early childhood education for handicapped children: Review and implications of research.* Washington, D.C.: Wynne Associates.

chapter 5.   children are curious

Childcraft. 1981. Chicago: World Book–Childcraft International, Inc.

Copeland, R. 1979. *How children learn mathematics.* (3rd Ed.). New York: Macmillan.

Dietz, M., and Sunal, D. 1976. Science. In *Curriculum for the preschool-primary child,* ed. C. Seefeldt. Columbus, Ohio: Charles E. Merrill.

Elkind, D. 1976. *Child development and education.* New York: Oxford University Press.

Flavell, J. H. 1963. *The developmental psychology of Jean Piaget.* New York: Van Nostrand.

Furth, H. 1969. *Piaget and knowledge.* Englewood Cliffs, N.J.: Prentice-Hall.

Good, R. 1977(a). The traditional sequencing of mathematics for young children should be changed. *School Science and Mathematics 77*(1), 53–58.

———. 1977(b). *How children learn science.* New York: Macmillan.

Kamii, C., and DeVries, R. 1976. *Piaget, children and number.* Washington, D.C.: National Association for the Education of Young Children.

———, and ———. 1978. *Physical knowledge in preschool education: Implications of Piaget's theory.* Englewood Cliffs, N.J.: Prentice-Hall.

Osborn, J., and Osborn, K. 1974. *Cognitive tasks: An approach for early childhood education.* Athens, Ga.: University of Georgia.

Payne, J. N. (Ed.). 1975. *Mathematics learning in early childhood.* (Thirty-seventh Yearbook.) Reston, Va.: National Council of Teachers of Mathematics.

Riechard, D. 1973. A decade of preschool science: Promises, problems, and perspectives. *Science Education 57*(4), 437–451.

Rosen, H. 1977. Genetic epistemology: Basic concepts and overview. In *Pathway to Piaget,* ed. Jerome J. Platt. Cherry Hill, N.J.: Postgraduate International, Inc. pp. 3–32.

Seefeldt, C. (Ed.). 1976. *Curriculum for the preschool-primary child.* Columbus, Ohio: Charles E. Merrill.

Wadsworth, B. 1978. *Piaget for the classroom teacher.* New York: Longman.

chapter 6.   children are creative

Aubin, N., Crooks, E., Hayden, E., and Walker, D. 1976. *Silver Burdett music early childhood.* (Teachers Edition.) Atlanta, Ga.: Silver Burdett.

Bayless, K. M., and Ramsey, M. R. 1978. *Music: A way of life for the young child.* St. Louis, Mo.: Mosby.

Beyer, E. 1961. Jump or jiggle. In *Poems to read to the very young,* ed. Josette Frank. New York: Random House.

Brissoni, A. 1975. Creative experiences of young children. *Art Education 28*(1), 18–22.

Burns, S. F. 1975. Children's art: A vehicle for learning. *Young Children 30*(3), 193–204.

Eisner, E. W. 1976. What we know about children's art—and what we need to know. In *The arts, human development, and education,* ed. Elliot W. Eisner. Berkeley, Calif.: McCutchan Publishing Corp.

Flack, M. 1932. *Ask Mr. Bear.* New York: Macmillan.

Foshay, A. W. 1961. The creative process described. In *Creativity in teaching,* ed. A. Miel. Belmont, Calif.: Wadsworth, pp. 22–40.

Francks, O. R. 1977. Genesis: The art of the young child. In *Early childhood education,* eds. Leonard H. Golubchick and Barry Persky. Wayne, N.J.: Avery Publishing Group.

Geisel, T. S. 1947. *McElligot's pool.* New York: Random House.

Getzels, J. W., and Jackson, P. W. 1962. *Creativity and intelligence.* New York: Wiley.

Herberholz, B. 1974. *Early childhood art.* Dubuque, Iowa: Wm. C. Brown.

Hilyard, I., and Jaye, M. T. 1971. *Making music your own.* Atlanta, Ga.: Silver Burdett.

Kaplan-Sanoff, M. 1977. Process and product art: New implications for education. In *Early childhood education,* ed. Leonard H. Golubchick and Barry Persky. Wayne, N.J.: Avery Publishing Group.

Kellogg, R. 1970. *Analyzing children's art.* Palo Alto, Calif.: National Press Books.

————, and O'Dell, S. 1967. *The psychology of children's art.* New York: C R M-Random House Publications.

Lansing, K. M. 1966. The research of Jean Piaget and its implications for art education in the elementary school. *Studies in Art Education 7*(2), 33–42.

Lowenfeld, V., and Brittain, W. L. 1970. *Creative and mental growth* (5th ed.). New York: Macmillan.

McClintock, M. 1958. *A fly went by.* New York: Beginner Books, Inc., distributed by Random House.

McCloskey, R. 1948. *Blueberries for Sal.* New York: Viking.

McDonald, D. T., and Ramsey, J. H. 1978. Awakening the artist: Music for young children. *Young Children 33*(2), 26–32.

Maguire, M. 1968. *My marvelous menagerie.* New York: Holt, Rinehart and Winston.

Marsh, M. V. 1970. *Explore to discover music.* London: Macmillan.

Miel, A. (Ed.). 1961. *Creativity in teaching.* Belmont, Calif.: Wadsworth.

Seefeldt, C. 1976. Art. In *Curriculum for the preschool-primary child,* ed. C. Seefeldt. Columbus, Ohio: Charles E. Merrill.

Sheehy, E. 1968. *Children discover music and dance.* New York: Teachers College Press.

Shelley, S. J. 1976. Music. In *Curriculum for the preschool-primary child,* ed. C. Seefeldt. Columbus, Ohio: Charles E. Merrill.

Smith, R. B. 1970. *Music in the child's education.* New York: Ronald Press.

————. 1963. The effects of group vocal training on the singing ability of nursery school children. *Journal of Research in Music Education 11,* 137–141.

————, and Leonhard, C. 1968. *Discovering music together: Early childhood.* Chicago: Follett.

Sparling, J. J., and Sparling, M. C. 1973. How to talk to a scribbler. *Young Children 28*(6), 333–341.

Stecher, M. B., McElheny, H., and Greenwood, M. 1972. *Music and movement improvisations.* New York: Macmillan.

Taylor, E. M. 1973. Teach music concepts through body movement. *Music Educators Journal 59,* 50–52.

Torrance, E. P. 1962. *Guiding creative talents.* Englewood Cliffs, N.J.: Prentice-Hall.

————. 1963. *Education and the creative potential.* Minneapolis, Minn.: University of Minnesota.

Wheeler, L., and Raebeck, L. 1972. *Orff and Kodàly adapted for the elementary school.* Dubuque, Iowa: Wm. C. Brown.

Wieder, C. G. 1977. Three decades of research on child art: A survey and a critique. *Art Education 30*(1), 5–10.

Winn, M. (Ed.). 1966. *The fireside book of children's songs.* New York: Simon and Schuster.

chapter 7.   children are talkative

Almy, M., Chittenden, E., and Miller, P. 1967. *Young children's thinking.* New York: Teachers College Press.

Barrett, T. C. 1965. The relationship between measures of prereading visual discrimination and first grade reading achievement: A review of the literature. *Reading Research Quarterly 1*(1), 51–75.

Betts, E. A. 1957. *Foundations of reading instruction.* New York: American Book Co.

Cazden, C. B. 1974. Play with language and metalinguistic awareness: One dimension of language experience. *International Journal of Early Childhood 6*(1), 12–24.

Chall, J. S. 1967. *Learning to read: The great debate.* New York: McGraw-Hill.

Chaparro, J. L. 1978. For the love of language. In *Claremont reading conference* (42nd Yearbook). Claremont, Calif.: Claremont Graduate School.

Chomsky, C. S. 1969. *The acquisition of syntax in children from 5 to 10.* Cambridge, Mass.: MIT Press.

Cohen, D. H., and Rudolph, M. 1977. *Kindergarten and early schooling.* Englewood Cliffs, N.J.: Prentice-Hall.

Copeland, R. W. 1979. *How children learn mathematics* (3rd Ed.). New York: Macmillan.

de Hirsch, K., Jansky, J. J., and Langford, W. S. 1966. *Predicting reading failure.* New York: Harper & Row.

DeVries, R. 1974. Relationships among Piagetian, I.Q., and achievement assessments. *Child Development 45*, 746–756.

Dimitrovsky, L., and Almy, M. 1975. Early conservation as a predictor of later reading. *Journal of Psychology 90*, 11–18.

Downing, J. 1970. Children's concepts of language in learning to read. *Educational Research 12*(2), 106–112.

Durkin, D. 1970. A language arts program for pre-first-grade children: Two-year achievement report. *Reading Research Quarterly 5*(4), 534–565.

————. 1978. *Teaching them to read* (3rd Ed.). Boston: Allyn and Bacon.

Durrell, D. D. 1958. First grade success story: A summary. *Journal of Education 140*, 2–6.

Dykstra, R. 1966. Auditory discrimination abilities and beginning reading achievement. *Reading Research Quarterly 1*, 5–34.

Editorial: Language in early education. 1974. *International Journal of Early Childhood 6*(1), 3–4.

Elkind, D. 1974. Cognitive development and reading. In *Claremont reading conference* (38th Yearbook). Claremont, Calif.: Claremont Graduate School, pp. 10–21.

————, Horn, S., and Schneider, G. 1965. Modified word recognition, reading achievement, and perceptual decentration. *Journal of Genetic Psychology 107*, 235–251.

————, Larsen, M., and Van Doornick, W. 1965. Perceptual decentration learning and performance in slow and average readers. *Journal of Educational Psychology 56*, 50–56.

Fasick, A. M. 1973. Television language and book language. *Elementary English 50*(1), 125–131.

Flood, S. E. 1977. Parental styles in reading episodes with young children. *The Reading Teacher 30*(8), 864–867.

Fox, S. E. 1976. Assisting children's language development. *The Reading Teacher 29*(7), 666–670.

Gates, A. I., and Bond, G. C. 1958. Factors determining success and failure in beginning reading. In *Research in the three R's,* ed. C. W. Hunnicutt and W. S. Iverson. New York: Harper and Bros.

Hall, M. 1976. Prereading instruction: Teach for the task. *The Reading Teacher 30*(1), 7–9.

Hess, R. D., and Croft, D. S. 1975. *Teachers of young children.* Boston: Houghton Mifflin.

Kaufman, A. S., and Kaufman, N. L. 1972. Tests built from Piaget's and Gesell's tasks as predictors of first-grade achievement. *Child Development 43,* 521–535.

Leeper, S. H., et al. 1979. *Good schools for young children* (4th ed.). New York: Macmillan.

Loban, W. 1963. *The language of school children.* NCTE Research Report No. 1. Champaign, Ill.: National Council of Teachers of English.

Lowes, R. 1975. Do we teach reading in the kindergarten? *Young Children 30*(5), 328–331.

Morrison, I. E. 1962. The relation of reading readiness to certain language factors. In *Challenge and experiment in reading, proceedings of the seventh annual conference of the International Reading Association.* New York: Scholastic.

Ollila, L. O. (Ed.). 1977. *The kindergarten child and reading.* Newark, Del.: International Reading Association.

Osborn, D. K., and Osborn, J. D. 1974. *Cognitive tasks: An approach for early childhood education.* Athens, Ga.: Early Childhood Educational Learning Center.

Paradis, E. E. 1974. The appropriateness of visual discrimination exercises in reading readiness materials. *Journal of Educational Research 67,* 276–278.

Platt, P. 1977. Grapho-linguistics, children's drawing in relation to reading and writing skills. *The Reading Teacher 31*(3), 262–268.

Robbins, E. L. 1970. Language development research. In *Interpreting language arts research for the teacher.* Washington, D.C.: Association for Supervision and Curriculum Development.

Robinson, H. M. 1955. Factors which affect success in reading. *Elementary School Journal 55,* 263–269.

Robinson, V. B., Strickland, D. S., and Cullinan, B. 1977. The child: Ready or not? In *The kindergarten child and reading,* ed. L. O. Ollila. Newark, Del.: International Reading Association. pp. 13–39.

Rude, R. T. 1973. Readiness tests: Implications for early childhood. *The Reading Teacher 26,* 572–580.

Rupley, W. H. 1977. Reading readiness research: Implications for instructional practices. *The Reading Teacher 30*(4), 450–453.

Sampson, O. C. 1962. Reading skills at eight years in relation to speech and other factors. *British Journal of Educational Psychology 32,* 14.

Samuels, S. J. 1973. Success and failure in learning to read: A critique of the research. *Reading Research Quarterly 8*(2), 200–239.

Schery, T. K. 1978. Theories of language development: Implications for teaching the language-disordered child. In *Claremont reading conference* (42nd Yearbook). Claremont, Calif.: Claremont Graduate School, pp. 69–77.

Schickedanz, J. 1978. You be the doctor and I"ll be sick: Preschoolers learn the language arts through play. *Language Arts 55*(6), 713–718.

Scott, R. 1969. Social class, race, seriation, and reading readiness: A study of the relationship at kindergarten level. *Journal of Genetic Psychology 115,* 87–96.

Simpson, B. F. 1972. *Multiple classification, class inclusion, and reading ability.* Final Report, Grant OEG-1-9-080046-0010(010), National Center for Educational Research and Development (Dept. of HEW, USOE). (ERIC Document Reproduction Services no. ED063606.)

Smith, F. 1979. The language arts and the learner's mind. *Language Arts 56*(2), 118–125, 145.

Strickland, D. 1972. Black is beautiful vs. white is right. *Elementary English 49,* 220–224.

Strickland, D. 1973. A program for linguistically different black children. *Research in the Teaching of English 1*(1), Spring. (Official bulletin of the National Council of English.)

Sullivan, D. D. 1976. Reading. In *Curriculum for the preschool-primary child,* ed. C. Seefeldt. Columbus, Ohio: Charles E. Merrill.

Tutolo, D. 1979. Attention: Necessary aspect of listening. *Language Arts 56*(1), 34–37.

Wadsworth, B. J. 1978. *Piaget for the classroom teacher.* New York: Longman.

Waller, T. G. 1977. *Think first, read later! Piagetian prerequisites for reading.* Newark, Del.: International Reading Association.

Whisnant, C., and Hassett, J. 1974. *Word magic: How to encourage children to write and speak creatively.* Garden City, N.Y.: Doubleday.

Yawkey, T. D. 1979. Let's pretend play as language learning. *Reading Improvement 16*(2), 130–133.

chapter 8.   children are dependent and independent

Artmann, S. 1979. Morale or mouthings: Care giver interaction makes the difference. *Childhood Education 56*(1), 31–32, 33–35.

Baruth, L. G., and Eckstein, D. G. 1978. *The ABC's of classroom discipline.* Dubuque, Iowa: Kendall/Hunt Publishing Co.

Broman, B. L. 1978. *The early years in childhood education.* Chicago: Rand McNally College Publishing Co.

Cohen, D. H., and Rudolph, M. 1977. *Kindergarten and early schooling.* Englewood Cliffs, N.J.: Prentice-Hall.

Curwin, R. L., and Mendler, A. N. 1980. *A complete guide to school and classroom management.* Reston, Va.: Reston Publishing Co.

Evans, E. D. 1975. *Contemporary influences in early childhood education.* New York: Holt, Rinehart and Winston.

Gallagher, J. J. 1973. The "quiet place": A means for behavior control. *Dimensions 2*(1), 6–7.

Hess, R. D., and Croft, D. J. 1975. *Teachers of young children* (2nd Ed.). Boston: Houghton Mifflin.

Hipple, M. L. 1978. Classroom discipline problems? Fifteen humane solutions. *Childhood Education 54*(4), 183–187.

Howell, R. G., Jr., and Howell, P. L. 1979. *Discipline in the classroom: Solving the teaching puzzle.* Reston, Va.: Reston Publishing Co.

Leeper, S. H., et al. 1979. *Good schools for young children* (4th Ed.). New York: Macmillan.

McCarthy, M. A., and Houston, J. P. 1980. *Fundamentals of early childhood education.* Cambridge, Mass.: Winthrop.

Osborn, D. K., and Osborn, J. D. 1977. *Discipline and classroom management.* Athens, Ga.: University of Georgia, Early Childhood Learning Center.

Read, K. E. 1976. *The nursery school* (6th Ed.). Philadelphia: Saunders.

Swanson, F., and Jenkins, R: L. 1969. From the other side of the teacher's desk. In *Discipline in the classroom.* Washington, D.C.: National Education Association.

Wallen, C. J., and Wallen, L. L. 1978. *Effective classroom management.* Boston: Allyn and Bacon.

Wenig, M., and Brown, M. L. 1975. School efforts + parent/teacher communications = happy young parents. *Young Children 30*(5), 373–376.

bibliography

chapter 1. good teachers are planners

Bingham, N., and Sanders, R. A. 1977. Take a new look at your classroom with Piaget as a guide. *Young Children 32*(4), 62–72.

Davidson, T., Fountain, P., Grogan, R., Short, V., and Steely, J. 1976. *The learning book: An integrated approach.* Pacific Palisades, Calif.: Goodyear.

Fondek, R. 1973. *Classroom capers.* Bellingham, Wash.: Educational Designs and Consultants.

Grand, C., and Gold, R. 1975. Kindergarten and the open classroom. *Childhood Education 51*(4), 211–213.

Hatcher, B., and Schmidt, V. 1980. Half-day is full-day kindergarten programs. *Childhood Education 57*(1), 14–17.

Hess, R., and Croft, D. 1975. *Teachers of young children* (2nd ed.). Boston: Houghton Mifflin.

Hilderbrand, V. 1976. *Introduction to early childhood education* (2nd ed.). New York: Macmillan.

Keith, J., and Schmidt, V. 1975. *Early childhood education in South Carolina* (2nd ed., rev.). Columbia, S.C.: South Carolina State Department of Education.

Learning centers children alive. 1973. Columbia, S.C.: South Carolina State Department of Education.

Leeper, S., Dales, R., Skipper, D., and Witherspoon, R. 1979. *Good schools for young children* (4th ed.). New York: Macmillan.

Mager, R. 1962. *Preparing instructional objectives.* Palo Alto, Calif.: Fearon.

Nations, J. E. (Ed.). 1976. *Learning centers.* Washington, D.C.: National Education Association.

Read, K. 1976. *The nursery school* (6th ed.). Philadelphia: Saunders.

Robinson, H. 1977. *Exploring teaching in early childhood.* Boston: Allyn and Bacon.

Rosen, H. 1977. Genetic epistemology: Basic concepts and overview. In *Pathway* to *Piaget* (Jerome J. Platt, Ed.). Cherry Hill, N.J.: Postgraduate International, Inc., pp. 3–32.

Stout, M. 1972. *The young child.* Englewood Cliffs, N.J.: Prentice-Hall.

Vance B. 1975. *Teaching the kindergarten child: Instructional design and curriculum.* Monterey, Calif.: Brooks/Cole.

Young, B. 1975. Take a fresh look around your kindergarten room. *Young Children 30*(3), 160–165.

chapter 2.   children are active

Arnett, C. 1976. *All active, all successful.* Bellingham, Wash.: Educational Design Consultants.

Dickerson, M. 1977. *Developing the outdoor learning center.* Little Rock, Ark.: Southern Association on Children Under Six.

Elkind, D. 1976. *Child development and education.* New York: Oxford University Press.

Gardner, D. 1964. *Development in early childhood: The preschool years.* New York: Harper & Row.

Gerhardt, L. 1973. *Moving and knowing: The young child orients himself in space.* Englewood Cliffs, N.J.: Prentice-Hall.

Kritchevslsy, S., Prescott, E., and Walling, L. 1969. *Planning environments for young children.* Washington, D.C.: National Association for the Education of Young Children.

Mackler, B., and Halman, D. 1976. Assessing, packaging, and delivery: Tests, testing, and race. *Young Children 31*(5), 351–364.

North, M. 1973. *Movement education.* New York: Dutton.

Orem, R. C. 1969. *Montessori and the special child.* New York: Capricorn.

———(Ed.) 1974. *Montessori, her method and the movement: What you need to know.* New York: Putnam.

Piaget, J. 1970. *Science education and the psychology of the child.* New York: Grossman.

Porter, I. 1969. *Movement education for children.* Washington, D.C.: American Association of Elementary-Kindergarten-Nursery Educators.

Schoedler, J. 1973. *Physical skills for young children.* New York: Collier-Macmillan, Threshold Division.

Smart, M., and Smart, D. 1967. *Children: Development and relationships.* New York: Macmillan.

Turner, L., and Turner, S. 1976. *More than just a game.* Palo Alto, Calif.: Peek Publications.

games

Alphabet Bingo. Trend Enterprises.

Balloon Game. Merit: Otto Maier Rauenburg.

Candy Land. Milton Bradley Company, 74 Park Street, Springfield, Mass.

Chutes and Ladders. Milton Bradley Company.

Color and Shape Bingo. Trend Enterprises.

Hi-Ho-Cherry-O. Western Publishing Co., 850 Third Avenue, New York, N.Y. 10022

Hickety Pickety. Parker Brothers, 90 Bridge Street, Salem, Mass.

Perfection. Lakeside Games, Minneapolis, Minn.

Picture Dominoes. Creative Playthings, Inc., Princeton, N.J.

Swiss Cheese. Milton Bradley Company.

Ting-a-ling Bingo. Cadaco, Inc., 310 W. Polk Street, Chicago, Ill.
What's Missing Lotto. Ed-U-Cards Mfg. Corp., 36–46 33rd Street, Long Island City, N.Y.
Winnie-the-Pooh. Parker Brothers, 90 Bridge Street, Salem, Mass.

chapter 3. children are full of pleasure

Aaron, D., and Winower, B. 1965. *Child's play.* New York: Harper & Row.
Lady Allen of Hartwood. 1968. *Planning for play.* Cambridge, Mass.: MIT Press.
Benninga, J. S. 1980. Egocentrism in the early childhood classroom. *The Educational Forum 45*(1), 113–120.
Blondel, B. 1973. Block building. *International Journal of Early Childhood* (OMEP) *5*(2), 186–190.
Boganoff, R. 1975. Sand and water are media for involvement. *Dimensions 3*(4), 66–69, 79.
Cartwright, S. 1974. Blocks and learning. *Young Children 24*(3), 141–146.
Elder, C. Z. 1973. Miniature sand environments. *Young Children 28*(5), 283–286.
Hartley, R., and Golderson, R. 1963. *The complete book of children's play.* (Rev. Ed.). New York: Thomas Y. Crowell.
Hirsch, E. S. (Ed.). 1974. *The block book.* Washington, D. C.: National Association for the Education of Young Children.
Jameson, K., and Kidd, P. 1974. *Pre-school play.* New York: Van Nostrand Reinhold.
Matterson, E. M. 1965. *Play and playthings for the preschool child.* Baltimore, Md.: Penguin.
Moore, S. G. 1977. Research in review: The effects of television on the prosocial behavior of young children. *Young Children 32*(5), 60–64.
Newman, E. A. 1971. *The elements of play.* New York: MSS Information Corp.
Palmer, E. L. 1972. Television instruction and the preschool child. *International Journal of Early Childhood* (OMEP) *4*(1), 11–15.
Riley, S. 1973. Some reflections on the value of children's play. *Young Children 28*(3), 146–153.
Seefeldt, C. 1972. Boxes are to build . . . a curriculum. *Young Children 28*(1), 5–11.
Stacks, E. B. 1960. *Blockbuilding.* Washington, D.C.: American Association of Elementary-Kindergarten-Nursery Educators (EKNE).
Strom, D. 1976. The merits of solitary play. *Childhood Education 52*(3), 149–152.
Suter, A. 1977. A playground—why not let the children create it? *Young Children 32*(3), 19–24.
Yardley, A. 1975. *Reaching out.* New York: Citation Press.

chapter 4. children are social

Allen, K. E. 1980. Mainstreaming: What have we learned? *Young Children 35*(5), 54–63.
Bingman-Newman, A. M., and Sanders, R. A. 1977. Take a new look at your classroom with Piaget as a guide. *Young Children 32*(4), 62–72.
Callard, E. D. 1978. Can children learn to love? *Childhood Education 55*(2), 68–75.
Dickerson, M. G., and Davis, M. D. 1979. Implications of P.L. 94–142 for developmental early childhood teacher education programs. *Young Children 34*(1), 28–31.
Goldman, A. 1978. The role of the teacher in the "treatment" of child abuse. *Dimensions 7*(1), 22–25.
Hollander, E. K., Saypol, J. R., and Eisenberry, M. 1978. Religious holidays in the public schools—no easy answers. *Childhood Education 55*(2), 84–88.

Jarolimek, J. 1978. Social studies for the elementary school: Where have all the flowers gone? *Childhood Education 55*(1), 26–31.

Klein, J. W. 1975. Mainstreaming the preschooler. *Young Children 30*(5), 317–326.

Lourie, R. S., and Schwarzbeck, C. 1979. When children feel helpless in the face of stress. *Childhood Education 55*(3), 134–140.

McLaughlin, J. A., and Kershman, S. M. 1979. Mainstreaming in early childhood: Strategies and resources. *Young Children 34*(4), 54–66.

Martin, L. A. 1978. How to reduce sex-role stereotyping. *Today's Education 67*(4), 59–61.

Miel, A. 1978. Social studies for understanding, caring, and acting. *Childhood Education 55*(2), 76–83.

Moore, S. G. 1977. Considerateness and helpfulness in young children (research in review). *Young Children 32*(4), 73–76.

———. 1979. Social cognition: Knowing about others (research in review). *Young Children 34*(3), 54–61.

Pagano, A. L. (Ed.). 1978. Social studies in early childhood: An interactionist point of view. (Bulletin 58.) Washington, D.C.: National Council for Social Studies.

Richards, B. 1976. Mapping: An introduction to symbols. *Young Children 31*(2), 145–156.

Riley, S. S. 1979. *How to generate values in young children.* Newport Beach, Calif.: New South Co.

Schenk, R. R. 1978. Some tools for day care teachers. *Dimensions 6*(4), 112–114, 126.

Schoyer, N. L. 1980. Divorce and the preschool child. *Childhood Education 57*(1), 3–7.

chapter 5.   children are curious

Althouse, R., and Main, C. 1974. The science learning center: Hub of science activities. *Childhood Education 50*(4), 222–226.

———, and Main, C., Jr. 1975. *Science experiences for young children.* New York: Teachers College Press.

Ashlock, R. 1967. What math for fours and fives? *Childhood Education 43*(7), 469–473.

Barron, L. 1979. *Mathematics experiences for the early childhood years.* Columbus, Ohio: Charles E. Merrill.

Bennett, L. 1978. Science and special students. *Science and Children 15*(4), 12–14.

Bradbard, M. R., and Endsley, R. C. 1980. How can teachers develop young children's curiosity? What research says to the teacher. *Young Children 35*(5), 21–32.

Burton, G. M. 1978. Helping parents help their preschool children. *Arithmetic Teacher 25*(8).

Galen, H. 1977. Cooking in the curriculum. *Young Children 32*(2), 59–69.

Ginsburg, H., and Opper, S. 1969. *Piaget's theory of intellectual development.* Englewood Cliffs, N.J.: Prentice-Hall.

Good, R. 1979. Children's abilities with the four basic arithmetic operations in grades K–2. *School Science and Mathematics 79*(2), 93–98.

Hammerman, A., and Morse, S. 1972. Open teaching: Piaget in the classroom. *Young Children 28*(1), 41–54.

Harbeck, M. B., and Marcuccio, P. 1978. A basic for the 1980's: Science in the lives of children. *Childhood Education 55*(2), 94–95.

Harlan, J. D. 1975. From curiosity to concepts: From concepts to curiosity. *Young Children 30*(4), 249–255.

Hill, S. A. 1979. Elementary school mathematics: More than the third R. *Childhood Education 55*(4), 215–220.

Hughes, R. 1979. What mathematical knowledge do Tom and Linda have when they enter school? *School Science and Mathematics 79*(4), 279–286.

James, J. 1974. When kids take over the kitchen. *Dimensions 2*(3), 74–77.

Johnson, B. 1977. Cup cooking offers highly individualized learning experiences for young children. *Dimensions 5*(4), 105–109.

Kamii, C., and Lee-Katz, L. 1979. Physics in preschool education: A Piagetian approach. *Young Children 34*(4), 4–9.

Kennedy, L. M. 1970. *Guiding children to mathematical discovery.* Belmont, Calif.: Wadsworth.

Liedtke, W. 1978. Rational counting. *Arithmetic Teacher 26*(2), 20–26.

Lovell, K. 1971. *The growth of understanding in mathematics: Kindergarten through grade three.* New York: Holt, Rinehart and Winston.

McAnainey, H. 1978. What direction(s) elementary school science? *Science Education 62*(1), 31–38.

McIntyre, M. 1976. The science learning center for preschool. *Science and Children 14*(3), 9–12.

O'Hara, E. 1975. Piaget, the six-year-old, and modern math. *Today's Education 64*(3), 32–36.

Trafton, P. 1975. *The curriculum.* In *Mathematics learning in early childhood,* ed. J. N. Payne. Reston, Va.: National Council of Teachers of Mathematics.

Yawkey, T. D. 1975. *Developmental mathematics and the young child: a Piaget rationale.* Washington, D.C.: U.S. Department of Health, Education, and Welfare, National Institute of Education. (ERIC Document Reproduction Service No. ED 121 452.)

chapter 6. children are creative

Clarke, E. C. 1979. The educational evaluation of children's artistic progress: More is better or is it? *Art Education 32*(1), 20–26.

Gainer, R. S. and Kukuk, E. 1979. Something to sing about. *Childhood Education 55*(3), 141–147.

Hallum, R., and Newhart, E. H. 1980. An interview with Hap Palmer. *Childhood Education 57*(1), 8–13.

Lewis, H. P. 1976. Peregrinations in child art. *Studies in Art Education 17*(2), 9–17.

Nesselwad, J. 1973. Practical tips insure successful art activities. *Dimensions 2*(1), 17–19, 24.

Rinehart, C. 1980. Music: A basic for the 1980's. *Childhood Education 56*(3), 140–145.

Robinson, G. 1978. Creativity: The child's search for self. *Dimensions 6*(4), 110–111.

Schwartz, J. and Douglas, N. 1975. Where is art education in early childhood today? *Art Education 28*(4), 6–10.

records

Jenkins, E. *Adventures in rhythm with Ella Jenkins.* Chicago: Adventures in Rhythm.

Palmer, H. *Hap Palmer record library.* Freeport, N.Y.: Educational Activities, Inc.

Silver Burdett Records. 1976. *Records that teach.* Atlanta, Ga.: Silver Burdett.

chapter 7. children are talkative

Blatt, G. T. 1978. Playing with language. *The Reading Teacher 31*(5), 487–491.

Bridge, C. 1979. Predictable materials for beginning readers. *Language Arts 56*(5), 503–507.

Buttery, T. J. 1979. Reading readiness for mainstreamed exceptional children in early childhood education. *Reading Improvement 16*(2), 118–122.

Evvard, E. C. 1979. How doth my grandson grow—in reading? *Childhood Education* 55(3), 283–285.

Forester, A. D. 1977. What teachers can learn from "natural readers." *The Reading Teacher 31*(2), 160–166.

King, E. M. 1978. Prereading programs: Direct versus incidental teaching. *The Reading Teacher 31*(5), 504–510.

Kirkland, E. R. 1978. A Piagetian interpretation of beginning reading instruction. *The Reading Teacher 31*(5), 497–503.

Lamme, C. C. 1979. Handwriting in an early childhood curriculum. *Young Children 35*(1), 20–27.

Nurss, J. R. 1980. Beyond letter recognition. *Dimensions 8*(4), 106–109.

Pickert, S. M., and Chase, M. L. 1978. Story retelling: An informal technique for evaluating children's language. *The Reading Teacher 31*(5), 528–531.

Price, E. H. 1976. How thirty-seven gifted children learned to read. *The Reading Teacher 30*(1), 44–48.

Roberts, K. P. 1976. Piaget's theory of conservation and reading readiness. *The Reading Teacher 30*(3), 246–250.

Ross, E. P., and Roe, B. D. 1977. Creative drama builds proficiency in reading. *The Reading Teacher 30*(4), 383–387.

Shaw, J. M. 1979. Exploring letters with young children. *Dimensions 8*(1), 12–16.

Smith, G. 1974. On listening to the language of children. *Young Children 24*(3), 133–140.

Stallard, C. K. 1977. Writing readiness: A developmental view. *Language Arts 54*(7), 775–779.

Strickland, D. S. 1979. On reading. *Childhood Education 56*(2), 67–75.

chapter 8.   children are dependent and independent

Bennett, T., and Milner, S. 1979. Child care center teaches parents too. *Dimensions 7*(2), 44–46.

Caldwell, B. M. 1977. Aggression and hostility in young children. *Young Children 32*(2), 4–13.

Dittmann, L. L. 1980. Project Head Start becomes a long-distance runner. *Young Children 35*(6), 2–9.

Donaldson, M. 1979. The mismatch between schools and children's minds. *Human Nature 2*(3), 60–67.

Duff, R. E., and Swick, K. J. 1980. Parent-teacher interaction: A developmental process. In *Readings in early childhood education*, ed. L. G. Baruth and E. Duff. Guilford, Conn.: Special Learning Corp.

Epstein, C. 1979. *Classroom management and teaching: Persistent problems and rational solutions*. Reston, Va.: Reston Publishing Co.

Farber, B. G., Hillard, S. W., and Hill, M. P. 1979. Fostering prosocial behaviors in children: What is the adult role? *Dimensions 7*(3), 77–80.

Galambos, J. W. 1969. *A guide to discipline*. Washington, D.C.: National Association for the Education of Young Children.

Ginott, H. G. 1975. *Teacher and child*. New York: Avon.

Hipple, M. L. 1975. *Early childhood education problems and methods*. Pacific Palisades, Calif.: Goodyear.

Jenkins, G. G. 1980. For parents particularly. *Childhood Education 56*(5), 291–293.

Marion, M. C. 1973. Create a parent-space—a place to stop, look, and read. *Young Children 28*(4), 221–224.

Nervius, J. R., and Filgo, D. 1980. Effective parenting: What can it teach the teachers? *Dimensions 8*(4), 110–115.

Rejai, M. 1979. On the failure of parents in the educational process. *The Educational Forum 43*(4), 435–437.

Stevens, J. H., Jr. 1978. Parent education programs: What determines effectiveness? *Young Children 33*(4), 59–65.

Tittle, B. M. 1978. Disruptive children? Check the compatability quotient of their teacher. *Dimensions 6*(3), 70–72.

index